The Prehistory of Orkney

I have been taught by dreams and fantasies
Learned from the friendly and the darker phantoms
And got great knowledge and courtesy from the dead . . .

EDWIN MUIR (1965) *I have been taught*

The Prehistory of Orkney

edited by Colin Renfrew *for Edinburgh University Press*

© Edinburgh University Press 1985
22 George Square, Edinburgh

Set in Linoterm Plantin
by Speedspools, Edinburgh, and
printed in Great Britain at
The Alden Press, Oxford

British Library Cataloguing
   in Publication Data
The Prehistory of Orkney
1. Man, Prehistoric—
   Scotland—Orkney
2. Orkney—History
I. Renfrew, Colin
941.1′32   DA880.06

ISBN 0 85224 456 8 (cloth)
       0 85224 506 8 (paperback)

Contents

Illustrations: Figures

Illustrations: Plates

Acknowledgements

The publishers wish to thank the following institutions and individuals
for permission to reproduce photographs, as indicated below.

In black and white

National Museum of Antiquities of Scotland: 4.1, 4.2, 4.3, 4.4, 4.5,
4.6, 4.7, 4.8, 4.9, 4.10, 4.11, 4.12, 4.13, 4.14, 7.1, 7.2, 7.3, 7.5,
7.6, 7.7, 7.8, 9.1, 9.2, 9.7, 10.4

Royal Commission on the Ancient and Historical Monuments of
Scotland: 6.3, 6.4, 6.5, 8.1, 8.2, 8.3, 8.11

Scottish Development Department (Crown copyright reserved): 3.1,
3.2, 3.3, 3.4, 3.5, 5.2, 5.3, 9.3, 9.4, 9.5, 9.6, 10.1

North of Scotland Archaeological Services: 8.6, 8.8, 8.10, 9 app.1

Nature Conservancy Council: 2.1, 2.4

Hunterian Museum, University of Glasgow: 7.4

British Library: 6.1, 6.2

Kirkwall Public Library: 8.5

Tankerness House Museum, Kirkwall (photo John Brundle): 5.4

University of Durham: 10.2, 10.3

Peter Gelling: 8 app.1, 2, 3, 4, 5, 6

John Hedges: 5.1

Professor Colin Renfrew: 5.6, 6.6, 8.7, 11.1

Drs Anna and Graham Ritchie: 6.7

In colour

National Museum of Antiquities of Scotland: 3, 12, 18, 20, 22

Scottish Development Department (Crown copyright reserved): 1, 2,
4, 7, 8, 10, 11, 13, 14, 19, 23

North of Scotland Archaeological Services: 9

Sigrid Kaland: 21

G. Moberg: 17

J. D. H. Radford: 24

Mick Sharpe: 5, 6, 15, 16

W. Vaughan: 25

1 Colin Renfrew **Introduction**

The prehistoric monuments of Orkney are justly famed for the abundantly rich picture they give of man's early past in this area. They constitute a complex which is not surpassed elsewhere in Britain – not even in Wessex, perhaps not even in continental Europe – for the wealth of evidence which it offers. For more than a century the two great stone circles, the Ring of Brodgar and the Stones of Stenness, in their spectacular setting on the Lochs of Stenness and of Harray, have been a romantic tourist sight. The great chamber tomb, Maes Howe, nearby, is one of the finest in existence. And the early prehistoric village at Skara Brae, excavated by Gordon Childe fifty years ago, is one of the few ancient sites whose name is known to a very wide public. From the Later Iron Age, the striking stone towers, the brochs, have always posed something of an enigma to scholars. And from the Viking period come not only the great cathedral of St Magnus and the church on Egilsay where he was martyred, but the foundations, on that rocky peninsula of land known as the Brough of Birsay, of what is often claimed as the Palace of Thorfinn, one of the first Norse Earls of Orkney.

These are just some of the sites which have for many years made Orkney celebrated among archaeologists and lovers of the past. Over the past decade or so, after many years of neglect, there has been a great upsurge of interest in and activity concerning early Orkney. Childe's famous excavation at Skara Brae has been re-opened and the new remains from it meticulously examined using a whole battery of modern techniques. Still older settlement remains have been found on the small and today rather remote island of Papa Westray. The spectacular site of the Stones of Stenness has been carefully examined, yielding new information and allowing for the first

I

time there the application of the radiocarbon dating technique. Tombs of this early period have now been excavated, with the careful recovery of a wealth of new data. For the first time moreover there is now a better indication of what was happening in Orkney in the Bronze Age. For the succeeding Iron Age, the origin of the brochs is now becoming clearer; and the rather obscure period in the early centuries AD, prior to the arrival of the Vikings, is today yielding some information about those enigmatic Picts who were displaced by the Norse invaders. And, at last, systematic and careful excavations of the Viking period, including a re-examination of the Brough of Birsay, are giving a proper archaeological background to sub-stantiate the story told in the Norse sagas.

The present book brings together the initiators of these and other recent projects in the Islands and offers to each the opportunity to give an up-to-date survey of the current state of our knowledge for each period in turn. In some cases the new discoveries have filled major gaps – for instance in the Bronze Age. In others they have served to reverse previously accepted views – that is perhaps the case with the brochs. And in the remainder they have yielded abundant new data which permit of much more detailed reconstruction than has hitherto been possible. It is my role as editor to offer a brief introductory survey, into which the more detailed discussions which follow can conveniently be placed.

THE DEVELOPMENT OF ORCADIAN STUDIES

The development of Orcadian prehistoric studies may be said to begin, in 1772, with the excavations by Sir Joseph Banks on the Bay of Skaill (not so far from the later discoveries at Skara Brae). Banks, after a disagreement about the practical arrangements, had withdrawn from Captain Cook's Second Voyage to the Pacific Ocean, and was instead embarked upon his own voyage of scientific investigation to Iceland. His work on Orkney (Lysaght 1974) may amount to little more than a passing curiosity in the history of archaeology, yet marks the beginning of systematic work in the islands.

Investigation did not advance significantly in the next few decades. The obvious standing monuments first attracted attention. Paramount amongst these were the two great stone circles between the Loch of Stenness and the Loch of Harray. Sir Walter Scott used these as the setting of one of the climactic scenes in *The Pirate* (1821), which is set in Shetland and in Orkney. The other two classes of monument already recognised in those early days were the stone towers or *brochs*, and the chambered constructions set below mounds, which were then termed Picts' Houses, although we today regard them as burial monuments.

At that time, the only obvious source of information was the scanty writings of Roman and later historical writers. The first did little more than mention the Orcades. And, prior to the Vikings, we learn very little of their inhabitants, at that time termed Picts. Adomnan, in his *Life of St Columba*, tells how that saint, while resident at the Pictish Court in north Scotland, sent one of his monks to visit the islands, but this is no more than a fleeting glimpse.

It was perhaps natural, then, that the Reverend George Barry, in his *History of the Orkney Islands* (1805), should regard as Pictish, and dating from around the time of St Columba in the sixth century AD, both the brochs and the Picts' houses. He placed these together in his classification, separating them from the standing stones, and from the earth mounds or tumuli, (most of which are today classed as bronze age). His work is of particular interest because he gives a detailed account and plan of the 'Picts' House' of Quanterness, re-excavated in the past decade and shown to be a splendid chambered tomb, dated to *c.* 3400 BC. He reported:

> So far as can now be discovered, there does not appear ever to have been, in any part of the building, either chink or hole for the admission of air or light; and this circumstance alone is sufficient to show that it had not been destined for the abode of men. The contents were accordingly such as might have been naturally expected in such a gloomy mansion. None of those things, which have been discovered in similar places, were found here; but the earth at the bottom of the cells, as deep as it could be dug, was of a dark colour, of a greasy feel, and of a fetid odour, plentifully intermingled with bones, some of which were almost entirely consumed. And others had, in defiance of time, remained so entire, as to show that they were the bones of men, of birds, and of some domestic animals. But though many of them had nearly mouldered to dust, they exhibited no marks of having been burnt; nor were ashes of any kind to be seen within any part of the building. In one of the apartments, an entire human skeleton in a prone attitude was found; but in the others, the bones were not only separated from one another, but divided into very small fragments.

Despite these evidences, Barry did not identify Quanterness as a tomb, and the distinction between broch and Picts' house was not yet made. It no doubt required a clearer chronological perspective, and this was supplied by the Danish Three Age System, published by Thomsen for the first time in English in 1848 (Ellesmere 1848) and more coherently in the following year by Worsaae (1849). This opened the way for one of the most important, and today underestimated, archaeological works of the nineteenth century, Daniel Wilson's *Archaeology and Prehistoric Annals of Scotland* (1851). Here he correctly identified the so-called Picts' houses as chambered tombs, and set them, along with the great stone circles, into the Stone Age, or Neolithic as it was later termed. He recognised that many of the burials from cists and tumuli should be classified as Bronze Age, and assigned the brochs to the Iron Age. He also successfully distinguished these things from the 'Scoto-Scandinavian relics', today called Viking. These crucial distinctions, with remarkably few modifications, have been followed and built on by nearly all later writers. They underlie the structure of this book.

3

Excavation was by now a popular pastime, and numerous chambered tombs and brochs were investigated, generally without adequate publication, by a number of enthusiastic antiquaries, amongst whom the most notable was George Petrie. The most striking single event of these years was undoubtedy the opening of Maes Howe in 1861, with the discovery of its remarkably perfect stone interior, and of the extensive runic inscriptions left there millennia after its initial use, by intruding Vikings.

The most impressive publication to arise in the mid-nineteenth century from work in Orkney, however, was a report not of excavation but of survey. It was undertaken by Captain F.W.L.Thomas, commanding a Royal Navy survey ship. Working in all weathers in the winter of 1849 he produced an excellent topographical map of that crucial isthmus of land, between the Lochs of Stenness and Harray, where are located the Ring of Brodgar, the Stones of Stenness and other monuments. He produced detailed plans of these, and of the remarkable chambered cairn on the Holm of Papa Westray. In his account (Thomas 1852) he was careful to distinguish between Picts' houses (i.e. chambered cairns) and Picts' castles or brochs. These distinctions were confirmed by the further excavations, mainly of brochs, conducted later in the century. But the broad outline of Orcadian prehistory had by then already been made clear in the pioneering synthesis of Daniel Wilson, and the survey of Thomas. The great stone circles had thus been recorded and set in their context alongside the chambered cairns (or Picts' houses) in the Neolithic, and the brochs in the Iron Age. Naturally the Norse origin of St Magnus' cathedral and the other early standing Christian buildings had never been in question. The Viking nature of the 'Scoto-Scandinavian' burial finds was now clear.

If the work of the mid-nineteenth century represents the first great phase of Orcadian archaeological research, the second undoubtedly came in the years between the two world wars. The leading figure was the distinguished prehistorian V.Gordon Childe. His excavations at the settlement of Skara Brae, from 1927 to 1931, again drew attention to the great richness of the Orcadian material, and to the excellence of its preservation, arising from the use of stone rather than wood as a building material. Initially Childe dated his finds at Skara Brae as Pictish – meaning Later Iron Age (i.e. the pre-Norse period, in the early first millennium AD). But he soon came to see that this was a serious misunderstanding, and that the appropriate context was Neolithic, nearly two thousand years earlier, as it then seemed. (With the benefit of radiocarbon dating we can now see that Skara Brae is actually three thousand rather than two thousand years earlier than Childe first thought.) Childe successfully corrected this misinterpretation, and went on to investigate several other sites, including two chambered cairns and the neolithic settlement at Rinyo on Rousay. He incorporated the Orcadian material into his two syntheses of the prehistoric period, *The Prehistory of*

. . . .

Scotland (Childe 1935) and *Scotland before the Scots* (Childe 1946). Important work on the chambered cairns of Rousay was carried out during this period, as well as the excavation of the brochs of Midhowe and Gurness, which resulted in abundant finds but unfortunately only brief or negligible publication. The important excavations at the major Norse site, the Brough of Birsay, likewise remain unpublished, and much valuable information was thus undoubtedly lost in an enterprise which had no more positive outcome than some of the less distinguished antiquarian diggings of a century earlier. Happily the current re-evaluation and re-excavation there opens the way to a fresh and well-documented understanding of this important site (see Curle 1982).

The immediate post-war period saw little archaeological activity in Orkney itself. It did, however, produce three major works of synthesis, which served to consolidate much that had been learned over previous decades. The publication of the Inventory volume for Orkney by the Royal Commission on Ancient Monuments (RCAMS 1946) documented in a scholarly way for the first time the great richness of the material, and this documentation was reinforced for the early period by the publication of the first volume, containing the Orcadian cairns, of Audrey Henshall's great work *The Chambered Tombs of Scotland* (Henshall 1963). In addition Dr F. T. Wainwright's edited volume (1962) *The Northern Isles* gave a balanced overview for both Orkney and Shetland, admirably summarising archaeo logical and historical knowledge at that time.

The third and current phase of archaeological research in Orkney began in the 1970s and continues with vigour today. It has been characterised by an approach which seeks to ask a whole series of new questions about the economy and society of early Orkney, and which has at its disposal a battery of new techniques to undertake this task. It is the contributors to this volume – together with several other colleagues – who have organised and conducted those various excavation projects which now allow a substantial reassessment of the Orcadian past. In doing so they have been aided by the application of radiocarbon dating, which has confirmed the essential justice of Daniel Wilson's early outline, and allowed the solution of several difficult problems. Those problems were initially made more difficult because many Orcadian sites – such as the mounds of burnt stone – are almost devoid of such artefacts as would allow them to be dated through typological comparison. This was, of course, precisely Gordon Childe's early difficulty at Skara Brae. Indeed one of the happy outcomes of radiocarbon dating in Orkney has been that so many of the broad chronological conclusions set out in the earlier syntheses prove to be essentially correct. The techniques of environmental archaeology have also now been enthusiastically applied (although here too we should note that Childe and his colleagues were precursors). Geomorphological studies and pollen analysis permit the reconstruction of the environment of the early inhabitants, and the study of plant and faunal remains allows the reconstruction of many aspects of their diet. The examination of human skeletal remains gives insights into population structure, and documents, among other things, the very short life expectancy during the neolithic period. The important results of recent surveys are mentioned here in the final chapter. All of this ferment of activity has made Orkney one of the most active areas of archaeological research in the British Isles, indeed in Europe. A happy outcome is that the law of diminishing returns has not yet set in. Quite to the contrary, the different projects undertaken have complemented each other, adding up to something very much more than a few disparate excavations. In Orkney, perhaps more than anywhere else in Britain, we have a well-documented picture for most of the phases of our prehistory. Of course there are many gaps, but the outcome of recent work has been to allow us to define much more clearly just where those gaps are.

A BRIEF OUTLINE

By way of introduction to the chapters that follow, it seems appropriate to offer a very concise outline, so that the reader can feel the logic of the development of the book. At the same time a number of the chief current issues can be stressed, for recent work has produced at least as many new problems as it has solved.

The story begins with an unpopulated and apparently treeless landscape. In their discussion of the Orcadian environments, Davidson and Jones survey the evidence from pollen studies and other sources which indicate that after the islands were severed from Scotland before 10000 BC, as a result of rising sea level at the end of the last ice age, the vegetation was one of heathland. The strength of the Orcadian winds seems to have prevented thick forestation, and the cover never became more dense than a scrub of birch and hazel. They go on to document the development of a more open herbaceous landscape in the Late Neolithic, and the onset of colder and wetter weather around 1900 BC. At this time, blanket bog began to form in some areas, and with it peat may have become, for the first time, available as a fuel. There was some further worsening of the climate around 1200 BC, and they suggest a marked deterioration around the beginning of the Iron Age at about 600 BC. It is against the background of these broad changes that the shifts in human settlement pattern must be read. But it is not yet clear to what extent climatic and vegetational change was responsible for the developments in social organisation and daily life which the finds document.

The first settlers seem to have come to Orkney a century or two before 3500 BC. Anna Ritchie in her chapter points out that we have no evidence for any hunter-gatherer population in the islands before the arrival of the first

6

farmers. The earliest settlement which we have at present is her own site, Knap of Howar on Papa Westray, but she stresses that other, perhaps simpler sites may yet be found.

The excavations of Clarke at Skara Brae, which he describes, have added a wealth of detail to the picture first established by Childe. For the first time we begin to have a clear picture of the neolithic economy, which was certainly an agricultural one. Indeed among the most interesting finds in recent years are the plough marks at his site, the Links of Noltland on Westray. The mass of radiocarbon dates now available has however heightened rather than removed one particular problem. The pottery and other finds at Skara Brae form a fairly well defined complex, a recurrent assemblage or 'culture', to use the archaeological jargon. Its most characteristic feature is the pottery, 'grooved ware', found at several sites. On the other hand the pottery found at Knap of Howar and at several other sites is of different form and decoration, and is termed 'Unstan ware', after the site where it was first identified. Previously the Unstan ware assemblage had been thought to be the earlier, but the radiocarbon dates now call the chronological distinction into question, and the explanation for the differences between the finds is not clear. This problem is touched upon not only by Anna Ritchie and Clarke, but by Henshall and Graham Ritchie in the chapters which follow.

The abundant evidence from the chambered cairns is reviewed by Henshall. It is clear now that they are contemporary both with Knap of Howar and its Unstan ware, and with Skara Brae and the grooved ware. The passage graves in the class which Henshall designates as the Maes Howe group are associated with grooved ware, while the long, compartmented cairns like those of Rousay and the recently excavated site of Isbister on South Ronaldsay sometimes have Unstan ware. Whatever the explanation of this distinction, we now have abundant evidence for the burial practices of the time, which, as Miss Henshall describes, in some cases involved excarnation – the deliberate de-fleshing of the bones, whether by exposure or temporary burial, prior to their definitive inhumation within the tomb.

The ritual monuments, most notably the Ring of Brodgar and the Stones of Stenness, are discussed by Graham Ritchie, the excavator of the latter site. The radiocarbon dates, as well as the grooved ware which he obtained, placed the monument close in date both to Skara Brae and to the tombs such as Quanterness which contained grooved ware. This allows him to take issue with my own suggestion that the two great henges represent the culmination, in a sense, of a process whereby the smaller and autonomous social groups of the earlier period, documented by the dispersed distribution of their local tombs, became linked in a more centralised society in the Later Neolithic, in which the great central monuments were conceived as playing a significant and central role.

The evidence for the Bronze Age, surveyed by Øvrevik, is still less abundant than for the other periods. But her excavations at Quoyscottie have now documented in detail the somewhat modest burial mounds of the Middle Bronze Age. And from the Later Bronze Age, as radiocarbon determinations now indicate, come the mounds of burnt stone, or burnt mounds, notably Liddle Farm and Beaquoy. They are now seen as domestic sites: cooking places or perhaps permanent settlements.

With the Iron Age and the brochs we are on firmer ground. Hedges is able to draw on the evidence of his important excavations of the brochs at Bu near Stromness and at the Howe of Howe Farm, to suggest that these monuments may have had a local origin within the Northern Isles. The sites of Jarlshof and Clickhimin in Shetland are relevant here, as is the new evidence of the iron age round house outside the neolithic chambered cairn at Quanterness. As Hedges rightly shows, some extravagant earlier ideas of invaders and migrations at this time may now be discounted. Moreover he has shown that the furnishings found within many of the brochs – which like those of neolithic Skara Brae are of stone – are not to be dismissed as later additions, but in some cases at least belong to the primary construction. The picture for this period, and for those which precede and follow it, is usefully supplemented in the appendix by Gelling on his excavations at Skaill in Deerness in the east Mainland of Orkney. It is sad to report that Peter Gelling died while this book was in press.

The period of the brochs merges gradually with that of the Picts. Anna Ritchie rightly stresses that the Pictish period is in the first instance defined historically, by written references dating between the third century AD and the ninth century, at which time the Pictish kingdom of Scotland was assimilated into the new Scottish kingdom. The Picts were no doubt the direct descendants of the broch people, but as the author explains, our knowledge of them has to come primarily from archaeological sources. Her own excavations at Buckquoy is one such source, as are the excavations in the late village surrounding the broch at Howe, described in the appendix by Neil. Now at last we have some solid archaeological material to set beside the rather shadowy historical references to the Picts.

Amongst British prehistorians it is conventional to regard prehistoric times as ending with the Roman period. But of course there was no Roman period in Orkney – despite some Roman imports among the brochs. We have few historical data for the Picts, and even the Norse period in Orkney is known primarily from the Norse sagas. The *Orkneyinga Saga* was written around 1200 AD, and it is to be appreciated (as it was intended to be) as much as a work of literature as of historical documentation. Morris is right, therefore, to remind us that in Scandinavia the Viking Age is generally seen as the last period of prehistory. The Scandinavian approach seems eminently suitable for Orkney, and we make no apology for including the Viking period within this survey of Orcadian prehistory. He is able to draw on his own work in the Bay of Birsay area, including his new excavations on the Brough of Birsay, on Anna Ritchie's work at Buckquoy, mentioned above, and on that of Sigrid Kaland at Westness on Rousay, where there is an important Viking cemetery.

With the Late Norse period in the thirteenth century, and the succession of the Scottish earls, historical records become more abundant. So too, of course, do standing buildings, primarily the great cathedral of St Magnus, founded by Earl Rognvald in 1137 AD and completed over the succeeding centuries. By the time the islands passed to the jurisdiction of the Scottish crown in 1468 they may be regarded as falling within the full light of history.

Acknowledgements. The idea of compiling a volume surveying the prehistory of Orkney was first proposed by Dr Graham Ritchie. This book owes much to his enthusiasm, and to that of Dr Anna Ritchie and of Mr Archie Turnbull, Secretary to the Edinburgh University Press. Dr Graham Ritchie kindly undertook the considerable task of compiling the bibliography. We are very grateful to Mr Turnbull and his colleagues at the Press for the care that they have exercised, notably in bringing disparate contributions together into a coherent whole and in the treatment of the illustrations.

2 D. A. Davidson, R. L. Jones **The Environment of Orkney**

THE PRESENT

Location, Geology and Topography. The seventy or so Orkney islands lie scattered astride latitude 59°N, within the North Atlantic Ocean, just to the north of Scotland (figure 2.1). Many of them are very small, some little more than skerries, so that exact agreement as to their total number (some authors place it as high as ninety) is difficult. Over one half of the land area (about 974 km²) of the archipelago occurs on the island called Mainland. The islands are composed almost entirely of gently-inclined Devonian (Middle Old Red Sandstone) flagstones and sandstones, together with a small quantity of volcanic rocks. In addition, there is a restricted outcrop of younger, probably Carboniferous, sandstones, lavas and tuffs (figure 2.2).

The island group is developed on an undulating plateau tilted north and east, with a major structural depression in its centre, containing Scapa Flow, and a residual massif in the south, forming the island of Hoy. There is a series of depressions in the plateau, from south-east to east, probably Tertiary river valleys that were subsequently overdeepened by Pleistocene ice. Inundations, principally in late Tertiary and Flandrian (Post-glacial) times, have filled these depressions to give the present pattern of islands, firths and straits. The post-glacial rise in sea level has also buried coastal peat beds, tombolos and bay-mouth bars or ayres (Mykura 1975). The legacy of the Ice Age is evident in the rounded configuration of the uplands, and in a widespread mantle of till at lower elevations. Flandrian deposits consist mainly of blown sand, which, for example, covers about one-third of the island of Sanday; and peat, which occurs principally on the eastern flanks of the west Mainland hills and in central Hoy (figure 2.3).

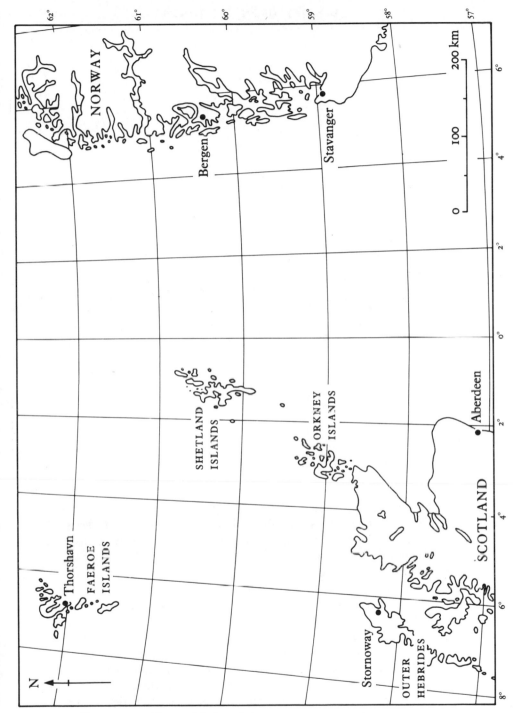

FIGURE 2.1. Geographical setting.

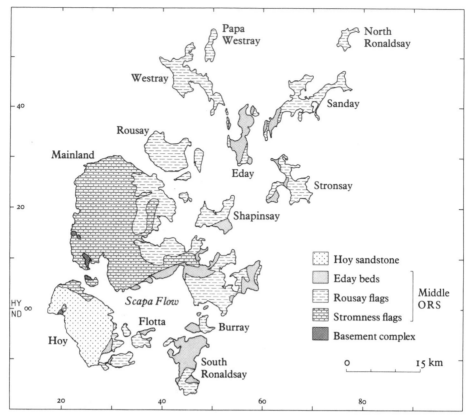

FIGURE 2.2. Solid geology. (From Mykura 1975, reproduced by
permission of the author and the Nature Conservancy Council.)

    The geological structure has a distinct effect on land form. The sides of
many hills are stepped, as a result of alternating hard and soft flagstone
strata, a mixture which also explains much varied cliff and rock platform
coastal topography (Mather, Ritchie and Smith 1975). Substantial parts of
Eday, Sanday, South Ronaldsay, and some of eastern Mainland have well-
developed ridge-and-scarp features cut in sandstone (Mykura 1975). Overall, the relief of the archipelago is moderate, considerable tracts of terrain
lying below 150 m OD. Western Mainland, together with much of Rousay, is
hilly, with elevations of up to 275 m OD. The only mountainous country is
located in Hoy where an altitude of 477 m OD is reached (plate 2.1).

    Perhaps the most important topographic feature, and one of un-
doubted significance to early man, is the coastline, whose total length is
about 800 km. The height and steepness of the coastline varies, with high
cliffs, low rocky shores and sandy beaches present in varying proportions.

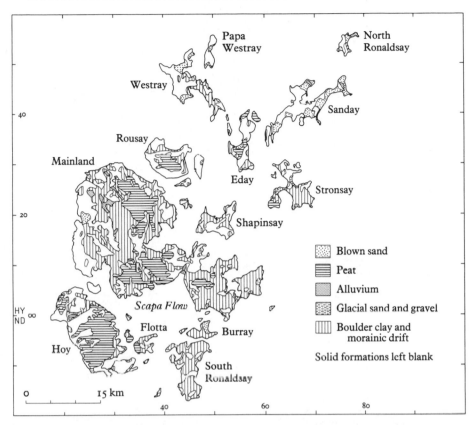

FIGURE 2.3. Surficial deposits. (Based on IGS Quaternary Map UK
(North), 1977, reproduced by permission of the Director, Institute of Geological Sciences. NERC Copyright reserved.)

High cliffs, comprising about 20 per cent of the coastline, occur mainly in
western Hoy, western Westray and on the west and south-east of Mainland.
Sandy beaches (including shingle) make up about 11 per cent and are most
common on the north isles. Approximately 70 per cent of the coastline,
however, is composed of low rock or boulder clay cliffs and low rocky shores
(figure 2.4). In the interior of the archipelago the shelter afforded by nearby
land masses gives rise to a low-energy geomorphic environment at the
coasts, while, around the fringes of the island group, exposure to the
prevailing west and south-west Atlantic winds produces spectacular cliff
scenery. Wind action is expressed in the areas of sand-dunes and sand-
sheets.

Flora and Fauna. Atmospheric conditions, especially salinity, together
with wind speed and frequency, have a significant effect upon plant and

13

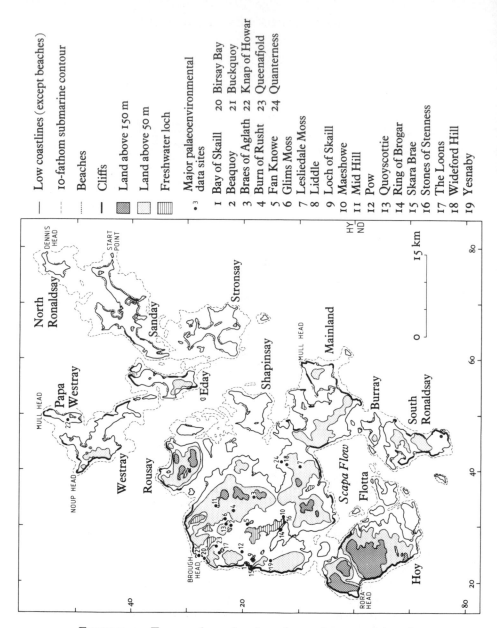

Key:

— Low coastlines (except beaches)
--- 10-fathom submarine contour
▦ Beaches
▮ Cliffs
▨ Land above 150 m
▨ Land above 50 m
▨ Freshwater loch
•3 Major palaeoenvironmental data sites

1 Bay of Skaill
2 Beaquoy
3 Braes of Aglath
4 Burn of Rusht
5 Fan Knowe
6 Glims Moss
7 Lesliedale Moss
8 Liddle
9 Loch of Skaill
10 Maeshowe
11 Mid Hill
12 Pow
13 Quoyscottie
14 Ring of Brogar
15 Skara Brae
16 Stones of Stenness
17 The Loons
18 Wideford Hill
19 Yesnaby
20 Birsay Bay
21 Buckquoy
22 Knap of Howar
23 Queenafjold
24 Quanterness

FIGURE 2.4. Topography and major palaeoenvironmental data sites. (Coastal types from Mather, Ritchie and Smith 1975, reproduced by permission of the authors and the Nature Conservancy Council. Palaeoenvironmental sites from Bramwell 1979, Caseldine and Whittington 1976, Clutton-Brock 1979, Donaldson, Morris and Rackham 1981, Evans and Spencer 1977, Godwin 1956, Keatinge and Dickson 1979, MacLean 1976, Moar 1969, Ritchie and Ritchie 1974, Sheldon 1979, Spencer 1975, Wheeler 1977, and authors.)

animal distributions. Wind effects are particularly well marked over 150 m OD, and the exposed nature of the islands partially determines the heights at which communities are found.

The last land link with the mainland of Scotland was severed by about 11000 bc, when the sea level in the Late Devensian period rose (A.G. Dawson, personal communication). The Orkney archipelago then became inaccessible to plants and animals unable to disperse across the Pentland Firth. Such physical isolation also meant that migrant prehistoric and historic peoples were forced to make a sea-crossing in order to reach the islands. Amongst the animals introduced by such settlers, was, according to Clutton-Brock (1979), the red deer.

At present, over one half of the Orcadian landscape is utilised in some form of agriculture, the characteristics of which will be examined in the following section. Most of the remainder of the vegetation is semi-natural, and, according to Bullard and Goode (1975), can be grouped into three main categories: grass heath, and tall herb and wetland communities within the agricultural zone; coastal plant communities; and upland vegetation in areas too poor for agriculture.

The degree of exposure is a major constraint on the height at which cultivation is possible. Where some shelter is available, farming may be practised at 100 m OD. Actual cultivation limits, and the extent of improved pasture, vary from locality to locality, a pattern which no doubt also existed in the past. In detail the limit of cultivation and the occurrence of improved pasture are influenced by a set of environmental, economic and social factors, but prime emphasis should be given to the labours of farmers over the centuries.

There is today no semi-natural woodland in the agricultural zone. The native status of many trees is uncertain, and will be discussed later. There are, however, a number of plantations containing a variety of deciduous species, notably where some shelter is afforded. Grass heath occurs mainly on steep slopes in the agricultural zone, and is dominated by grasses, sedges and ericaceous species, together with supplementary herbs. In the upper parts of valleys, tall herb and fern vegetation is encountered, while flushes and mires, many base-rich, occur in similar locations. Extensive areas often occur in the valley mires and in damp patches on agricultural land.

The smaller islands frequently possess a cover of grass heath, of which crowberry (*Empetrum*), thrift (*Armeria*) and sea-plantain (*Plantago maritima*) are important members. Along the coastline, salt-marsh is restricted to sheltered locations at the head of bays and behind ayres. Sand-dunes are likewise not extensive and tend to be of the 'single ridge' type. There are, however, quite widespread areas of dune pasture (machair), known locally as links. This pasture is especially widespread in the north isles and is usually dominated by creeping fescue (*Festuca rubra*), sand sedge (*Carex arenaria*) and carnation-grass (*C. flacca*). In the zone where climatic and soil conditions make cultivation impossible, three main vegetation types exist: first, heath, grassland and subarctic 'fell-field'; second, montane woodland and scrub (localised on Hoy), and consisting mainly of rowan (*Sorbus aucuparia*), birch (*Betula pubescens*), hazel (*Corylus avellana*), aspen (*Populus tremula*) and willow (*Salix* spp.); third, peatlands, divisible into blanket bog which occurs on the higher Mainland hills but is best developed on Hoy, and mires which occur in topographic depressions throughout the uplands. As Bullard and Goode (1975) point out, vegetation restricted to high altitudes further south in Britain is developed at successively lower altitudes northwards because of worsening climatic conditions. Much semi-natural Orcadian vegetation, even at low altitudes, has montane characteristics.

Any analysis of environmental conditions has to take careful account of human agency. Thus, present-day climatic or soil conditions can be evaluated in terms of current agriculture on Orkney. Problems arise when any palaeo-environmental assessment is attempted, since data on former environmental conditions and past economies are fragmentary at best. It is conventional in such analyses to describe present-day climatic and soil conditions, and this can be justified on the argument that many of the environmental problems faced by modern farmers have had to be tackled since prehistoric times. Also, the palaeobotanical evidence, to be presented later, suggests that a largely non-wooded environment has been in existence for about 6000 years. This would imply that soil types have not been completely transformed over this period, though it will be shown that some significant changes have occurred.

Comparative environment stability over the last five millennia should not be assumed to indicate an unchanging relationship between nature and man. Major changes have taken place even within the last 200 years. The old agriculture was the run-rig system. The enclosure movement in the early nineteenth century brought consolidated holdings, new agricultural machinery, new crops and stock, and a six-course rotation system. In recent decades the amount of land under cereals or roots has been drastically reduced, so that the typical farm is now 88 per cent grass, 7 per cent oats, 3 per cent barley and a mere 1 per cent each of turnips and potatoes (R. Miller 1976). The introduction of new seed mixtures combined with the heavy application of fertilisers give present-day Orkney a very green landscape. These agricultural and associated technological changes mean that the significance of environmental conditions has varied markedly over the last two centuries. Today, new drainage techniques are being applied, so that low-lying, poorly-drained areas are being claimed for agriculture. In contrast, the use of horses permitted marginal land to be cultivated in the past, which has had to be abandoned when tractors replaced them. The present-day population of Orkney is only a fraction of that of former times. Higher population pressure in the recent historical past meant that more marginal land had to be utilised. It is not enough, therefore, to establish a dynamic relationship between land use, technology and environmental resources; the variable of population pressure must also be introduced into the equation.

Climate. In terms of the physical environment, climate has the greatest impact on the economic life of Orkney, a situation which no doubt also prevailed during prehistory. The salient feature of the climate is the high frequency of strong winds, the effects of which are marked – given the lack of shelter, the overall humid environment with no distinctive wetter or drier periods, and the small annual range of temperature. These characteristics result from the high latitude of Orkney and the strong maritime influence.

TABLE 2.1. Number of days with gusts of 39 mph (17.2 m sec^{-1}) or more at Kirkwall Airport, 10-year means from 1963 to 1972 (from Plant and Dunsire 1974, 73).

JANUARY	15.5	MAY	6.7	SEPTEMBER	8.1
FEBRUARY	12.1	JUNE	4.7	OCTOBER	13.4
MARCH	15.0	JULY	4.8	NOVEMBER	18.0
APRIL	9.7	AUGUST	4.1	DECEMBER	18.3

Total 130.4

In describing the Orcadian climate, one inevitably begins with wind. Anemograph data are available only for Kirkwall Airport and have been analysed by Plant and Dunsire (1974). They note that wind directions are fairly evenly spread around the compass, with the highest frequencies in the quadrant between south and west. An increase in easterly winds is evident in the spring and early summer. Figures for the incidence of gales (over 39 mph/17.2 m sec^{-1}) highlight the dominance of wind in the Orcadian environment (table 2.1). As can be seen from this table, gales are a very frequent occurrence from October until March. Averaged over the year there is a 35.7 per cent chance of a gale on any one day.

The average annual rainfall ranges from *c.* 800 mm in the southern and eastern areas to over 1000 mm on the uplands of Rousay, Hoy and western Mainland (Macaulay Institute for Soil Research, 1978). The monthly and annual totals recorded at Kirkwall Airport are given in table 2.2. The driest period is from April to July. The monthly rainfall totals may not appear very high, but more important is the persistent nature of rainfall in influencing outdoor work. Plant and Dunsire (1974) compute the number of hours during a working day (0700 to 1700 hours GMT) when rainfall is sufficiently intensive to disrupt or prevent outdoor work (table 2.3). These figures,

17

when combined with the incidence of gales, highlight the frequent impossibility of outside work, especially during the months from November to March.

TABLE 2.2 Monthly totals of rainfall (in mm) recorded at Kirkwall Airport, 22-year means from 1951 to 1972 (from Plant and Dunsire 1974, 11).

JANUARY	101	MAY	54	SEPTEMBER	81
FEBRUARY	74	JUNE	57	OCTOBER	112
MARCH	74	JULY	56	NOVEMBER	116
APRIL	52	AUGUST	84	DECEMBER	118

Total 979

A small temperature range, both on a daily and an annual time-scale, is characteristic of Orkney. Figures are given in table 2.4 to illustrate the small annual range of mean daily temperatures on a monthly basis, whilst the differences between the maximum and minimum monthly averages are also small. The small temperature ranges also mean that frost is not common. The average numbers of days with air frost at Kirkwall Airport in January and February are 8.0 and 10.1 respectively. The average date of the first air frost is 20 November and the corresponding date for the last air frost is 23 April for the same station (Plant and Dunsire 1974).

TABLE 2.3. Number of hours of rain falling at some time during the hour at a rate of 0.5 mm hr^{-1} or more between the hours of 0700 and 1700 hours GMT at Kirkwall Airport (from Plant and Dunsire 1974, 21).

10-year mean, 1963-72

JANUARY	56.3	MAY	29.8	SEPTEMBER	41.6
FEBRUARY	38.7	JUNE	24.7	OCTOBER	57.5
MARCH	47.1	JULY	28.6	NOVEMBER	75.0
APRIL	34.6	AUGUST	37.3	DECEMBER	66.7

Total 537.9

10-year mean as percentage of total working time

JANUARY	18	MAY	10	SEPTEMBER	14
FEBRUARY	14	JUNE	8	OCTOBER	19
MARCH	15	JULY	9	NOVEMBER	25
APRIL	12	AUGUST	12	DECEMBER	22

Total 15

The Orkney climate, especially the elements of wind and dampness, places severe stress on agriculture. The present-day absolute emphasis on pasture has reduced the risk of losing locally-grown feedstuffs, but this in turn means that fodder has to be imported. The reduction in hay production in contrast to the rise of silage has also reduced the effect of weather on agriculture. Even so, an unusually wet summer, as in 1979, can cause serious hardship. Before the present 'Green Revolution' as described by Ronald Miller (1976), the traditional mixed type of agriculture would have been more at the mercy of the weather, despite greater diversification. Crop failure, when wet autumns prevented the harvesting of crops or the drying of hay, was endemic in such a physically marginal climate. Presumably such weather fluctuations have existed at least as far back as 1800 BC, when an increase in climatic oceanicity seems likely to have occurred (Keatinge and Dickson 1979). These authors also suggest another climatic change in Orkney about 3800 BC, when onshore winds began to increase. Thus wind may well have presented a serious hazard to farming since neolithic times.

TABLE 2.4. Monthly means of daily maximum temperature, daily mean temperature and daily minimum temperature in degrees Celsius at Kirkwall Airport, from 1951 to 1972 (from Plant and Dunsire 1974, 26, 27, 28). Tables 2.1, 2.2, 2.3 and 2.4 are reproduced by kind permission of the Director-General of the Meteorological Office.

	maximum	mean	minimum
JANUARY	5.3	3.6	1.9
FEBRUARY	5.5	3.4	1.4
MARCH	6.9	4.6	2.3
APRIL	9.2	6.2	3.2
MAY	11.3	8.5	5.6
JUNE	13.9	10.9	7.8
JULY	14.9	12.2	9.4
AUGUST	15.0	12.3	9.7
SEPTEMBER	13.8	11.2	8.7
OCTOBER	11.3	9.2	7.1
NOVEMBER	7.9	6.0	4.1
DECEMBER	6.1	4.4	2.7

Soils. The nature of Orcadian soils can be linked to four factors: the superficial deposits (which are largely glacial tills); the strongly maritime climate; the gently rolling landscape for much of the archipelago; and the influence of man. As described in the previous section, an outstanding feature of the Orkney climate is the effect of a moderate rainfall total of *c.* 800 mm on the lower areas, combined with low evaporation rates. Thus gleying is a dominant soil process in gently-sloping and low-lying areas. Poor drainage also influences extensive areas of hill peat on the uplands of west Mainland, Rousay and Hoy. The incidence of strong winds inhibits the growth of trees. Well-drained forest soils are therefore absent; instead, the norm is for soils to suffer at least some drainage impedance and to be developed under heathland or grassland.

TABLE 2.5. The ten soil associations of Orkney and their parent materials (from Macaulay Institute for Soil Research 1978, 24-5). Table 2.5 and figure 2.5 are reproduced by kind permission of the Macaulay Institute for Soil Research, and the authors.

STROMNESS. Drift derived from sandstones and breccias of the Middle Old Red Sandstone and rocks of the granite-schist complex of the Moinian

LYNEDARDY. Drift derived from flagstones and sandstones of the Middle Old Red Sandstone with rocks of the granite-schist complex of the Moinian

THURSO. Drift derived from strata of the Stromness Flags and the Rousay Flags of the Middle Old Red Sandstone

CANISBAY. Drift derived from strata of the Stromness Flags, the Rousay Flags and the Eday Beds of the Middle Old Red Sandstone

FLAUGHTON. Drift derived from sandstones of the Eday Beds of the Middle Old Red Sandstone

DARLEITH. Drift derived from basic lavas and intrusions

DUNNET. Drift derived from strata of the Upper Old Red Sandstone

RACKWICK. Fluvioglacial sands and gravels derived from strata of the Upper Old Red Sandstone

BOYNDIE. Fluvioglacial sands

FRASERBURGH. Shelly sand

The Soil Survey for Scotland soil maps for Orkney were published in 1982. The survey was executed by Mr F. Dry and the full results of his research are not available at the time of writing. However, an interim report has been published, from which the following description of the soils derives (Macaulay Institute for Soil Research 1978). Superficial deposits cover about 85 per cent of Orkney, with till and peat the most extensive. In areas such as Sanday, North Ronaldsay, and the Bay of Skaill, wind-blown sand is dominant. Rae (1976) interprets the till as being the result of variations in glacier flow over Orkney. The Soil Survey recognise four types of till:

(1) a moderately fine-textured till which occurs throughout the islands, but is most extensive in such areas as east Mainland, South Ronaldsay, Shapinsay, Stronsay, Westray and in particular parts of west Mainland,

(2) a coarse or moderately coarse-textured till which occurs mainly on Hoy,

(3) a moderately coarse or medium-textured till which is common throughout west Mainland,

(4) a morainic till which occurs locally on Mainland.

These tills are further subdivided according to lithological type and age, when linked with the remaining parent materials types (different kinds of sands), provide the basis for the ten soil associations which have been identified. A soil association is a characteristic soil pattern related to parent material and relief.

The Thurso, Canisbay, Dunnet and Fraserburgh Associations are the most extensive, though peat is also widespread (figure 2.3). For mapping purposes, the Soil Survey subdivides soil associations into soil series. These series encompass the following range of major soil groups and subgroups: podzols, peaty podzols, non-calcareous gleys, peaty gleys, brown calcareous soils, oroarctic podzols, calcareous gleys and saline gleys. The first five types are the most widespread.

The spatial pattern of some of these soils is illustrated in figure 2.5. Figure 2.5a presents a topographic extract for the area between Finstown and the outskirts of Kirkwall in the east Mainland. A gently sloping coastal strip along the southern shores of the Bay of Firth gradually rises in an open basin form to Wideford Hill (225 m), Keelylang Hill (220 m), Hill of Lyradale (176 m) and Hill of Heddle (135 m). There is a marked correlation between soil types and drainage conditions. On the upper slopes of these hills, peat is dominant (figure 2.5). Peat also occurs in poorly-drained footslope as well as depressional localities. A hydrologic sequence of soils is evident, for example on the northern slopes of Wideford Hill and Keelylang Hill. Peat on the summit areas is followed by peaty podzols on the upper slopes. Middle slopes may well suffer from an excess of water leading to the formation of peaty gleys, as demonstrated by these slopes on Wideford Hill and Hill of Heddle. Drainage conditions improve on the lower slopes of Wideford Hill – round Quanterness farm. This is reflected in the presence of freely- and imperfectly-drained podzols. The final extensive members of the hydrologic sequence are the non-calcareous gleys which occur in the most low-lying and gently sloping localities. In summary then, the hydrologic sequence is from peat on hill summits, ranging through peaty podzols and peaty gleys on upper and middle slopes to freely and imperfectly drained podzols on the best drained localities. On footslopes or in hollows, non-calcareous gleys and peats predominate. This spatial patterning is evident on much of Orkney, though there are obvious deviations in areas of high relief (for example, Hoy) or where blown sand is extensive. A critical issue is the extent to which soil conditions have changed since prehistoric times.

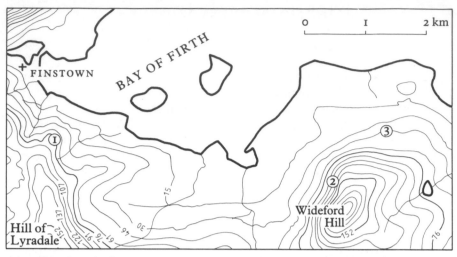

(a) Chambered cairns: 1 Cuween, 2 Wideford Hill, 3 Quanterness

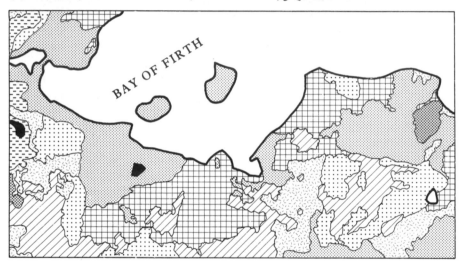

(b)

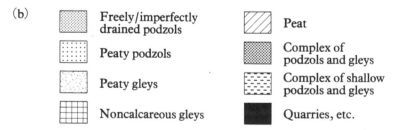

	Freely/imperfectly drained podzols		Peat
	Peaty podzols		Complex of podzols and gleys
	Peaty gleys		Complex of shallow podzols and gleys
	Noncalcareous gleys		Quarries, etc.

FIGURE 2.5. (a) Topography and cairn location between Finstown and Kirkwall, Mainland. (b) Soil types in the Finstown–Kirkwall area. (Reproduced by permission of the Macaulay Institute for Soil Research and the authors.)

THE PAST

Introduction. During the last dozen years, knowledge of the prehistoric environment of Orkney has increased markedly, chiefly as a result of investigations either at or close to archaeological sites on Mainland. These investigations have been mainly palaeobotanical, with the aim of reconstructing vegetational history, and using the evidence to try to say something about climatic conditions, soil types and the effects of human activity. However, other techniques, such as molluscan analysis, and the examination of bones from archaeological sites, have widened the range of data, and provide an insight into prehistoric resource exploitation and palaeoenvironments. A range of sediments and finds have been dated by radiocarbon, and a detailed chronology built up to accompany the picture of ecological change (table 2.6).

Early Research. Before 1969, when Moar presented evidence of Late Devensian (late last glacial) and Flandrian (present interglacial) vegetation, the only palaeobotanical data consisted of records of tree remains in island peats (Traill 1868); a cursory examination by means of pollen analysis of a number of organic deposits by Erdtman (1924), which revealed woodland sometime during the Post-glacial; and a pollen and macrofossil study of samples obtained from the Maes Howe ditch during Childe's 1955 excavation. The latter were discussed by Godwin (1956), and the results indicate a largely open landscape where human influence was present.

Late Devensian to Middle Flandrian Landscapes. Moar (1969), at Yesnaby and The Loons on Mainland, concluded that the Orkney landscape between about 12000 and 8000 bc, was barren, consisting of open grassland and heath. This became better developed during the climatic warming of Late-glacial Zone II time – the so-called Allerod or Windermere Interstadial (Coope and Pennington 1977). Grasses (Gramineae), sedges (Cyperaceae), juniper (*Juniperus*), least willow (*Salix herbacea*), saxifrages (Saxifragaceae), sorrel (*Rumex*) and crowberry (*Empetrum*) were important constituents of the flora (table 2.6). Moar suggested that the early Post-glacial period was first characterised by an increasing density of heathland as the climate improved. At first, juniper dominated this heathland, then crowberry. Gradually, birch began to colonise, and was joined by hazel, to form scrub vegetation (Pollen Assemblage Zone F III at The Loons) (table 2.6). Pollen of oak (*Quercus*), elm (*Ulmus*) and alder (*Alnus*) were recorded, but these trees were not thought to be native to Orkney, although pine (*Pinus*) may have been present on the islands.

The north-eastern part of the Scottish mainland seems to have been dominated by tall herb communities and birch-hazel scrub in the mid-Flandrian (H. J. B. Birks 1977; Peglar 1979). Remains of birch, hazel and willow are quite widespread in Orkney peats. No oak or alder has been

23

British Pleistocene stage	Other sub-divisions	Radiocarbon date ad/bc / Calendar date AD/BC	Nature of vegetation	
INTERGLACIAL · FLANDRIAN	LATE FLANDRIAN (L, A, I)	Present	Agricultural land, machair, fen, tall herb and fern communities, dwarf-shrub heath dominated by heather, blanket peat with cotton grass.	
		1000 ad / 1030 AD		Blanket peat formation begins
		0 ad / 60 AD	Pasture land with grasses and ribwort. Arable land with mugwort, crucifers and cereals.	
		1000 bc / 1250 BC	Heathland dominated by heather. Machair with sea plantain and bucks-horn plantain.	
	MIDDLE FLANDRIAN (C, A, L, G)	2000 bc / 2530 BC	Tall herb and fern communities including umbellifers and polypody.	Scrub decline begins
		3000 bc / 3785 BC		
		4000 bc / 4845 BC		
		5000 bc / c 5900 BC	Birch-hazel scrub. Tall herb and fern communities.	
	EARLY FLANDRIAN (T, S, O, P)	6000 bc		Scrub development begins
		7000 bc		
		8000 bc	Denser heathland with juniper and crowberry.	
GLACIAL · DEVENSIAN	LATE DEVENSIAN LATE-GLACIAL	9000 bc	Open grassland with mugwort. Heathland with crowberry. Denser grassland. Better developed heathland with crowberry and juniper.	
		10 000 bc	Open grassland with sorrel and mugwort. Heathland with crowberry.	

TABLE 2.6. Chronology and vegetation types during the Late Devensian and Flandrian. (Chronological scheme after West 1977. Vegetational and radiocarbon data from Caseldine and Whittington 1976, Erdtman 1924, Godwin 1956, Keatinge and Dickson 1979, Moar 1969, and authors. Radiocarbon/calendar date calibration from Clark 1975.)

recovered, and records for pine are dubious.

Also from Mainland, Keatinge and Dickson (1979) have presented detailed evidence for mid-Flandrian vegetation changes. Their earliest pollen assemblages (in Zones GM-1 at Glims Moss and LS-1 at Loch of Skaill), together with radiocarbon assays, confirm and extend Moar's findings, indicating the presence until about 3800 BC of birch-hazel woodland or scrub, with willow, ferns and tall herbs also present. Slight indications of pine, oak, elm and ash are assumed to be the result of long distance transport of grains, from the Scottish mainland and/or Scandinavia. Alder pollen values rise c. 5900 BC and the elm curve declines about 3800 BC (table 2.6). Both trends, and a decline in pine values, are attributed by Keatinge and Dickson to vegetational changes on the Scottish mainland. The decline in pine, for example, may have been a reflection of the reduction in the north-western pine forests around 2600 BC as demonstrated by H.H.Birks (1975).

Initial Replacement of the Scrub. Evidence from Mainland shows that birch-hazel scrub began to be replaced by more open vegetation about 3500 BC. Pollen Assemblage Zones GM-2 and LS-2a at Glims Moss and Loch of Skaill respectively, have high values of Gramineae, ribwort (*Plantago lanceolata*) and a variety of other herbaceous taxa (Keatinge and Dickson 1979) (table 2.6). Keatinge and Dickson point out that such pollen taxa may be representative of the fen vegetation and nearby tall herb and fern communities, but suggest that in view of their substantially increased representation, a more likely explanation is to be found in vegetation disturbance. If such disturbance, involving human clearance of the scrub vegetation, occurred, it would have required less effort than traditional neolithic forest clearance which usually took place in denser woodland. Because of the relatively open nature of the early- and mid-Flandrian Orkney vegetation, where there were many naturally-occurring plants associated with a non-forested environment, it is difficut, on palynological evidence alone, to assert with confidence that the presence of such taxa is a result of human activity, However, when there is well-documented archaeological evidence, as is the case for the Orcadian Neolithic, it is reasonable to infer that high values of grass, ribwort, and a range of their herbaceous pollen taxa including cricifers (Cruciferae) and mugwort (*Artemisia*) reflect agrarian practices, probably of a predominantly pastoral kind. Moar noted that the ribwort pollen curve began to rise as birch-hazel scrub gave way to more open vegetation (Pollen Assemblage Zone F IV), and suggested neolithic agricultural activity as a possible cause.

At the Loch of Skaill, sea plantain and bucks-horn plantain (*P. coronopus*) in the pollen record for about 3800 BC suggest that machair may have begun to develop. Blown sand has been found below occupation layers dated to 3800–3300 BC at Skara Brae (D.V.Clarke 1976a and b). Also,

Keatinge and Dickson report mineral material, whose source may be aeolian, in organic sediments at Loch of Skaill and Pow. Such material may have been a response to increased on-shore wind speeds. The mineral material has a neolithic age, and, if not wind-blown, may be inwash from surrounding slopes, where scrub clearance had taken place.

Molluscs provide corroborative evidence of the replacement of woodland by more open vegetation in the mid-Flandrian. In what is considered to be a neolithic context at Skara Brae and Buckquoy, Spencer (1975) reports that land snails, including *Carychium* and *Discus*, indicative of woodland and occurring in buried soil, are replaced by taxa such as *Vallonia excentrica* and *Pupilla muscorum* in the overlying shell sands. Evans (1977) suggests that the buried soil at Skara Brae is more or less contemporary with the earliest neolithic occupation, and proposes, on molluscan evidence, that it supported a vegetation including grassland and scrub woodland, an interpretation which is consistent with the gleyed nature of this palaeosol. There also seems to have been a degree of neolithic woodland clearance prior to sand accumulation in this locality. At Knap of Howar on Papa Westray, a neolithic settlement contains a midden (dated *c.* 3600 BC), which occurs over a buried soil and under blown sand. Molluscs are present and their ecology, according to Spencer (1975), is consonant with neolithic scrub clearance, which probably gave rise to the blown sand.

It is also possible that a climatic change about 4400 to 3800 BC, referred to earlier, may have been influential in vegetational modification. There is botanical evidence for lower temperatures at this time, a phenomenon also suggested by *Coleoptera* (beetles) (Osborne 1977). If such climatic change meant increased wind speeds, these could have initiated natural, or accelerated human, changes in the vegetation cover, as Keatinge and Dickson suggest, by means of physical damage and salt-spray effects.

The peak of the main Flandrian sea-level rise is recorded by a flooding of the sea into the Bay of Skaill at about 4900 BC. An intertidal reed (*Phragmites*) peat has been identified, which implies that the bay was once a freshwater loch. Invasion by the sea, with the formation of a sandy beach, and the initiation of sand-blow is dated sometime between 4600 and 3800 BC. The deposition of these calcareous sands caused an abrupt change in soil formation and probably had much to do with the formation of considerable areas of open vegetation, perhaps even before the first neolithic settlements.

The Later Neolithic Environment. A number of other sites provide environmental evidence and radiocarbon assays to confirm neolithic activities in Orkney. However, such evidence almost certainly post-dates the initial clearance of birch-hazel scrub, and suggests a predominantly open landscape dominated by herbaceous vegetation, the archaeological context of which is Late Neolithic (table 2.6). At Lesliedale Moss, sediments dated to about 2300 BC have low tree and shrub pollen totals, and considerable herbaceous and dwarf-shrub values, particularly of ribwort, sorrel, members of the rose family (Rosaceae), and heather (*Calluna*), suggesting agrarian, probably mainly pastoral, practices in the locality (Davidson, Jones and Renfrew 1976; R. L. Jones 1979).

Around Maes Howe a similar, virtually treeless landscape is depicted about 2600 BC, a finding supported by pollen analyses at the Stones of Stenness (Caseldine and Whittington 1976). At Maes Howe, Pollen Assemblage Zone MNH-1 reflects mixed agricultural practices, probably with a pastoral bias – there is a substantial amount of ribwort pollen, but also that of cereals. At Stenness, oat (*Avena*) and wheat (*Triticum*) pollen, and barley (*Hordeum*) macrofossils (MacLean 1976) have been identified.

At the Quanterness chambered tomb (Renfrew 1979), the earliest radiocarbon date is 3420 ± 110 BC (Q-1294) from the lowest stratum in the tomb. There are bone records of red deer, horse, sheep, ox and pig from neolithic strata which document the pastoral element in the economy at this time. Sheep bones are most frequent, and if their presence is not solely the result of a funerary tradition, their occurrence strengthens the case for the presence of an open and rather sparse vegetation (Clutton-Brock 1979). Bird-bone data from Quanterness indicate that buzzard (*Buteo buteo*) and goshawk (*Accipiter gentilis*), usually woodland inhabitants, were present in the Neolithic (Bramwell 1979). This may support the contention that some areas of scrub woodland survived, although both birds will occupy open terrain if an adequate food supply is available. Frequent birch and willow charcoal of neolithic age have been reported from Quanterness (Sheldon 1979). Fish remains from the same site indicate substantial use of intertidal and deeper water marine resources, in addition to those provided by farming. The fish bones also suggest, notably by the presence of remains of the currently Mediterranean/Atlantic distributed corkwing wrasse (*Crenilabrus melops*), that the Orkney sea temperatures in the Neolithic were slightly higher than those of the present (Wheeler 1979).

Bronze Age Environments. Archaeological evidence of Early Bronze Age dwellers in Orkney is scanty. Pollen diagrams covering this time, for example, Lesliedale Moss and Maes How (Davidson, Jones and Renfrew 1976; R. L. Jones 1979) and Glims Moss (Keatinge and Dickson 1979) reflect a lowering in the scale and intensity of farming which, however, remained mixed. There was also some regrowth of scrub vegetation. Evidence has been obtained from blanket peats at Burn of Rusht, Mid Hill and Braes of Aglath, of renewed agricultural activity which began about 1800 and lasted until *c.* 400 BC, hence spanning the Middle and Late Bronze Age and Early Iron Age (Keatinge and Dickson 1979). At these blanket peat sites, a pre-peat vegetation of open birch-hazel woodland with a well-developed ground flora of tall herbs and ferns, was replaced by grassland, where ribwort, members of the buttercup and daisy families (Ranunculaceae and Compositae) were frequent. The decline in scrub woodland occurs at the peat-soil interface, where carbonised woody material was recorded. Peat began to form at Burn of Rusht, Mid Hill and Braes of Aglath between 1800 and 1300 BC. A similar pollen spectrum is recorded from the base of blanket peat at Wideford Hill (Assemblage Zone WH-1) (R. L. Jones 1979), and although there are no radiocarbon dates for this profile, its age is probably analogous to the other blanket peat sites. Possible reasons for the inception of blanket peat growth have been explored by Moore (1975) and others, and may involve either natural or human factors, or a combination of both. There may have been a colder and wetter climatic phase beginning about 1900 and heightening around 1200 BC, according to Frenzel (1966), which would have favoured peat growth in suitable locations (table 2.6). Moore suggested that tree-felling would have led to an increase in the volume of groundwater, a rise in water-table and the accumulation of organic matter above existing soils. Whatever the cause of blanket peat formation in Orkney, the palynological evidence allows the inference that grazing pressure increased on the Mainland hills around 1900 BC. The blanket bog was probably the first peat to be utilised as fuel – the valley mires were not really suitable for this purpose (Keatinge and Dickson 1979). Hence, prior to the formation of blanket peat, brushwood, or some alternative combustible such as turf or seaweed was likely to have been used as fuel by prehistoric peoples.

Other sites support the notion that Middle and Late Bronze Age times were important agriculturally. At Loch of Skaill, there is a decline in hazel pollen and an increase in indicators of arable farming about 1300 BC. From the Bay of Birsay, a radiocarbon assay of 1606 ± 190 BC (GU-1222) from a midden overlying a buried soil confirms a similar Bronze Age context (Donaldson, Morris and Rackham 1981). Carbonised naked barley, together with a wide range of animal and fish bones at this site reflect a major dependence on the local environment for food.

The preliminary report on the soil survey of Orkney stresses the important role of man in influencing soils (Macaulay Institute for Soil Research 1978). The cultivation and husbandry of widely-distributed natural peaty gley and peaty podzol soils led to the development of a thick topsoil in particular locations. The application of seaweed and farm manure assisted in soil accumulation; and paring, whereby turf first used as bedding for animals was later applied to fields, may also have been important. This process leads to the formation of man-made or plaggen soils, which also occur in extensive areas of north-east Europe (de Bakker 1979). There is evidence to suggest that plaggen formation was already under way in prehistoric Orkney. At the site of Skaill, in Deerness, P. Gelling has identified an intricate pattern of plough marks in a buried soil. Limbrey (1975) has investigated this soil and she describes it as a buried podzol. She suggests that the land surface during the Late Bronze Age, or possibly earlier, had been ploughed and fertilised. The age of this buried soil may have to be revised in the light of radiocarbon dating from the Skaill site. The soil was, however, buried by wind-blown sand before Viking times. Indeed, changes in soils are intimately connected with coastal changes in the Orkneys. A change in sea level of as little as ± 1.0 m would have a marked effect on both the drainage conditions of coastal plains, and on the configuration and extent of lochs, which are at present separated from the sea by a slight drop in elevation. The critical issue is the detailed pattern of sea-level changes during the Flandrian in Orkney, and evidence of these is sparse. As noted earlier, it is generally accepted that the Orcadian coast is one of submergence, with a gradually rising sea level producing the present intricate archipelago. A buried soil at St Peter's Pool, Deerness is mantled by stratified beach deposits at c. 1 m OD (Limbrey, personal communication). If this soil, like that at nearby Skaill, is of Bronze Age date, then a subsequent rise in sea level is suggested. Other tantalising evidence is occasionally present along the shores of some of the lochs, where small, cliff-like notches, about 0.5–1.0 m above OD occur (plate 2.2). Such features are present at Tankerness (HY524093), and Loch of Harray (HY 308139). At Tankerness (Lamb, personal communication), prehistoric structures were discovered during a period when water-level was low in the loch. The obvious implication is that drainage conditions in coastal situations, with feedback along the low-lying loch shores, have deteriorated over the last few millennia.

The other relevant components of coastal change are accretion and erosion. Shingle bars (ayres) have formed at the head of many bays, often impounding bodies of water (oyces) (plate 2.3). The formation of ayres and oyces reflects a gradual lowering of land relative to sea. One effect of ayre formation is to impede drainage in tributary areas, where the extension of peat, and peaty gley or gley soils is thus encouraged.

The other accretionary coastal component is wind-blown sand (plate 2.4). As noted above, sand-blow probably began about 3800 BC. However, it is likely that aeolian deposits in Orkney (figure 2.3) have evolved over a number of time-spans, and not necessarily in a synchronous manner. Such blown sand must, as Donaldson, Morris and Rackham (1981) suggest for the Bay of Birsay, have reduced the coastal agricultural zone where it formed dunes. However, it did also spread as sheets, which provided useful tracts of land for farming, notably pastoral.

A range of archaeological sites provide evidence of Middle and Late Bronze Age environmental conditions. These include Maes Howe, the Stones of Stenness, the 'burnt mounds' of Liddle, Beaquoy and Fan Knowe, and the barrow cemetery of Quoyscottie. At Maes Howe, from

PLATE 2.1. Glacial trough, South Burn, Rackwick, North Hoy.
(Courtesy of the Nature Conservancy Council.)

PLATE 2.2. The eastern edge of the Loch of Tankerness. The loch may
once have had a slightly higher level, as suggested by the small
raised platform currently being eroded. (D.A.Davidson.)

PLATE 2.3. The formation of a shingle bar (an ayre) at the mouth of the
Graemeshall Born in Holm has led to the development of a small
loch (an oyce). Scapa Flow is in the background. (D. A. Davidson.)

PLATE 2.4. Machair at Mae Sand on Westray. (Courtesy of the
Nature Conservancy Council.)

about 2000 BC to the end of the Bronze Age, there is pollen evidence (from Assemblage Zones MHN-2 and MHS-1 of the ditch sequences, together with that from the lower peat layer on the mound platform) of predominantly herbaceous vegetation, although with some limited, temporary resurgences of hazel scrub (Davidson and Renfrew 1976; R. L. Jones 1979). Agrarian activity was varied and included growing. The West Ditch Terminal at Stenness provides a similar sequence of landscape history, with presumed Bronze Age agrarian phases of varying intensity envisaged by Caseldine and Whittington (1976). Thermoluminescence dates signify that the burnt mounds of Liddle, Beaquoy and Fan Knowe, were formed between c. 1000 and 400 BC (Huxtable, Aitken, Hedges and Renfrew 1976). Pollen re-covered from soils and peat buried beneath these monuments (R. L. Jones 1975) indicates the local existence of some scrub woodland, a substantial proportion of heather-dominated heathland, and a fairly low level of agri-cultural activity. As such events pre-date the mounds, they are assumed to represent earlier Bronze Age practices, during which time the landscape was recovering after the rather intensive late neolithic husbandry. The pollen spectra from beneath the barrow cemetery at Quoyscottie are fairly similar to those from beneath the burnt mounds (R. L. Jones 1977). The landscape was open, and there was agrarian activity, including some cereal growing. At Liddle, peat infilling part of the structure has a radiocarbon date of 1185 ± 110 BC (SRR-525) at its base. The pollen record from this peat indicates that human influence was greater than during the time recorded in the buried soil at the site.

In terms of environmental history, the climatic deterioration referred to earlier may be relevant in a Middle and Late Bronze Age context. According to Stuart Piggott (1972), its major impact in Britain may have come around 1300 BC. Cultivation limits were then probably lowered, principally perhaps due to an increased bog and heath cover, which reduced the area available for easy cultivation (S. E. Øvrevik, this volume). Peat seems to have been widely used at burnt mound sites. If, as envisaged earlier, blanket peat formation became widespread around 1800 BC, some would have been available for combustion in the first millennium BC. Alternatively, the resurgence of scrub woodland indicated by the pollen diagrams covering this period could have given a source of fuel. Ritchie and Ritchie (1974) report birch and hazel charcoal associated with a Bronze Age site at Queenafjold, Mainland, which lends some support to this hypothesis. There is evidence of significant heathland clearance around the burnt mound sites prior to the inception of farming. At Liddle, arable farming and disturbed soils are indicated, while grazing was practised too, as part of a mixed economy.

The Iron Age Environment. The agrarian practices of Middle and Late Bronze Age times appear to have continued in the Iron Age, according to various pollen diagrams. A well-documented worsening of climate occurred about 600 BC, when conditions became wetter (Godwin 1975). This must have led to a further restriction of available agricultural land with a corresponding increase in bog and heath vegetation. This is borne out by the pollen record, as also is a fair amount of husbandry. For example, at Glims Moss and Loch of Skaill, peaks in ribwort and mugwort pollen in Assemblage Zones GM-3 and GM-4, and LS-2, may, according to Keatinge and Dickson (1979) represent iron age agricultural activity. The expansion of heather at the start of Pollen Assemblage Zone GM-4 at Glims Moss could have also been a result of widespread heath formation at this juncture, although, as Keatinge and Dickson point out, its local growth on the mire may have been mainly responsible. Assemblage Zone LM-3 at Lesliedale Moss indicates little tree and shrub pollen, and much of dwarf-shrubs and herbs, many of the latter perhaps representing agricultural activity. Similarly, Assemblage Zone WH-2 at Wideford Hill has a majority of heathland and grassland pollens referable to this time period (Davidson, Jones and Renfrew 1976; R. L. Jones 1979).

At the archaeological sites, a number of palaeobotanical and radiocarbon findings relevant to the Iron Age landscape have been made. The upper peat layer on the mound platform at Maes Howe has a heather-dominated pollen assemblage, and contains cereal and other agrarian indicator pollen. At the Ring of Brogar, radiocarbon dates for the basal organic deposit in the ditch have a mean of around 400 BC, and the associated pollen assemblages cover the last part of the first millennium AD. The environmental mosaic was evidently rather different hereabouts. Varied farming activities are portrayed, but there is less heathland pollen, than, for example, at nearby Maes Howe (R. L. Jones 1979). Supplementary environmental data for this period comes from the Quanterness settlement, or 'Round House', whose average age in its first phase is c. 700 BC, and in its second phase, about 200 BC. Bones of cattle, sheep and deer were recorded, indicating a subsistence economy, perhaps with a pastoral bias (Clutton-Brock 1979).

The Pre-Norse and Norse Environment. Some of the available palynological data undoubtedly covers the pre-Norse and Norse periods, and a limited amount extends towards the present. However, its collection was not specifically concerned with the environment of historical time. Hence the sampling strategy for pollen analysis tends to mitigate against detailed palaeoecological inferences. General trends at this time may be discerned with reference, for example, to Pollen Assemblage Zone LM-3 at Lesliedale Moss which indicates a further expansion of heathland, very low tree amounts and phases of agricultural activity of a mixed nature. More detail is forthcoming from Pollen Assemblage Zone MHS-2 at Maes Howe. This begins in the Pictish period about 300 AD, and continues beyond 725 AD into

Norse time. It portrays much heathland and a balance of arable and pastoral farmland (Davidson, Jones and Renfrew 1976).

The best pre-Norse and Norse environmental data comes from several archaeological sites in the Bay of Birsay (Donaldson, Morris and Rackham 1980) and from nearby Buckquoy (A. Ritchie 1977). At Birsday, pre-Norse and Norse material has been radiocarbon assayed, mainly to the later part of the first millennium AD. Charcoal of birch, hazel and willow/aspen may indicate the local presence of scrub woodland until Norse time, but molluscan evidence from Buckquoy suggests grassland close at hand (Evans and Spencer 1977). There were plenty of domestic animals, including cattle, sheep and deer at both sites, while Birsay yielded macrofossils of barley and oats, denoting arable farming in the locality. Marine mammals, fish and wildfowl also formed an important part of pre-Norse and Norse diets in this region, according to the bone remains.

CONCLUSION

The Orcadian landscape of today is developed on numerous fairly small islands. Their topography is sculptured in relatively soft rocks, and is generally subdued, principally as a result of Tertiary and Pleistocene geomorphological processes. Save in certain exposed coastal areas, this means that the geomorphic environment is a fairly low-energy one. For instance, there are no major river systems on the islands. The climate of the archipelago is also influenced by the small size of its component land masses, by general maritime features, notably the North Atlantic Drift; and by strong winds which give rise to marked problems of exposure.

The soils are predominantly peaty podzols, peaty gleys and gleys, and there is a substantial extent of blown sand and peat. Within the limit of cultivation, the soils are often drained and fertilised, so that over one half of the islands' area is cultivated primarily for pasture. Most of the remaining vegetation is semi-natural, has many montane characteristics due to the exposure factor, and consists mainly of grass and heath communities, together with wetlands. Trees are conspicuous by their absence.

The palaeoenvironmental record implies that during the tenure of the Orkneys by prehistoric and historic peoples, which began about 3800 BC, a number of major environmental facets have remained substantially unchanged. However, the effects of the successive cultural groups have been considerable, notably in respect of vegetation disturbance and soil change as a result of agricultural practices. Pollen evidence indicates that by c. 5900 BC, a climax vegetation of birch-hazel scrub with an understorey of tall herbs and ferns clothed the islands. Palynological and molluscan data shows that this began to be replaced about 3800 BC by more open vegetation. Such vegetation change was probably brought about by neolithic settlers. It is also possible that an overall climatic deterioration that began about 3800 BC and has continued until the present (aided by means of increased on-shore winds that caused physical damage to plants), intensified salt-spray and initiated sand-blow. By about 2600 BC, in the Late Neolithic, there was virtually no tree cover remaining, and the landscape was one of predominantly herbaceous and dwarf-shrub heath vegetation within which mixed farming, perhaps with a pastoral bias, was being practised. Indeed, by 2600 BC the major semi-natural components of the Orcadian vegetation seem to have begun to resemble those of the present. By about 1300 BC, there would have been even more similarity, as now peat growth became extensive on the uplands, and heathland vegetation covered more areas. Farming was carried on, however, notably in Middle and Late Bronze Age times, and in the succeeding Iron Age and Norse Period, but there is little doubt that the amount of available agricultural land was reduced considerably as climatic deterioration and soil exhaustion rendered much marginal upland unworkable. A number of palaeosols, whose types are similar to present-day soils, have revealed evidence of cultivation and fertilisation, which seems to have begun in neolithic and intensified in bronze age time in selected localities.

Finds of artefacts and bones associated with particular cultures have afforded clues to diet and economy, as well as providing additional environmental data. Imprints of barley on pottery, macrofossils of cereals, bones of oxen, sheep, deer, pigs and goats, together with those of fish and sea birds support the notion of a mixed economy in an open landscape, where arable and pastoral farming, fishing and hunting were tapping a large number of environmental resources as a means of subsistence (Childe 1962; Davidson, Jones and Renfrew 1976). The bulk of the palaeoenvironmental evidence points to the major landscape components of relief, climate, soil type and vegetation cover as having changed relatively little since neolithic time. However, it is clear that successive cultural groups have brought about significant modifications to certain areas, notably by means of agricultural land use in the vicinity of their settlement and funerary sites.

3 Anna Ritchie **The First Settlers**

The islands of Orkney were supporting a permanent human population at least five and a half thousand years ago. These inhabitants had an astounding skill for building in stone, and many of their tombs and some of their houses have survived in remarkable condition. They practised mixed farming, exploited the sea for food as well as transport, made their own pottery and tools and created a self-sufficient economy that remained the basis of Orcadian life down to recent times.

The simple question of exactly when man first came to live in Orkney is frustratingly difficult to answer. Commonsense suggests that the islands must have been explored by people based on the Caithness coast long before anyone took the final step of crossing the Pentland Firth to set up permanent home, but the archaeologist is dependent upon material traces for information and such exploration need leave few tangible clues. Moreover, it is along the Orcadian shores that one might expect to find the earliest evidence of human activity, and those shores have changed dramatically over the last six thousand years; gradual submergence and cliff erosion have combined to destroy the fringes of the early landscape. The tombs and settlements that survive tell us of long-established neolithic communities, not of their pioneering forebears, and we know nothing of the foraging visits by mesolithic fishermen that may have created a store of knowledge about the islands many years before colonisation began.

Claims have nevertheless been made for the presence in Orkney of mesolithic communities (Laing 1974, 25), based on surface finds of flint tools which Lacaille has described as possessing an 'archaic aspect' (1954). This material is insufficient as evidence of a truly mesolithic phase of activity and is best seen, as Lacaille saw it, as an archaic survival in a post-mesolithic context. Mesolithic economy in Scotland is thought to have been based on fishing, plant collection and hunting in that order of importance (Mellars 1976), and, although the fishing was good, the attraction of Orkney must have been marginal for plant collection and non-existent for hunting. A beautiful flaked flint axe found on Fair Isle (Lacaille 1954, 274, fig.121) is almost certainly an imported heirloom. At present the most northerly evidence of mesolithic activity is provided by the flint tools from Freswick Bay in Caithness (Lacaille 1954, 185, fig.72; A.Morrison 1980, 164, fig.7.8). The chronological overlap between mesolithic and neolithic sites indicated by radiocarbon dates (A.Morrison 1980, fig.7.11) provides one aspect of the context in which an intermingling of flint-working traditions could have occurred. Recent studies have emphasised the advantages of a mesolithic life-style, and it is clear that, if their handling of natural resources were efficient, the effort involved in food-production would not necessarily appear attractive to indigenous food-gatherers, and a mesolithic way of life could easily survive alongside a technically more advanced neolithic system. This is particularly true of littoral communities, where the exploitation of fish and shellfish resources is not limited by the seasonal factors governing the availability of most plants and animals (Evans 1975, 105) and where, in the winter months, red deer become an additional local asset (Mellars 1976, 377).

On present evidence, then, it would seem that Orkney presented a virtually empty landscape to neolithic man, empty at least of permanent human settlement, as the earliest neolithic settlers gazed across the Pentland Firth. For Orkney is clearly visible from Caithness, and even from further south on the mainland of Scotland, while Fair Isle is at least sometimes a visible stepping-stone between Orkney and Shetland. It was almost certainly in skin-boats that the first settlers arrived in the Northern Isles, for they are far more seaworthy than dug-outs and more suited to the difficult seas of the Pentland Firth (P.Johnstone 1980, 27, 132), but it is also likely that rafts played an essential role, especially in transporting livestock. There is some evidence to suggest that sea temperatures around Orkney were warmer in neolithic times than today (Wheeler in Renfrew 1979, 149), but even so the sea voyage from Caithness to the islands must have been a cold and hazardous enterprise. It may even have been the local mesolithic fishermen who, in their skin-boats, ferried the early neolithic farmers and their animals across the Pentland Firth (P.Johnstone 1980, 132).

An unusually clear picture has survived of this early period, but there are of course still problems, some very basic and others the more refined questions that result from an already large store of information. The attraction of Orkney as a place to settle and the extent to which the Orcadian environment imposed modification of the settlers' life-style are crucial factors in understanding the process of colonisation. Clark has stressed the importance of fishing as a factor in encouraging sea travel and the discovery of new lands (G. Clark 1980, 99–100). At the same time, appreciation of the various factors is limited by the scant information available about early neolithic settlements on the mainland of Scotland, to provide a yardstick against which Orkney may be measured. Nevertheless, the basic requirements of neolithic man are clear: land suitable for mixed farming, building materials for permanent settlements, natural food resources and a reasonable climate. He was prepared to trade or exchange if necessary for portable goods.

The climate and landscape of Orkney were not only suitable but, in comparison with the northern mainland of Scotland, preferable, and what the islands lacked in timber for building was amply recompensed by the quality of their stone. There was suitable stone for axes, and a supply of beach pebble flint and chert that was adequate, if far from ideal, for smaller tools. Materials for making pottery were to hand. The major drawback is likely to have been the lack of wood, not so much in size and quantity but in variety. Early man is known to have appreciated the different qualities and potential uses of the various woods and wood barks available in the Temperate forest (G. Clark 1980, 42), and the neolithic craftsman in Orkney is likely to have felt frustrated at being unable to obtain locally the ideal woods for his purpose – such as pine for arrow shafts. Supplies of birch and hazel were available, and knowledge of the flexible and water-resistant qualities of hazel bark is demonstrated by its use at Rinyo to line drains (Childe and Grant 1939, 18). Post-sockets for roof-supporting timbers at Knap of Howar indicate posts up to 120 mm in diameter, but there is no way of identifying the wood or of determining whether this timber was home-grown, imported or derived from driftwood.

It is unlikely that the islands were already populated by the larger wild animals; Clutton-Brock has pointed out that any mammals present in Orkney before the arrival of man must either have swum there or have survived from the cold conditions that prevailed before the islands were cut off from the mainland of Scotland (1979, 113). This relict fauna would not have included cattle, sheep, pigs or even red deer, and although the latter are good swimmers it is thought that they too were introduced by man and either kept in a domestic context or released to breed naturally (Renfrew 1979, 120). Once in Orkney, deer could have swum to the smaller islands without human help. The practical difficulties for the early settlers of transporting livestock across the Pentland Firth must have been daunting, even assuming that they would wait for good weather and calm seas before setting out with the young animals lashed to their rafts. From neolithic times onwards, the cattle and sheep of Orkney have differed from those in

Caithness (Noddle 1978), demonstrating the success of early stock-breeding in Orkney. An additional factor in isolating the animal population of Orkney may well have been the increase in wind-speeds around 5000 BP postulated by Keatinge and Dickson (1979), which would have made sea voyages even more difficult.

The earliest radiocarbon dates from settlement sites and pollen diagrams suggest that food-producing communities were fully established in the Northern Isles by about 3500 BC. It is inherently unlikely that developed settlements such as Knap of Howar and Skara Brae should represent the homes of the first pioneering colonists; these sites are the products of a confident farming society. Typological analysis of the surviving pottery from tombs and settlements led Henshall to the conclusion that none belonged to the primary colonising phase, although the immediate origin of the colonists in Caithness is clear from the development of the Orkney-Cromarty class of tomb (Henshall 1963, 61, 117). Sea-level changes and coastal erosion have undoubtedly destroyed some of the evidence of the earliest Orcadians, but the recent discovery of extensive structural remains beneath the sand at Links of Noltland on Westray has demonstrated that there are still sites to be found.

Since we cannot yet identify the very earliest colonists, it is impossible to trace the route by which they arrived on the southern shores of the Pentland Firth, whether by way of the east or west coasts of mainland Scotland. Nor, at this remove, can we give them a name. Their skeletons allow us to picture them as physically very similar to ourselves, their average height only a few centimetres shorter than our own, but their life expectancy much briefer: a recent study of the remains of some 340 men, women and children buried in the tomb at Isbister on South Ronaldsay revealed that few adults had survived beyond their twenties (Hedges 1983a).

Similar figures were obtained from the burials at Quanterness (Renfrew 1979, 162–3) and, if they can be taken as normal, they raise some fascinating questions about neolithic society. What was the status of the few people who reached old age (around 50 years)? There would be enormous problems over transmitting knowledge and organising long-term building projects amongst such a young population, unless the elders wielded considerable authority and were venerated for their experience and wisdom. This point is particularly germane to later neolithic times when projects such as the construction of the great henge, the Ring of Brodgar, or the design and building of Maes Howe chambered tomb, demanded large-scale deployment of labour over a long period as well as sophisticated engineering and architectural expertise.

The earliest settlers need not have been tomb-builders, and there may have been a primary phase, as yet undetected in the archaeological record, during which a very limited range of neolithic activities was practised.

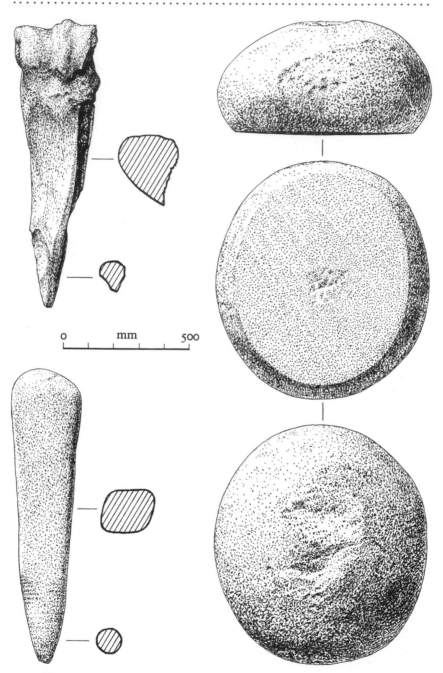

o   mm   500

FIGURE 3.1. Bone gouge, stone borer and stone grinder
from Knap of Howar.

40

There is perhaps a glimpse of this earlier life-style at Knap of Howar, with the unique survival of a tool that is more appropriate to a food-gathering community than to the level of food-production demonstrated by the rest of the economic evidence. This is a stone tool of which three examples were found on the floor of house 2 and which is best interpreted as a seed grinder. It is a circular, fine-grained stone about 90 mm in diameter, with a lower surface ground perfectly flat and a convex upper face bearing a pair of hammered indentations (figure 3.1). The flat lower surface is characterised by a central pitted hollow from 13 to 40 mm across. There are close ethnographic parallels for this tool among food-gathering societies in Africa and Australia, as well as archaeological parallels in the Later Stone Age of southern Africa (R.Inskeep in A.Ritchie 1984; Goodwin and van Riet Lowe 1929, 165–6). In the latter context, the stones were used in conjunction with a larger lower stone of trough-like form, and they relate to the grinding of wild seeds rather than cereals. The purpose of the central pit is to catch the edge of flat seeds and turn them over. D.L.Clarke has emphasised the insignificance of seeds in the mesolithic plant diet of Temperate Europe compared with that of mesolithic communities further south (1978, 30), but Orkney could not match the annual abundance of roots, nuts, berries and fungi of the Temperate forest, and must have presented a local ecology at variance with that of the true forest zone. During the initial human settlement of Orkney, wild seeds may well have made a useful contribution to the plant diet. It has been argued that there were large open areas of herbaceous vegetation already available to the first colonists (Keatinge and Dickson 1979, 604), and these included plants, such as *Rumex*, the seeds of which are known to have been used as food in prehistoric times.

SETTLEMENT AT KNAP OF HOWAR

Knap of Howar lies on the west coast of Papa Westray (NGR HY483518), one of the most northerly of the Orkney islands. The name of the site is tautologous, meaning knoll of mounds, and it is probably a good description of the appearance of the site prior to the first excavations in 1929, when it was covered by sandy hillocks. Coastal erosion had revealed an extensive midden and walling, and excavations by William Traill, the landowner, and William Kirkness uncovered two substantial stone-built houses (plate 3.1). No dating evidence was found and the high standard of the masonry was thought to indicate contemporaneity with Iron Age brochs (Traill and Kirkness 1937, 314). The site was reluctantly accepted into guardianship by the Office of Works in 1937, and its remote location and the lack of information about its date and character made it a little-visited monument. Further excavations were undertaken in 1973 and 1975 by the Department of the Environment in order to obtain dating evidence and to consolidate collapsed areas of walling (A.Ritchie 1984). The basic sequence is simple.

PLATE 3.1. House 1 before re-excavation in 1973.

A layer of midden some 0.4 m thick represents the primary phase of activity on the site but, apart from the remains of stone paving to the south of house 1, there was no trace in the excavated areas of any contemporary building (period I). The two surviving houses were then built on top of the earlier midden, house 1 first and then house 2, and an upper layer of midden some 0.20 m thick was contemporary with their occupation (period II). Both the archaeological evidence and the radiocarbon dates demonstrate that there was no cultural and no significant chronological difference between the two main periods of activity on the site. A series of nine radiocarbon dates places the occupation within the period between about 3700 and 2800 BC. The recent work involved the re-excavation of the interiors of both houses, the dismantling of some 8.5 m of collapsed house wall, the excavation of about 36 m² of midden outside the houses and of 15 test-pits, each 1 m², designed to trace the extent of the midden deposit. Kirkness had taken many photographs during the original excavation (the negatives are now in the National Monuments Record of Scotland), and these were often helpful in determining the extent of that excavation and of subsequent disturbance.

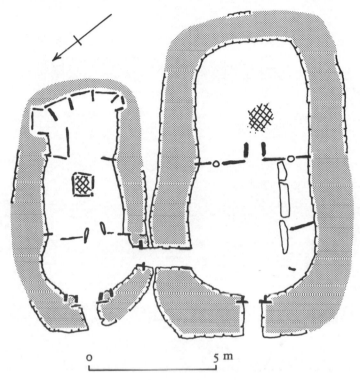

FIGURE 3.2. Plan of the neolithic houses at Knap of Howar.

House 1 was clearly the main dwelling house and had remained in use throughout period II (figure 3.2). It is rectilinear in plan with rounded corners both internally and externally, and its overall floor-area measures 10 m by 5 m. The wall is 1.5 m thick and was built with an inner and outer drystone facing, one stone thick, and a core of midden material. The inner wall-face was laid directly on the natural subsoil, whereas the outer face was built on top of the period I midden, and it appears that the primary midden cleared from the area within the house was used as core-material for the wall. The wall survives to a height of 1.60 m, and the entrance has survived intact at the W end of the house (plate 3.2). It consists of a paved and lintelled passage, 1.70 m long through the thickness of the wall, with door jambs and a sill stone at the inner end. A second passageway in the N wall leads through the walls of both buildings into house 2, with the door jambs at the latter end. House 1 is divided into two rooms by a line of four upright

PLATE 3.2. The main door into house 1, looking across Papa Sound
to Westray.

slabs and, originally, two timber posts. The outer room was paved and
furnished with a low stone bench or platform along the s wall, and nothing
remained of the original floor deposit except inside the passage connecting
the two houses. The inner room had not been cleared as thoroughly in the
early excavations, and a thin skin of original floor deposit survived, together
with a hearth in a shallow hollow and a massive trough quern. The floor was
unpaved and grooving in its surface suggested that a low wooden bench may
once have lined its walls. A small aumbry had been incorporated into the N
wall (colour plates 1, 2).

House 2 was built immediately alongside house 1, but their walls
touched only at the point of the conjoining passage. Although built in the
same way with a midden-filled wall, this house is smaller, less regular in
plan and appears to have fulfilled a different function. Internally it measures

PLATE 3.3. House 2 as seen from the main doorway, with cupboards
built into the back wall of the innermost room.

7.5 m by 3 m and survives to a maximum height of 1.26 m, and it is divided
by upright slabs into three rooms. The outer room was featureless apart
from the two doorways, one through the s wall into house 1 and the other
through the w end-wall. The latter main entrance consisted of a paved
passage, 1.5 m long, but, although one lintel at least was still in position at
the time of the original excavation, the roof of the passage no longer
survives. The internal wall-face on either side of the main entrance exhibits
a post-and-panel technique not employed at the other doorways. Both
entrance passages had been deliberately and carefully blocked in antiquity.

The small innermost room (plate 3.3) had apparently been used primarily for storage, for built into the wall were five 'cupboards' and three
shelves or aumbries, and there were two pits in the floor. The central room
appears to have been the main working area, for it contained two successive

PLATE 3.4. The middle room in house 2 with its two successive hearths.

hearths and associated floor deposits up to 200 mm thick, undisturbed by the original excavators (plate 3.4). The primary hearth was 0.65 m by 0.70 m with a substantial stone kerb and boulder floor, but the secondary hearth was of the same shallow pit type as in house 1. Although the ash from the hearths was analysed, it proved impossible to identify the fuel; it is unlikely that there was suitable peat for fuel in neolithic times, and timber was scarce, but there would have been plenty of driftwood and local brushwood, and there are good alternatives to wood for burning, including dried animal dung, turf and seaweed.

It is likely that both buildings had a hipped timber-framed roof, perhaps supported by partial corbelling of the walls at eaves level as well as by the tall upright slabs bonded into the walls and the wooden posts in house 1. They were filled with sand when first uncovered, and there does not seem to have been a significant amount of stone slabs in the filling to suggest the sort of flagstone roof-covering still in use on vernacular buildings. A simple covering of turf or thatch must be assumed. Wall foundations and paving found in the early excavations outside the main entrance into house 1 (Traill and Kirkness 1937, 310–11, fig. 1) may represent the remains of a yard or annexe, but erosion had destroyed most of this feature; it does, however, underline the fact that the site may not be as complete and discrete a unit as its surviving remains imply. The missing structures of period 1 may well have been lost into the sea.

The houses were flanked on either side by midden deposits, not in heaps but spread out to a uniform thickness of some 0.35 m over an area of about 500 m². The lower level of midden belonged to the primary period of occupation, before the surviving houses were built, while the upper level represented the domestic rubbish that accumulated during the use of those houses. The content of the two midden levels was virtually identical, indicating that there had been no change in lifestyle. The midden was rich in artefacts and organic debris, with the important exception of plant remains; one of the effects of spreading out the rubbish instead of allowing it to accumulate in piles was to expose much of it to the air, thus reducing the chances of survival for grain, seeds and even pollen. Wet sieving in the sea yielded a few carbonised grains of hulled barley, but this method was chiefly useful for the recovery of fishbones. A variety of fish were caught, indicating both inshore and offshore fishing. Young saithe, ballan wrasse and rockling were probably caught from the shore, while large saithe, cod, ling and other deep water fish are more likely to indicate line-fishing from boats 2–5 miles out to sea. There was an equally diverse exploitation of shellfish resources in which limpets were predominant but oyster, winkles, cockles and razor shell were also significant; some at least of these shellfish are likely to have been used for human consumption rather than as fishbait, but their contribution as a food source was negligible. The shells were certainly crushed to make a strengthening filler for pottery fabric. Amongst the oyster debris there were noticeably fewer bottom shells than top shells, perhaps because bottom shells are more friable and easier to crush, and, in the 1930 excavation, a pile of ground razor shells was found beside the great trough quern in house 1. Both the shellfish and the evidence from land and freshwater mollusca indicate that there has been considerable change in the environment of Knap of Howar since neolithic times. Today the site lies above a rocky shore and was, prior to the original excavation, covered by almost 3 m depth of wind-blown sand. At the time of its occupation in the late fourth millennium BC, the site appears to have been separated from a sandy shore by an extensive sand-dune system, and it probably lay in pasture-land with small freshwater pools in the vicinity. It is conceivable that Papa Westray was still joined to Westray, for the sound between the two is today very shallow in the Aikerness area. The surviving bird bones include both freshwater and sea species and, although birds were clearly not an important item in the diet, the oil obtainable from birds such as the guillemot, razorbill, puffin and great auk would have been invaluable for domestic use, especially for lighting.

As the evidence survives, Knap of Howar possessed a predominantly pastoral economy based on rearing cattle and sheep, but cultivation of cereal crops may have been more extensive than the record suggests. Soil conditions were distinctly adverse to the preservation of organic material other than bone, and to the few grains of barley found in the midden may be added three pollen grains of wheat from a buried soil horizon broadly contemporary with the site. Two querns found in house 1 may have been used to grind grain among other materials; if so, the grain is more likely to have been grown locally than to have been imported. If they have been correctly interpreted, the seed grinders suggest a methodical approach to the collection of wild plants as a food source, and they may have been used in conjunction with the querns.

Cattle and sheep appear to have been reared in equal proportions and both show evidence of fairly recent domestication: the cattle were large and closely related to the aurochs, and the sheep were a primitive form bearing poor wool. Most animals were killed young as a source of meat, hides and bone for tools. There were a few large pigs. There is little evidence of hunting among the animal bones, only a few deer, and the seal and whalebone are likely to have been derived from carrion.

The faunal evidence suggests a self-supporting farming unit, and this impression is strengthened by an artefact assemblage in which there are no detectable imports, either from outside Orkney or even from outside the Papa Westray–Westray area. The excavations have yielded a large number of artefacts, and these are likely to be a small proportion of the true total; much of the midden and the midden sealed in the house walls remains intact, and it is difficult to estimate how many finds were inevitably overlooked in the early excavations. The largest surviving but perhaps least comprehensible class of material consists of flint and chert, of which about 700 pieces were recovered, one-seventh showing traces of working, including knives and scrapers. This material is derived from the beach, where it is still washed up from marine deposits and, although the nodules can be quite large, the artefacts and debris are characteristically small, often retaining patches of cortex.

The pottery has been studied and drawn by Miss Audrey Henshall, who found parts of at least 78 pots, of which about 13 are Unstan-type bowls, about 41 are simple bowls either plain or bearing restrained decoration and about 9 are bowls with cordons or shoulders. Most are round-based but there is some evidence to suggest a few flattened bases. Unstan ware is named after the chambered tomb at Unstan on mainland Orkney, in which

1. This house, at Knap of Howar on the small island of Papa Westray, is the oldest recorded building in Orkney. Radiocarbon dates suggest that it was built about 3500 BC.

2. Knap of Howar, Papa Westray. The neolithic date of the two-house farmstead was established only during re-excavation in the 1970s. A BBC team is shown filming the excavation of the larger house.

was found a number of very distinctive shallow pottery bowls bearing finely executed decoration. Compared with the tomb pottery, the Unstan bowls from Knap of Howar are small and thin-walled, a feature which Miss Henshall considers to be perhaps of chronological significance. Their decoration is characterised by firm incised or stab-and-drag lines, together with rows of stabs. Such vessels were presumably drinking-bowls. They provide a distinctive cultural context for the site, in which the bulk of the pottery may be seen as plainer domestic Unstan ware, but there are complications. A number of features, especially the cordons and the shouldered vessels, are alien to the classic Unstan tradition and relate more to grooved ware. Moreover, only the cordons relate specifically to Orcadian grooved ware, as distinct from grooved ware generally. The social implications of this pottery evidence are at present difficult to evaluate. Petrological analysis of the pottery together with archaeological evidence of deposits of unfired clay demonstrate that all the pottery was made locally and, although four groups of pottery fabric have been distinguished, none can be correlated with any differences of style in the finished product.

A small polished stone axe, 53 mm long, was found in the primary midden, and analysis of the stone by thin sectioning resulted in its identification as a fine-grained dolomite which, like the clay for the pottery, could have been derived from a local source on Papa Westray. Polished stone axes have been found in several Orkney-Cromarty tombs, including one from Isbister on South Ronaldsay which is very similar to that from Knap of Howar.

The rest of the stone artefacts include two querns and hammerstones derived from beach pebbles, together with two unusual tool-types which may help to identify a characteristic artefact assemblage: the seed-grinders described earlier and a type of borer. There are six of the latter tool, all elongated pebbles 100–172 mm long on which one end shows intensive wear (figure 3.1).

Among the bone artefacts are both common and distinctive tools, from bone awls, pins and a needle to a small bone spoon, a whalebone spatula, a blubber knife and two examples of a unique dimpled bone gouge. Both whalebone and antler were used to make perforated mallets which must be seen as prototype maceheads, an artefact that in stone belongs to grooved ware assemblages (Roe 1968). Many of the bone tools are connected with leather-working, reflecting the importance of animal skins for clothing; at this period, the sheep were too primitive to supply adequate wool for textiles, and garments such as tunics and perhaps trousers would be made from soft calf-skin, while the hairy sheepskins would make good bedding as well as cloaks.

The identification of Knap of Howar as the home of makers of Unstan ware provided the first glimpse in Orkney of the domestic life of the people

49

who buried their dead in stalled cairns. Unstan ware was not a purely funerary type of pottery but was also the fine tableware of the living. The range of associated equipment is predictably wider in the domestic context than among the gravegoods, although few contemporary burials have survived undisturbed. The nearest excavated stalled cairn to Knap of Howar is Holm of Papa Westray North (ORK 21), one of the three chambered tombs on the tiny uninhabited holm off the east coast of Papa Westray; it was partially excavated in 1854, and has recently been re-excavated by the author on the grounds that it is the most likely candidate to have been Knap of Howar's family mausoleum. Study of the material is still in progress: not only human bones but a wide variety of animal and bird bones, with a remarkable emphasis on fishbones and deer antlers that suggests very strongly that there were totemistic ideas behind the way in which the tomb was used. In view of the fact that the only other excavated tomb on the Holm is of Maes Howe type (ORK 22), known elsewhere to have been used by the makers of grooved ware, the discovery of grooved ware outside the newly excavated stalled cairn is of special interest.

There are very close architectural links between Orkney-Cromarty chambered tombs and the houses at Knap of Howar. Upright stone slabs are used to form burial compartments in the tombs and to divide the houses into 'rooms', and low benches furnish both the tombs and the houses, built sometimes in stone and in some cases probably in wood. The internal plan of house 2 is particularly close to that of the tripartite tomb of Bigland Round on Rousay (ORK 2), and there are identical details in their construction; the cairn at Bigland Round was stripped entirely, revealing not only an inner wall-face but also upright slabs set at ground level both radially and concentric to the chamber. Excavation of the wall of house 2 at Knap of Howar, on either side of the entrance, uncovered an inner wall-face and upright radial slabs within the outer casing, the purpose of which was presumably to strengthen the wall (plate 3.5). The entrance had been carefully blocked with stones, and similar blocking has been found at several tombs, including Bigland Round.

ORCADIAN SOCIETY

Knap of Howar on Papa Westray is one of four neolithic settlements in Orkney which are well-preserved and which have been excavated to reveal considerable information about the way of life that they represent: the others are Skara Brae on mainland Orkney, Links of Noltland on Westray and, least well-preserved, Rinyo on Rousay. These last three settlements belonged to people using grooved ware, whereas the decorated pottery from Knap of Howar links the site with the makers of Unstan ware, and this cultural distinction is reiterated, apart from certain basic common elements, in the rest of the associated artefacts, including house-types as well

PLATE 3.5. The entrance in house 2, showing the inner wall-face and
upright slabs within the house wall.

as portable equipment. In chronological terms, Knap of Howar ought not to
be treated separately from the three grooved ware settlements, because the
later radiocarbon dates from Knap of Howar are contemporary with the
earlier dates from Skara Brae. Nevertheless, these settlements represent
two distinct and apparently separate cultural traditions, though not necessarily separate ethnic groups. In his discussion of the problems surrounding
the relationship of the makers of Unstan ware and of Orcadian grooved
ware, Renfrew postulated an evolution of grooved ware from Unstan ware
which began on the mainland of Orkney and then spread to the islands,
although he emphasised that this is a hypothesis that has yet to be proved
(1979, 207). The case for the chronological priority of Unstan ware rests
primarily on the radiocarbon dates. Renfrew discounted rightly (1979, 208)
the late date from Knap of Howar of 2131 ± 65 bc (SRR-452), which is a

re-run on a sample which previously had given an even more aberrant date of 3756 ± 85 bc (SRR-347); neither date can be regarded as reliable, and the acceptable radiocarbon date range for this site is 2820 ± 180 bc (Birm-816) to 2300 ± 130 bc (Birm-815), or about 3700–2800 BC. Although there is overlap, these dates as a group are earlier than those again as a group from grooved ware sites.

A major problem in deriving grooved ware from Unstan ware is, as Renfrew admitted (1979, 207), the existence of comparable grooved ware communities in southern England. D. V. Clarke has, however, argued that the contrasts in the artefact assemblages associated with the northern and southern grooved ware groups are increasing as new material is discovered, and that these contrasts are not explicable in terms of environmental differences (1976b, 240). At the same time, the links within Orkney between Unstan ware and grooved ware in terms of their respective artefact assemblages are also increasing. Stone maceheads are a grooved ware artefact, yet their antler and whalebone prototypes occur in an Unstan ware context at Knap of Howar. There are features in the pottery from the latter site that are alien to the Unstan tradition, particularly the use of applied cordons, but, as this is at present the sole domestic site in Orkney with Unstan ware, such features may be alien only to funerary pottery. Outside Orkney, Unstan ware has been found in a domestic context at Northton on Harris, along with characteristic Hebridean wares and simple undecorated bowls (Simpson 1976, 222), demonstrating that mixed pottery assemblages are possible.

There is a clear need for more Unstan ware settlements in Orkney before there can be any solution to the problem of the relationship between the makers of Unstan ware and of grooved ware. At present the differences between their associated artefact assemblages remain as striking as, and probably more significant than, the differences in pottery styles. None of the characteristic Skara Brae artefacts appears at Knap of Howar, and similarly there are distinctive tool types at present peculiar to the latter site (seed grinders and bone gouges). House-types are a major area of contrast, and it would be helpful to know whether the Knap of Howar houses are truly representative of a type that was built elsewhere in Orkney. If a real change in house-type could be demonstrated, it could help to explain the development of the Maes Howe type of tomb, for the architectural similarities between the Knap of Howar houses and Orkney-Cromarty cairns are so strong as to suggest that tombs were built as houses for the dead, emulating the houses of the living.

There are many details lacking from the impression of life in early neolithic times that survives in the archaeological record, even such basic details as whether flour was made into bread, and yet that blurred impression is familiar. Whatever barbarities existed in social behaviour and tribal ritual of which no trace remains, practical daily life can have been little different from the basic Orcadian pattern that survived until recent times. The economic realities of survival for the small farmer-cum-fisherman in a cold and demanding environment were as much a governing factor in the nineteenth century AD as in the thirty-fifth century BC.

4 D. V. Clarke, Niall Sharples Settlements and Subsistence in the Third Millennium BC

Though few in number, some of the known sites of the third millennium are quite exceptional in terms of the quality and range of the material preserved. Most of our information comes from the three villages at Skara Brae on Mainland (Childe 1931; Clarke 1976a), Rinyo on Rousay (Childe and Grant 1939; 1947) and Links of Noltland on Westray (Clarke, Hope and Wickham-Jones 1978). Recent excavations at Pierowall Quarry, Westray, have revealed a badly damaged structure. Chance finds at three other sites on Mainland – Dingieshowe, Sands of Evie (Stevenson 1946, 142–3) and Saevar Howe (Farrer 1864, pl.1.4) – and one on Sanday – Bay of Stove (RCAMS 1980, 16, no.70) – may represent further settlements but no structures have been positively identified (figure 4.1). Of these, Skara Brae is undoubtedly the best surviving prehistoric settlement in northern Europe and the continuing excavations at Noltland suggest that there too the structures will be similarly well preserved.

Before looking at these sites in more detail let us enter a *caveat*. Orkney and its remains form part of a wider province embracing Shetland and the northern mainland of Scotland. Neither of these areas has yet produced structures comparable to those found on Orkney but artefacts found in Caithness at Freswick (L. Scott 1951, 73) and Keiss (unpublished finds in National Museum of Antiquities of Scotland) and at Jarlshof in Shetland (e.g. Hamilton 1956a, 23 and 28, fig.13.3) suggest that such sites might yet be recognised. With only a small number of finds from these two districts, the emphasis naturally falls on the similarity between these objects and examples discovered on Orkney. When we have settlements comparable to Skara Brae and Noltland in other areas of northern Scotland, the differences

54

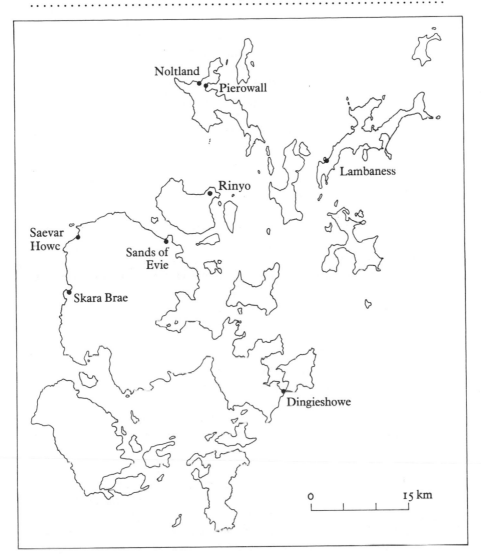

FIGURE 4.1. Grooved ware sites in Orkney.

between the various villages may well assume an equal importance for more general interpretations. This point is relevant to our consideration of the finds from Orkney. In attempting to relate finds from several sites, emphasis is first given to points of similarity and the more we discover the more confident one is that what they represent is membership of a social grouping embracing a number of individual sites. Once this relationship between sites has been established then, by analysing the differences between or

55

within sites, we will begin to gain an understanding of the social systems operating within the larger grouping already defined. No serious study has yet been directed towards identifying, quantifying and explaining such differences in the rich assemblages from Orkney and we will not be able here to offer more than a few unsubstantiated hints. Nevertheless it is important to remember these differences and their potential when reading a chapter such as this one which largely concentrates on points of similarity.

If a concern with similarity underlies any recognition of particular groupings within Orkney, and indeed in contiguous areas, it is harder to place these Orcadian groups in a wider, British context. It has been generally accepted for over forty years that the pottery recovered at sites like Skara Brae and Rinyo forms part of a potting tradition, found throughout Britain and known as Grooved Ware (figure 4.2) (the term is something of a misnomer since much of the decoration, particularly in Orkney, comprises plastic ornament rather than grooving). Within the substantial corpus now available, various styles have been defined (Wainwright and Longworth 1971, 235–44) but the overall unity of the pottery has never been seriously or at least convincingly questioned. What this ceramic tradition means in human terms is, however, far from clear. Earlier views that it indicated a 'culture' (Piggott 1954, 321–46: admittedly involving other material in the description of the culture but wholly dependent on the pottery for the original formulation) have now been modified to a 'sub-culture' (Wainwright and Longworth 1971, 268). The term 'sub-culture' is, we are told, 'normally employed to describe a part of the total culture of a society which is distinctive of a segment of that society, e.g. an ethnic group, a social class group or a regional group'. Whether one adopts the culture or sub-culture view, the evidence from Orkney, other than that of the pottery, is not readily reconcilable with the evidence from farther south. It would be a mistake to suppose that these problems of integration and understanding are in any way restricted to Orcadian material, although this does show the difficulties in their extreme form. Comparable quandaries exist in analysing any of the British evidence for this period (Bradley 1982).

Despite these inherent difficulties in analysis, a great deal of information is available about the grooved ware groups (we retain the term for convenience). The most remarkable and immediate feature is that settlement, as far as we can tell, was concentrated in villages. Villages are today a commonplace in our experience but in third-millennium-BC Britain such settlements were extremely rare – where the evidence exists, the picture is almost entirely that of the single farmstead with ancillary buildings as at Knap of Howar (figure 4.3). Even in areas like Shetland, where the evidence for this period is especially well preserved, the houses, although not particularly distant from one another, nevertheless appear to stand within their own plots of land (Whittle 1980). The Orcadian sites provide a

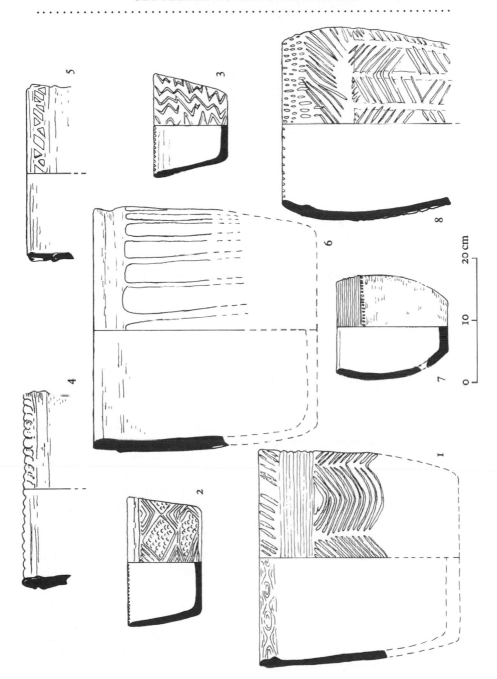

FIGURE 4.2. Grooved ware from Britain: 1 Clacton; 2–3 Greeting
St Mary; 4–6 Skara Brae; 7–8 Durrington Walls.

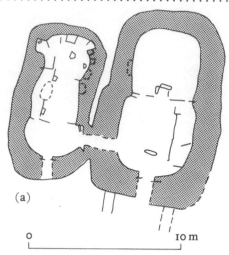

(a)

0   10 m

FIGURE 4.3. Village and farmstead: (a) Knap of Howar;
(b, *facing*) Skara Brae (at same scale).

marked contrast to this image. The houses cluster together, linked by passages rendered necessary by the semi-subterranean nature of the houses' construction. Ancillary buildings lie adjacent to but not interspersed amongst this central nucleus of houses.

THE SETTLEMENTS

This pattern can be best seen at Skara Brae where the fine preservation of the later-phase village has removed some of the ambiguities associated with the more ruined remains at Rinyo; at Links of Noltland excavation has not yet been sufficiently extensive to locate with confidence the domestic area. The second phase village at Skara Brae consisted of at least six houses (more may have been lost through coastal erosion), all except one linked by a main passage running the length of the village. The one exception, house 7, is entered from a separate passage running at right angles to the main passage.

Each of these houses is closely comparable in terms of construction techniques, size and internal layout, and all are surrounded by midden material. This material is not rubbish dumped by the inhabitants of the houses which it surrounds. The creation of the midden heap is the first stage in the construction process. Since structures of the earlier village have been located below these houses this midden material must have been carefully stored elsewhere for future use; the West Midden at Noltland which extends over an area of at least 1100 m² may well represent material stored in just this way but never used. The processes involved in constructing the later-phase village at Skara Brae are complex but in essence they seem to

(b)

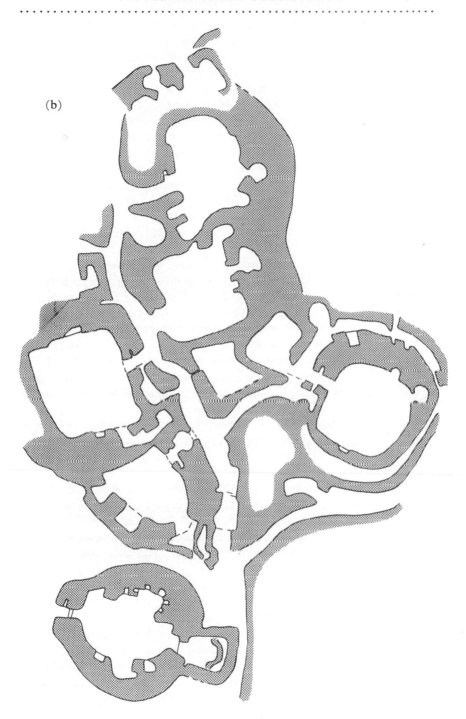

have involved the creation of a mound of midden material which had previously decayed, a period in which this material was allowed to consolidate and finally, the setting of houses into previously left or newly excavated depressions. All the evidence from the recent excavations at Skara Brae points to this basic sequence but we do not know if the midden dome which we can now see is the result of a single major operation or, perhaps more likely, the product of several such operations as additional houses were built. Certainly, the passages, which are similarly set in channels cut or left in the midden heap, were not all built at the same time (D. V. Clarke 1976a, 17). We have no evidence to show whether the houses were similarly constructed in phases though their plans strongly suggest this possibility. There must have been a strong desire for semi-subterranean houses if recourse was made to artificial means in order to create them in the absence of a suitable natural alternative. We see the same processes at the other settlements: at Rinyo the slope of the hillside was cut back and augmented by the use of midden material, and at Noltland a high sand dune was dug into and the hollow lined with midden against which the walls of the structure were set. It is difficult, particularly in the case of the structure at Noltland, to believe that the use of this technique was dictated solely by practical considerations such as improved weatherproofing of the houses. Indeed, structure 8 at Skara Brae, a workshop, is entirely freestanding and shows that a semi-subterranean situation was not thought appropriate for all buildings. Nevertheless, the use of this technique does seem to have produced particularly stable structures, as the preservation at Skara Brae and Noltland shows, and afforded protection to the inhabitants, especially against animals. Whether or not it was a reason for adopting this form of construction, this image of close-set houses linked by passages and surrounded by midden or other material creates a strong impression of a group with a highly developed sense of community.

The individual houses at Skara Brae and Rinyo, by their similarity, do much to reinforce this impression of a close-knit community. All consist of a single room (plate 4.1), square with rounded corners and, although there is some variation in size, 4.5–6 m², the differences do not appear great enough for any significance to be interpreted from them. The walls, constructed of drystone masonry with a midden core, have sufficient thickness to accommodate cells entered from the main chamber. Entry to each house was by a single, low, narrow doorway in the wall adjacent to the passage. Inside, the main items of furniture, the skeletons of which survive in stone at Skara Brae, were arranged in the same pattern in each house. In the centre was a large stone-lined hearth (plate 4.2), on the wall opposite the entrance a substantial dresser (plate 4.3) and on both side walls box beds (plate 4.4), originally with pillars to support a canopy. A number of clay-luted stone tanks, about 300 mm² and of a similar depth, have been set into the floor

PLATE 4.1. House 1 at Skara Brae.

PLATE 4.2. Stone-lined hearth.

PLATE 4.3. A dresser.

PLATE 4.4. A box bed.

PLATE 4.5. Stone tank, originally luted with clay.

PLATE 4.6. A cupboard.

PLATE 4.7. Interior of a cell.

(plate 4.5). At various points around the walls there are cupboards, the largest generally occurring above the beds (plate 4.6). Finally, each house has a number of cells which vary in size but can be entered only from within the chamber (plate 4.7; colour plate 3).

That we can speak with confidence of the interior arrangements of houses over four thousand years old is remarkable, and depends not only on the unusual quality of the flagstone used in these buildings but also on the preservative nature of the surrounding midden material; in the best pre-served houses at Skara Brae the walls still stand to a height of over 3 m. Even so there are some major points for which we have very little evidence, especially the method of roofing the houses. Discoveries in house 1 at Skara Brae, during the early excavations in the middle of the nineteenth century, suggest that it may have had a roof supported on whalebone rafters although no confirmatory evidence was discovered in any of the other houses. Cer-tainly a roof of turf or thatch supported on whalebone or timber rafters seems considerably more likely than a corbelled stone roof but no serious study has as yet been undertaken to determine the range of possibilities. Equally, we should not be misled by the presence of the major items of furniture into believing they represent the whole picture. Some pieces are clearly only the basic frame while others present varied problems of inter-pretation. The beds, for instance, must be envisaged as containing material such as mattresses made of bracken (cf. Rymer 1976) and bedclothes of

3. Skara Brae, house 7. The stone dresser, which no doubt displayed to visitors the most prestigious possessions, faces the doorway, with hearth and bench between.

4. Links of Noltland, Westray. When this excavation is complete it is expected to reveal a domestic settlement with similarities to Skara Brae. It dates from the third millennium BC.

animal skins. The canopies above the beds are more difficult since we do not know their purpose; if they were simply designed to protect the bed from water dripping from the roof then animal skins would probably have been sufficient although not necessarily the most practical solution; whereas if they were to increase the storage capacity within the house wood, or less likely stone, would require to have been used. The hearths pose a different kind of problem since there is no difficulty in envisaging their function and appearance. The question is rather what kind of fuel was burnt. Childe, the major excavator of Skara Brae, influenced probably by the present Orcadian situation had no doubt that it was peat but more recent studies suggest that the growth of peat suitable for burning did not begin in this area of Orkney until after the settlement had been abandoned (Keatinge and Dickson 1979). An adequate supply of fuel is, of course, a pre-requisite for subsistence. In Orkney at that time, with peat unavailable and wood only in the form of drift, a variety of materials were probably collected for this purpose. Among the more obvious things are animal dung, still in use until quite recently on northern isles such as Sanday and North Ronaldsay (Fenton 1972), and seaweed (Fenton 1978, 206–9: the glassy, slag-like material known as cramp, found on many Orcadian sites, may well be the accidental product of this use of seaweed) but other items such as whale and seal bone (Heizer 1963, 188) may also have been used. No doubt most fires involved a combination of fuels reflecting only their periodic availability.

Greater speculation is involved in trying to understand the use of the cells and of the clay-luted boxes set into the floors. At first sight the cells seem straightforward enough as providing extra storage space in a unit in which all activities had to take place within a single room. However, there is a considerable variety both in size and form and in the number present in each house. Accessibility to some of them seems to have been made deliberately difficult, a point given emphasis by the discovery, in one in house 1 at Skara Brae, of 2400 beads, pendants, pins and a whale vertebra dish containing red pigment. Others, apparently one in each house, have drains running from them under the floor of the house. These drains are carefully constructed so that those running from individual houses join a main drain carrying the material outside the area of the settlement; at Rinyo traces of a bark lining survived in some sections of the drains. Although not analysed, the material found in the drains is not inconsistent with the use of the cells as lavatories. We can then offer at least three possible uses for the cells as storage areas, as safes and as lavatories. The clay-luted boxes, on the other hand, exhibit such uniformity that a single common purpose may be supposed although there is little to indicate what that purpose might have been. There are generally three or four boxes in each house and the careful luting with clay implies that they were intended to contain water. Perhaps they did no more than enable the household to keep a supply of fresh water

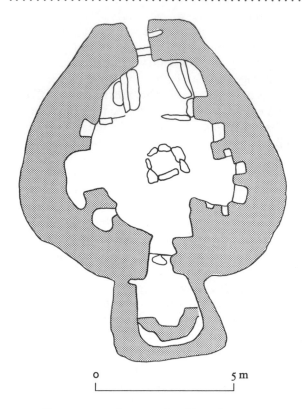

o   5 m

FIGURE 4.4. Structure 8 at Skara Brae.

for domestic purposes within the house even though a single large tank might have met the need better. However, if as seems likely the limpets found in such large numbers on these settlements were collected for use as fish bait the boxes might have had another purpose. Some use of limpet as bait requires that the limpet be soaked for about a week to soften it so that by using the tanks in rotation it would be possible to maintain a supply of fresh bait (D. V. Clarke 1976b, 243–4). These boxes are not closely comparable to the larger tanks found in the burnt mounds of Bronze Age date.

At least two structures however, one at Skara Brae and one at Noltland, do not conform either in plan or in the internal arrangement of their fittings to the pattern seen in the houses. That at Skara Brae, structure 8, is separate from the main village and not surrounded by any accumulation of midden (figure 4.4). Its maximum internal width and length are both 6 m, but in plan it is much more oval than the houses. On the south side there is a porch protecting the entrance through walls over 2 m thick; presumably this remarkable thickness compensates for the absence of a protective midden

66

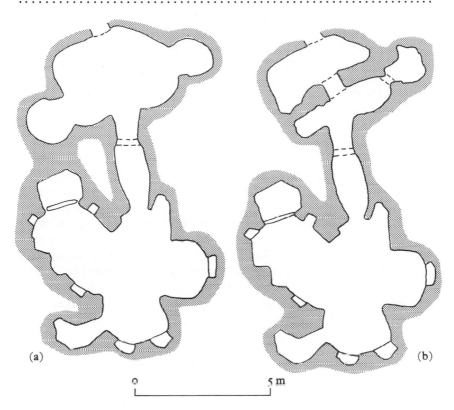

(a)   (b)

0   5 m

FIGURE 4.5. Structure at Links of Noltland.

surrounding it. Although there is a hearth in the centre and cupboards and cells in the walls, the dresser and beds are absent. Instead the walls are deeply recessed and the southern end of the building is largely partitioned off by upright slabs. Childe, in his description of this structure, noted that objects similar to those he had found in the houses were rare but that the partitioned area contained heaps of burnt volcanic stone and that on the floor were numerous small scrapers, cores and rejected flakes of black chert. 'Clearly then', he concluded, 'a flint-knapper had worked in the hut'. Whether or not it was used exclusively for the working of flint and chert, there can be no doubt that we have here a workshop rather than a house. The presence of heat-damaged volcanic stones and an apparent flue in the north end of the structure raises the possibility that the chert was being subjected to heat pre-treatment before being worked. Such a technique is well documented in the ethnographic record and involves the heating and controlled cooling of the chert nodules to improve their flaking qualities, with the use of heated volcanic stone a prime means of attaining the required temperatures. The second building, which is at Noltland, seems also to be set beyond the domestic area but is otherwise not closely comparable to the workshop just described (figure 4.5) Since excavation is not yet complete, interpretation of such matters as its function are clearly impossible but its remarkable nature merits a brief description here, if only to give emphasis to the point that the architectural uniformity already described, while real enough, is unlikely to be anything like a complete picture. It is set into a midden-lined hollow dug into a high sand dune and consists of two rooms of different shape and size linked by a narrow connecting passage some 3.5 m long. Overall the maximum dimensions of the complex are some 12 m long by 7 m broad. The smaller of the two rooms close to the entrance was rectangular with a single cell opening off each side wall. Subsequently one of these cells was sealed off and the room subdivided by a wall across it. Unlike any other Orcadian grooved ware structures, the entrance to this building has been given emphasis by being outlined in the interior with large slabs stuck onto the dry stone walling with yellow clay. The other, larger room has an irregular, lobate plan with the central area surrounded by large recesses. It does not seem to have been modified in any way during its use. The whole structure was subsequently infilled, the smaller chamber, the passage and a cell off the main chamber being packed with midden whereas the larger chamber contained large stone slabs, midden and sand. The whole process was carefully done and involved such things as building an arc of upright slabs to block off the entrance to the large room and the removal and replacement of the roofing slabs of the passage. As well as many artefacts, the midden material contained numerous skulls, a completely articulated skeleton of an otter and large wedges of compacted fish and rodent bone with no midden admixture. Lying on the rubble infill of the main chamber were two cattle skulls and an apparently articulated eagle skeleton. Although, in combination, the overall plan, the use of more than one room and the deliberate infilling find no parallels at other grooved ware sites, many of the individual elements are closely comparable to those found at Skara Brae and Rinyo (colour plate 4).

This wealth of information about the architectural environment of the inhabitants of these settlements can perhaps form a basis for imagining what life was like for an individual, but what can it tell us about the broader social structure? Largely using the evidence of the tombs it has been argued (Renfrew 1976; 1979, 199–223) that we have here the evidence for a 'segmentary society'. This involves groups (i.e. villages in this case) which are clearly defined, operate largely independently and exercise control over their productive resources. None of the groups or segments will be significantly larger than any of the others so that each, despite individual differences, is largely comparable to the others. This structure, however, was, Renfrew argued, modified around 2700 BC by centralising tendencies assuming the form of leadership controlling several groups and reflected in the archaeological record by the construction and use of the henges at Stenness and Brodgar and the monumental tomb at Maes Howe. A more recent study (Hodder 1982, 218–28) is a brief attempt to integrate the settlement and tomb evidence and in particular draws attention to the similarity in the use and arrangement of space in both the houses and tombs, a point which may have some validity notwithstanding the very considerable misuse of the data from which it is argued. With only three partially excavated villages there is not a sufficient base of settlement data by which these hypotheses might be tested. However, while no evidence from the grooved ware settlements is fundamentally at variance with the concept of a 'segmentary society' there is as yet nothing from these sites to support the idea of the emergence of a centralising tendency. Work on constructing the later phase village at Skara Brae was certainly taking place about this time but apart from minor design modifications in the interior fittings no significant changes can be discerned. There is, of course, no reason why the changes in social structure envisaged by Renfrew should be reflected on individual sites. Yet the chronological overlap between Unstan and grooved ware groups (D. V. Clarke 1983) and the marked differences of their assemblages is not explicable in terms of a segmentary society.

Further, the idea of a segmentary society with its implied egalitarianism needs to be treated with caution. Are, for instance, relations between groups to be structured on a different basis in such a society from those within groups? Equally problematic is how disputes between groups were mediated, for the settlements show no evidence of resort to physical aggression, at least in an organised way. Indeed if independent action was largely the norm for these groups, the maintenance of a uniform tradition on an inter-settlement basis for some 500 years or so becomes quite remarkable. It cannot be explained simply in terms of immigrants arriving with a package of traditions and practices already formed which the communities merely perpetuate. The long sequence at Skara Brae creates a firm picture of an innovating and adapting group not unwilling to adopt new practices in changing circumstances. Much of this is irreconcilable with the concept of a segmentary society and it does suggest that the idea will need considerable development to take account of the accumulating evidence from the settlements.

Whatever the generalised nature of the society of which these settlements formed a part, it is possible to make some suggestions concerning the social organisation within the settlements. Most of these will, however, be based on Skara Brae and this dependence on a single site makes them very tentative. There can be no doubt that life was both communal and organised – as the central nucleus of semi-subterranean houses linked by narrow passages would require. But the sense of community was not so strong that it involved a large, shared dwelling-place, such as are found among some early farming groups in continental Europe. Certainly, the domestic area seems to have been particularly well-defined but within that area there was further subdivision based on a family unit. Each of the houses seems best suited to a small group, perhaps involving only two generations, and is certainly not suitable for any kind of extended family grouping. This combination of a sense of community combined with a recognition of separate groups within the community is also reflected in some of the architectural features. The well-constructed doorways at the end of the passages undoubtedly served a very practical purpose but they also emphasise the division between the domestic and non-domestic areas. The presence of similar doors, controlled from within each house, equally acknowledge the presence of separate units within the community. Thus the architectural solutions adopted in the construction of the village can be interpreted as both supporting the cohesiveness of the community and as accepting the need for individual groups to distance themselves from that community from time to time.

It has already been noted that the difference in size between the houses is not particularly great, certainly not enough for a difference of status between the occupants to be inferred with any confidence. Nevertheless, such differences may well have been pointed out in more subtle ways. Anyone entering the houses had their view wholly dominated by the large dresser on the opposite wall (plate 4.8). This piece of furniture, as with modern examples, is designed so that its upper parts have a display area. It is not too fanciful, therefore, to suppose that the objects ranged on the shelves were intended in part as a statement of the status of the occupants. Certainly, the positioning and form of the dresser could not have been better designed for such a purpose. It is interesting to note that the dresser in more recent Hebridean black-houses seems to have had a similar role (Stoklund 1980, 131). Childe, in his discussion of the houses at Skara Brae, drew attention to another parallel with the Hebridean houses involving the arrangement of the beds. He noted that one was always larger than the other and that the larger was always on the right of the fireplace relative to the door. Such an arrangement is found in the Hebridean houses with the larger bed belonging to the man and the smaller the woman. Indeed, the hearth, with its centrally dominant position, was in the Hebrides an important means of demonstrating to the visitor his status in the eyes of the occupants. As the focal point of social activity within the house the seating position around the hearth accorded to the visitor reflected his relationship to the family. Now we know next to nothing about such provisions in the Orcadian houses which we are here discussing but it is interesting that the one item which may reasonably be interpreted as a seat, a large stone block in house 7 at Skara Brae, was positioned in what, on the Hebridean analogies, would

PLATE 4.8. View from the doorway of house 7 at Skara Brae.

be socially the most important position between the hearth and the dresser opposite the door. Of course, these interpretations can be no more than plausible suggestions but they do show that houses cannot be regarded merely as buildings providing protection from the elements but as items reflecting a wide range of economic and social functions some of which have only symbolic forms. Indeed Stoklund concluded 'in many ways the house is a reflection of the society around it. Where we find a very homogeneous building tradition and interior design we can with some certainty conclude that there is a high degree of cultural integration, a harmony regarding the goals, norms and values of life' (1980, 122). Just such a situation as this is found in the Orcadian grooved ware settlements. Moreover, where the scope for variations in the design is small, as in this case, studies of more recent dwellings suggest that the symbolic function is strongest. If then the total integration of these groups is well developed, as the evidence seems to suggest, it is not perhaps surprising that symbols indicating status should prove so elusive in the archaeological record.

THE ECONOMY

In contrast to the structural remains, the evidence for the economy of these settlements can only be interpreted in terms of the whole community. The data come in large measure from the midden heaps in which the rubbish from individual houses cannot be distinguished. Variations within the midden deposits are certainly discernible – at Noltland, for instance, large quantities of beads and bead-making debris have been recovered from one area but such material is almost wholly absent in the other excavated areas – but their significance is still far from clear. We can, then, only provide a broad sketch of the economic activities without much indication of how they were organised. It must be supposed, however, that the highly integrated nature of these settlements is indicative of a considerable degree of co-operation at community level. Certainly, one would expect the differences between these settlements and the isolated farmsteads characteristic of most early farmers in Britain to be reflected in their economic organisations, although it is difficult to distinguish those differences in the evidence available.

Quite the most important feature of the Orcadian settlements is the tremendous diversity of the environment which they could exploit. The land, already largely cleared of trees except for dwarf and isolated examples, was capable of supporting a rich pasture while, in the areas of machair at least, the light sandy soils were easily ploughed. The seas surrounding the islands were rich in many forms of marine life, probably of even greater variety than that found today. Indeed the animal and bird life exploiting this marine environment would have more than compensated for the absence of some land animals brought about by the island situation. Nor need the lack of trees have been as big a disadvantage as might at first appear. The erosion by rivers of the virgin forests of North America would have brought many large trees to the eastern seaboard of that continent and these, having subsequently floated across the Atlantic would provide a ready source of driftwood on Orkney beaches. Some of the wood, which includes actual artefacts (plate 4.9), recovered from a waterlogged midden at Skara Brae has been identified as spruce and this can only reasonably be interpreted as coming from North America. Similar finds have been made at several sites in north and west Scotland and one, at Stanydale in Shetland, provides some indication of the quantities available. There the excavator found spruce in the form of charcoal and, on the basis of the post holes, concluded that some 700 m of dressed timber would have been required to roof the structure (Calder 1950, 192). The richness of the environment and the quantities of material that it could provide is worth emphasising since there is no evidence that the inhabitants of these settlements were involved in any struggle for survival. Indeed, in the one case where we seem to have evidence of a temporary shortfall in the supply of a raw material, namely flint at Skara Brae, they seem to have been able to adapt easily to the use of the locally available, but inferior, chert.

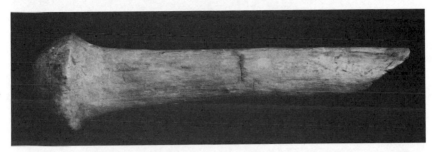

PLATE 4.9. Wooden handle from Skara Brae (203 mm long).

The food supply came largely from agricultural activities although their interpretation is made difficult by the differential survival of the evidence, which is heavily biased towards the products of animal husbandry. In the absence of any evidence to the contrary it has until recently been assumed that grooved ware groups were not involved in cereal production but were instead wholly concerned with pastoralism. Large quantities of carbonised grain, mainly barley, were, however, recovered from the earliest middens at Skara Brae but were otherwise absent in the excavated middens. Not too much is perhaps to be made of this absence since comparable finds remain rare (cf. M. Jones 1980) and a large number of factors are involved in controlling whether such material becomes incorporated in rubbish deposits. Although similar finds have not been recovered at the other settlements, confirmatory evidence in the form of ploughmarks has been discovered at Noltland (plate 4.10). The area so far exposed is small but sufficient to show that the area had been intensively cultivated for some time. The ploughing had been done by a light plough or ard, which scratches rather than turns the soil, but whether the traction involved was human or animal is uncertain. A considerable quantity of domestic refuse has been found in the plough soil and it seems clear that one of the important functions of the community's midden was as a fertiliser on the fields. The use of seaweed is also likely and would not be particularly surprising since its employment as manure is well documented in the recent past for large areas of Scotland, particularly Orkney (Fenton 1974). Insufficient work has yet been done at Noltland for us to be able to judge the size of the fields but in one trench a small length of a boundary ditch associated with the ploughing was exposed. Although it had been re-cut, this ditch went out of

PLATE 4.10. Ploughmarks at Links of Noltland.

use before the ploughing ended, implying that the fields were realigned from time to time. The size of this ditch, which is comparable with one that seems to be associated with the ploughing at Rosinish on Benbecula (Shepherd and Tuckwell 1977), is such that it could only have served to mark off the individual field; it certainly would not have been sufficient to deter animals from entering the field. No indications of a fence were found associated with this ditch and just how animals were kept away from the growing crop remains unclear. However, the fill of the ditch contained a number of large stones, as did that at Rosinish, and these may represent the final traces of a seaweed fence. Such fences were relatively common in the coastal areas of Denmark (Rasmussen 1974, 393–95) and were usually built using a base of heavy stones. Such fences could have a height in excess of 2 m and are reported to have lasted for generations. Incontrovertible evidence of their use would certainly be difficult to recover in the archaeological record, except in exceptional circumstances, so that it cannot at the moment be regarded as anything other than a suggestion. Nevertheless, the problem of protecting the crops was real enough and some solution must have been found.

The animal husbandry seems to have involved roughly equal proportions of cattle and sheep with only a very small number of pigs. Some at least of the cattle were extremely large, with a size rivalling that of their wild predecessor the aurochs, the bones of which might anyway be present amongst the assemblages. On the basis of the bones recovered at Skara Brae, a large percentage of the cattle were slaughtered at the end of their first year. It has often been supposed that such slaughtering represents a lack of adequate supplies of winter fodder but it is possible to reinterpret it as evidence for a dairy based system (Legge 1981, 180). No byres for housing cattle over the winter have so far been recognised among the structures and the construction techniques of the houses preclude the possibility of animals and humans sharing the same accommodation, which was a practice common in the more recent past. The sheep were small, the Soay is perhaps their nearest modern equivalent, and they are unlikely to have produced much in the way of wool; the absence of clearly identifiable weaving equipment among the artefact assemblages perhaps supports this view. The relatively large quantities of sheep present is an unusual feature in the economy of these Orcadian sites. In early farming communities elsewhere in Britain cattle or pigs, either separately or together, would normally dominate the faunal assemblage (Tinsley and Grigson 1981, 225). Only around c. 1000 BC do sheep begin to increase in importance. Clark (1952, 121) has suggested that this is because sheep are more suited to an open environment and whereas in mainland Britain this had to be created, it already existed even before the first settlement of Orkney. Another exceptional feature of Orcadian husbandry practices is the opportunistic relation-

PLATE 4.11. One of the articulated deer skeletons at Links of Noltland.

ship with red deer. At Skara Brae this species accounts for only about 1 per cent of the animal bones recovered and such a situation is best interpreted as occasional hunting. However, at Noltland deer bones are altogether more numerous including the discovery of some fifteen completely articulated skeletons (plate 4.11). Since deer are likely to have been brought to Orkney by man (Clutton-Brock 1979, 113) this bone debris is unlikely to represent the casual slaughter of an indigenous herd. This is not to suggest that the deer were being farmed in the same way as cattle or sheep but nevertheless a herd on an island the size of Westray could only have been viable with man's continuing control and protection. The absence of antler tools in any quantity suggest that the deer were being regularly exploited for food and skins. Presumably the much larger size of Mainland on which Skara Brae is situated prevented the inhabitants there from exploiting the deer in a similar manner.

The other important source of food, as far as we can judge, was collected from the sea in the form of fish and marine molluscs. Large quantities of bones and shells have been recovered in the recent excavations at Skara Brae and Noltland, but understanding exactly what this debris means is more difficult. Limpets are by far the most numerous molluscs at both sites, something which has customarily been interpreted as indicating that they were eaten in large quantities by the inhabitants of these settlements; but their low calorific value and the fact that in the historical past such food has only been resorted to in times of extreme hardship suggests that an alternative explanation should be sought. The most obvious is that they were collected for use as fish bait, such usage being well documented in the recent past in many parts of Scotland. Some shellfish, particularly oysters and crab, would certainly have formed part of the diet but the impression is that they were collected to provide variety rather than as a staple. Fish are likely, however, to have been much more important although again the situation is less straightforward that it might at first sight appear. A preliminary examination of the fish bones suggests that although some are from large specimens most are small and from species living close to the coast. Boats would certainly have been used but it is unlikely that trips were made far from the coast except on rare occasions. Almost no equipment used to catch these fish has been discovered at any of the sites. Yet whether all this fish was for human consumption must be open to question. In the nineteenth-century excavations at Skara Brae a stone mortar was found filled with crushed fish bone suggesting to the excavator that it had once been fish meal. In times of great hardship this has certainly formed part of the human diet in Scotland but its more common use is as feed for cattle.

The problems we have just mentioned concerning the use of fish and shellfish become even more acute in considering the remains of other wild

PLATE 4.12. Bone point made from the humerus of an adult gannet (128 mm long).

animals and birds, the bones of which are found at these sites. Most if not all could certainly have been eaten, but the desire for other forms of raw material which they could provide may have been an even greater motivation in their capture. The need for skins, oil, feathers and pelts rather than meat may well have been the main reason for hunting whales, seals, seabirds and otters. The bones of all these species have been found in relatively small quantities but there may be a number of factors preventing us from appreciating their real importance. Whale and seal bone which has not been fashioned into artefacts is extremely rare but it has already been noted that such bone provides a good source of fuel and there can anyway have been little incentive to carry bone back from the point where the carcase was beached without some use being made of it. But the relatively small quantities found have caused most observers to suppose that it represents the exploitation of stranded animals. This may well be the case with species such as killer whale and walrus as well as the rorquals which sink once they have been killed (Tønnessen and Johnsen 1982, 6) but other species such as pilot whales are relatively easily caught (cf. Joensen 1976). Equally, adult gannets are almost wholly represented at Skara Brae by humeri which have been fashioned into bone points (plate 4.12). Undoubtedly, this bone has been specially selected for this tool because of qualities which are now difficult to determine but it is unlikely that gannets were caught solely to obtain this bone. The problem is that the vagaries of preservation allow us to see only individual aspects of what is undoubtedly a multi-facetted exploitation of the environment in terms of raw materials. Even with such straightforward material as shell from birds' eggs which must have been collected for food, a question arises with the identification of some of it as probably that of eider duck. These are still numerous in Orkney today but we can only speculate whether the collection of their eggs also involved the obtaining of eider-down.

Most of the objects found at these sites are made from one of three raw materials: pottery, stone and bone. The range of artefact types is considerable but, as we have noted earlier, only the pottery finds ready parallels elsewhere in Britain. The usual explanation for the wide range of other

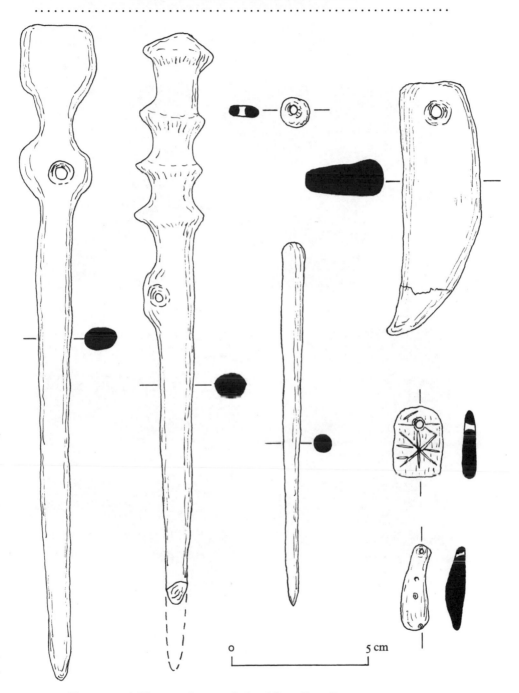

FIGURE 4.6. Pins, pendants and a bead from Skara Brae.

PLATE 4.13. Carved stone objects from Skara Brae.

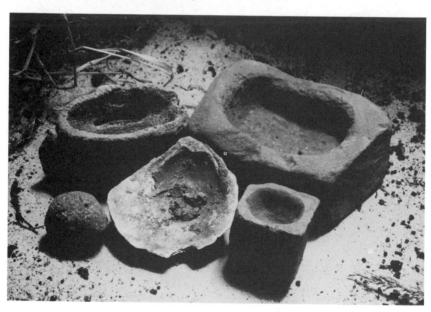

PLATE 4.14. Stone and bone pots containing red colouring matter from Skara Brae.

artefacts is that they reflect the special environmental conditions found in Orkney, although detailed studies of the objects do not substantiate this view to any great extent. Certainly the flint and chert because of its scarcity had a more restricted use than in other areas of Britain since it was employed solely in the working of wood and bone. In other words, wood and more particularly bone together with larger objects made of the local stone formed the main tool kit. Insofar as we can interpret the function of most of these objects they seem largely to have been employed in the butchering of animals and the processing of their products. The pottery is also to be associated with this group of objects in terms of its use for cooking and storage. There is, however, an equally large group of material including pins, beads, pendants (figure 4.6), some remarkable carved stone objects (plate 4.13) and even bone and stone pots in which red colouring matter was mixed (plate 4.14). The function of this group of objects is much less obviously practical and although bone remains the most important raw material a wider variety, including shell and jet, is utilised than in the case of the tools.

How then can all these strands of information be brought together and what general picture do they provide of the society and economy in the third millennium BC? We are dealing here with communities which, while not unchanging, essentially maintained a stable life-style with its associated traditions for a period exceeding 500 years. This continuity, however, should not be interpreted as backwardness; rather all the evidence suggests that they were groups living in harmony with an environment which they used but did not over-exploit. Apart from rare occasions, this rich and diverse environment was capable of supporting them in a manner sufficiently easy to allow time for a wide range of activities not closely related to survival. The diet was remarkably varied including some items, such as venison and oysters, now regarded as luxuries. This in some ways enviable existence was achieved by small communities, perhaps involving not more than ten or fifteen families, with a considerable measure of self-sufficiency. Presumably the communal sharing of routine tasks which is implicit in the structural integration of these villages provided an opportunity for the development of individual skills of benefit to the community. There is, however, no evidence of craft specialisation in the sense that an individual pursued a task exclusively and depended upon exchanging the products with others in order to maintain himself. Yet the image of independent communities should not be pushed too far. Some raw materials, for example haematite which is only found in Orkney in two veins on the north coast of Hoy, are sufficiently rare in their occurrence for it to be reasonably supposed that they were obtained by contacts with other groups. Regular contacts would anyway be required for the obtaining of marriage partners and without such meetings the remarkable cultural uniformities which we have been describing would be difficult to explain over such a long time-span. Much needs to be done before we can bring this inter-settlement network into clearer focus and begin to understand its social and economic roles. In particular, we need to define more clearly the full range of materials which a settlement might reasonably obtain acting independently within its immediate environment. Only then will it be possible to assess the significance of the wider network. Enough has already been done to show that these aspirations need not be mere pipe-dreams.

5 Audrey S. Henshall **The Chambered Cairns**

Chambered cairns are found in many parts of western Europe, and are the earliest structures still surviving in the landscape. They were built as burial places; essentially they were rooms, normally closed, to which access could be had for burials and other purposes, and they were generally covered by a cairn. Chambered cairns vary greatly in design from one area to another, and some are of astonishing size and elaboration. Until modern times they have generally been objects of awe and superstition, an attitude which has done much to protect them from demolition. The mechanics of the spread of chambered cairns through Spain, France, Britain, Ireland, Denmark, and other parts of Europe, have long been, and continue to be, discussed. It is clear from the diversity of plans, of burial rites, and of the material culture of their users, that it was not a simple matter of emigration and colonisation from a single centre. One of the most intriguing questions is why some early farming communities buried their dead in stone chambers and others did not. The building of even a modest tomb must have entailed considerable physical and economic strain on a neolithic society, and the structures were clearly much more than just burial vaults.

These tombs are known to have been used for very long periods, often many centuries. Their most important functions were probably as foci for social and religious ceremonies concerned with the wellbeing of the communities they served: we may guess at ancestor worship and rituals to ensure fertility of animals and lands. It is ironic that these aspects of the significance of the tombs are, by their nature, those which elude us, for archaeological studies are based on material remains. The tombs may also have served as important territorial markers for the societies that built them.

Nonetheless, in those areas where they were the established burial place, chambered cairns provide a great deal of information about the earliest farmers. Obviously the structures themselves, their plans and building techniques, deserve study. Also their distribution, both on an international scale and in relation to the immediate environment, gives an indication of the early settlement patterns and the lands which were exploited. Then there is the skeletal material recovered from the chambers by excavation, the physical remains of the people who were buried in them and who lived in the habitation sites such as those described in chapters 3 and 4. The pathology of their bones gives an insight into living conditions, and if the material allows, demographic analysis may shed light on social organisation and economics. Faunal remains included in the tombs, by accident or intention, provide evidence on the environment, and on the economy of the communities concerned. It was usual for objects of daily use to be left with the burials or in the filling which finally sealed the tombs. The objects which survive are mainly pottery sherds and stone and flint tools, all of prime importance in any assessment of the origins and contacts of any group of tomb builders, and of their material equipment. Radiocarbon dates taken from bones or vegetable matter can be used, if conditions are favourable, to date the building and period of use, and also the objects within them. As yet only the first steps have been taken in establishing a firm chronology for European tombs and in particular for Orcadian tombs.

The far north of Scotland has a remarkable concentration of chambered cairns, and, for their land area, the Orkney and Shetland Islands have the greatest concentration of all. But the Orcadian cairns are of outstanding interest for other reasons: the variety of size and plan, the elaborate designs and structural excellence, the number which are relatively complete, and the detail with which they have been studied. The earliest tombs are likely to have been built by the first neolithic inhabitants of the islands, and it is clear that they came across the Pentland Firth from Caithness, though the date at which this happened is uncertain, probably in the early centuries of the fourth millennium BC. It is likely that the history of chambered cairns in the islands spans over a thousand years, and during this time a variety of tomb designs developed, partly in ways unique to the islands and partly in response to new ideas reaching the islands from the mainland. The extent to which the culture of the distinctive late neolithic Orcadian grooved ware communities (including the design of their tombs) was due to development within the islands is a matter of debate.

The study of Orcadian chambered cairns really began about the middle of last century with the investigations at a number of sites by George Petrie, James Farrer, R. J. Hebden and F. W. L. Thomas. Following a lull, work began on the Royal Commission's Inventory of the ancient monuments of Orkney in the 1920s and 30s (RCAMS 1946), and in the 1930s there were the series of remarkable excavations by C. S. T. Calder on Eday, and J. G. Callander and W. G. Grant on Rousay. After the war V. G. Childe excavated at two outstanding monuments, Maes Howe and Quoyness, and soon afterwards S. Piggott published his synthesis and interpretation of the information to date (1954, 232–56). A catalogue of sites and their contents, with references, was published in 1963 (Henshall 1963, 183–253, also 1972, 562–3; for Orkney, the code numbers used in these volumes will be quoted in italics, while sites in Caithness and Sutherland also published in Henshall 1963 or 1972 will be prefaced by CAT and SUT respectively). A number of additional sites have been recognised since 1972, and are listed on p. 115. There have also been two excavations of outstanding importance in recent years, at Quanterness (*43*) by C. Renfrew (1979) and at Isbister (*25*) by R. Simison (J. W. Hedges 1983a).

THE ORKNEY–CROMARTY GROUP

The distribution and architectural development of passage-graves in Scotland was discussed in 1972 (Henshall 1972, 201–6, 257–64). In general terms the earliest small and simple passage-graves of international type, consisting of a circular or polygonal chamber with entrance passage, gave rise, in the Highlands and Islands, to several rather more elaborate plans, the whole group being known as the Orkney–Cromarty group, abbreviated here to OC. One chamber plan had a pair of opposed upright slabs set transversely to the axis to divide an antechamber from the main chamber. An extension of this idea, using a second pair of slabs as a portal to an inner section of the chamber, produced a chamber of three parts. This tripartite chamber plan is common in Caithness, and, the easily quarried sandstones and flagstones providing an excellent building material, the walls of the passage and chamber were of masonry rather than the large blocks of stone usual to the south and west, and quite high false-corbelled vaults were erected over the main part of the chamber. The access passage was on the axis of the chamber, and the whole was generally covered by a relatively small round cairn.

A number of excavated sites in Orkney have this same basic tripartite plan, for instance Bigland (*2*) (figure 5.1), Kierfea Hill (*26*), Knowe of Craie (*27*), all three on Rousay, and Huntersquoy (*23*), Sandyhill Smithy (*47*) on Eday. The cairns are of modest size, from about 8 to 12 m in diameter, revetted by a single, or more often a double, wall-face of dry masonry. The passage leads into a chamber some 3.4 to 4.8 m long. All the chambers have lost their roofs but as the surviving transverse slabs are of modest height the roofing is likely to have been about 1.5 to 2.0 m above the floor. The dry-built side walls should probably be envisaged as oversailing in their upper courses above the tops of the upright slabs, and linked by a row of lintels, such as partly survived at Knowe of Lairo (*28*). This last is a

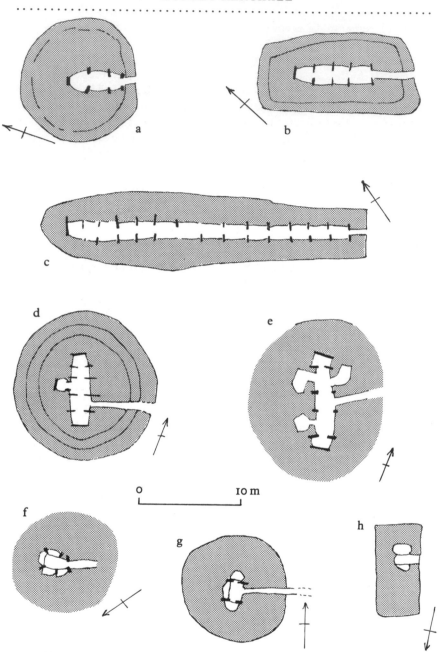

FIGURE 5.1. Simplified plans of the tombs of the Orkney–Cromarty group: (a) Bigland, Round; (b) Knowe of Yarso; (c) Knowe of Ramsay; (d) Unstan; (e) Isbister; (f) Calf of Eday, SE; (g) Huntersquoy (lower chamber); (h) Dwarfie Stane.

large chamber, 5.2 m long, with the paired transverse stones in proportion, 2.1 m high, and the roof 4.1 m above the floor; curiously the chamber and passage are built on a sinuous axis. Among the unexcavated cairns there are similar chambers ranging from small to large, though when incompletely exposed they cannot always be distinguished from stalled chambers. At least one tripartite chamber as large as Lairo is known in Caithness (CAT 70).

A desire for longer chambers led to an increase in the number of compartments. In Caithness only two of these longer stalled chambers are known, but in Orkney the idea was fully exploited leading to the construction of some very remarkable monuments, although a few four-compartment chambers are no longer than the largest tripartite ones. Among the sites with full excavation reports, Knowe of Yarso (32) (figure 5.1) has an interesting chamber plan which is essentially tripartite, the long inner compartment being subdivided in its lower part by a pair of short transverse slabs with a sill stone between them; the innermost section had been divided horizontally by a shelf resting on a scarcement in the side walls.

On a stretch of the south coast of Rousay, only 3½ miles long, there are four other stalled chambers, three of them the longest so far identified. Blackhammer (3), Knowe of Rowiegar (31), Midhowe (37) and Knowe of Ramsay (30) (figure 5.1) in ascending order of size, ranging from seven to fourteen compartments and from 13 to 26 m long. They were described as 'stalled' by the excavators who first revealed this type of chamber, for, even in their roofless state, they do indeed have the appearance of long narrow byres with their series of paired tall transverse stones and the passageway down the centre. At Midhowe (figure 5.3) the best preserved, the tallest transverse stones are over 2 m high, and the side walls still stand 2.5 m high. The innermost compartment is subdivided in the same way as at Knowe of Yarso. The size of these chambers, together with their close distribution, astonishes every visitor. The Rousay stalled chambers, including two unexcavated sites elsewhere on the island, are covered not by round but by rectangular cairns, this change presumably being a practical way to encase the chamber with the minimum of stonework for its support, and to provide a ramp for manoeuvring the lintels into place. At Blackhammer the passage approaches the chamber at right angles to the axis, an arrangement found at a few other sites.

One of the best known Orcadian tombs is Unstan (or Onston, 51), in Stenness (figure 5.1). The chamber of five compartments is of average length, but interestingly is covered by a round cairn. Like Blackhammer, the passage enters the long side of the chamber thus allowing two end compartments both of which have had shelves, and a kerb across their entries. Another feature to note is a cell accessible from the opposite side of the chamber to the passage. The cell is entered between a pair of low portal stones, it has a back-slab but dry-built walls, and is roofed by a capstone at a height of only 1.26 m. When the tomb was excavated in 1884 the finds included sherds of distinctive shallow bowls with decorated collars (a form misleadingly described as carinated in archaeological literature). These became the type-specimens for Unstan Ware, discussed later.

The most recently excavated chamber, Isbister on South Ronaldsay (25, J. W. Hedges 1983a, 1–31, 301–2) (figure 5.1) is exceptional in several respects but closest to Unstan. There are four pairs of transverse slabs giving five segments to the chamber, as the passage enters the chamber from the side. Yet the two middle pairs of slabs project so little beyond the chamber wall that the appearance is more of a large rectangular area with a special area divided off at each end. Access to the end-sections is restricted by the greater projection of the two end pairs of transverse slabs and the positioning of a kerb between them. The difference of the end-sections is emphasised by the side walls at ground level being set back from the line of the main chamber walls, by the flagged floor, and by a flagstone shelf in each. The chamber is also provided with three side cells entered by short passages; the cells are similar to that at Unstan except they are entirely dry-built, and are roofed even lower, at only 1 m. As originally built, the chamber was under an oval cairn of the minimum size to enclose the chamber and cells. The retaining wall of the cairn still reaches a height of 1.9 m at one side, so the cairn seems to have been in the form of a drum with a vertical masonry facing (plate 5.1, colour plate 5).

The quality of the craftsmanship in these cairns induces the greatest respect for their builders. The dry-stone masonry is neat and regular, and at some sites the retaining wall-face of the cairn has been decoratively treated. A projecting basal course is not unusual, and at three Rousay sites the stonework above this is either set slanting in opposite directions on either side of the entrance, to be reversed at the back of the cairn, or set in two bands each slanting in opposite directions and separated by a wide horizontal course, or set in opposed slanting panels reminiscent of the opposed hatched triangles which decorate the collars of some Unstan bowls. The narrowness of the cairn casing in relation to the height of the chambers indicates that a number of sites besides Isbister must once have had vertical retaining walls of considerable height, and these were presumably designed to be seen. The wall-face survived for almost its full height at Isbister because the cairn was covered by an outer rubble mound which sloped down to a boundary wall some 5 to 9 m outside the retaining wall. The large upright slabs forming the ends and divisions of the chambers, the skeletons of the structure, were handled with skill and were so carefully selected and set that they normally remain in position even at badly ruined sites. Often the transverse slabs have slanting upper edges to complement the corbelling of the wall-head above them.

Besides the shelves in some end compartments, some (but not all) of

PLATE 5.1. The chamber at Isbister, showing the south end compartment and, on left, the slab of the passage roof.

both the tripartite and the stalled chambers have been found to be equipped with low benches, set along the side walls between the transverse slabs. At Knowe of Craie (27) one of the benches was of solid stone construction similar to those found at one Caithness chamber (CAT 69). Otherwise the benches consist of a slab, bonded into the side wall and supported by stones on edge set on the floor. It is evident that these are original features, but their positioning seems curiously erratic: in two chambers they are along both walls, in one in the inner compartment only, in one long chamber along part of one side only. Failure to identify remains of shelves in some end compartments where projecting stones were clearly intended for their support, as at Knowe of Yarso (32), suggests that some shelves, and some benches too, may have been of wood.

A second variant of the tripartite chamber developed in Orkney, and is named after the cairn at Bookan. At Huntersquoy on Eday (23) and at Taversoe Tuick on Rousay (49) (figure 5.5) the cairns are extraordinary structures with two chambers one above the other, covered by a round cairn, the whole built as a unit. These two-storeyed tombs are sited on slopes, with the upper chamber entered from the uphill side, the flags forming its floor being the capstones of the lower chamber, entered from the downhill side. The upper chamber at Huntersquoy was tripartite in plan. Space for the lower chamber required quarrying back into the clay and underlying rock of the hillside. The plan is based on the tripartite arrangement, but the long axis of the chamber lies along the contour of the hill and thus at right angles to the passage, presumably to reduce effort during construction. Thus the chamber has two end-compartments entered between pairs of transverse slabs, and a central compartment with the low passage entering one side, the 'burial area' lost because of the position of the passage being provided by a recess above its inner end. The lower chamber at Taversoe Tuick is similar, but the upper chamber is irregular, and probably should be regarded, like the miniature chamber outside the cairn which will be mentioned later, as a simplification of the lower chamber plan. The walls of all these chambers are of the highest quality dry masonry, concave in plan between the divisional slabs. All the recesses of these two subterranean chambers have a slab shelf, at each site two of them resting on a solid masonry platform or bench (colour plate 6).

Two separate almost intact chambers, on Calf of Eday (9, 10) (figure 5.1) also belong to this Bookan sub-group, having much in common with the subterranean chambers already described, including round cairns, cutting back into a hillslope, and the provision of benches or shelves in the recesses. However, the divisional slabs projecting from the walls are not strictly paired. The appearance of the terminal compartments at Huntersquoy and Taversoe Tuick is reproduced at Calf of Eday (9) by additional paired upright slabs narrowing the entrance to the recesses, and in one case there is also a kerbstone. The Bookan chamber was a more regular version of this last plan. The surviving roofs of the Bookan group chambers are low, constructed either by large slabs spanning the whole chamber, or by slabs covering each recess and supporting slabs spanning the central area. Although the plans seem distorted and curious, they are ingeniously designed. It is notable too, that, of the variety of chamber plans available in Orkney, it is this type of chamber which appears in Shetland, being the progenitor of the large number tombs in those islands. The reasons may be largely practical, due to the intractable building stone and to the economic difficulties of the early stages of colonisation of those islands.

One extraordinary monument, the Dwarfie Stane (*13*)(figure 5.1), has attracted the attention of visitors and the speculation of antiquaries since the sixteenth century, and indeed its classification as a chambered tomb is periodically questioned. A small chamber has been hewn in a rectangular erratic block of sandstone, itself a remarkable feature lying in a desolate moorland valley on the island of Hoy. The chamber, no more than 0.76 m high, consists of a central passage with a compartment on either side, each marked off with a low sill, one of these compartments being further distinguished by vestigial projecting jambs. The plan appears to be a simplification of the Bookan-type plan, Huntersquoy providing the closest parallel, the idea of carving the chamber out of the solid rock being an extension of the rock-cutting undertaken for four Bookan-type chambers.

At a few sites there are two chambers under one cairn. At the two-storey cairns the chambers, which have been classed respectively as a Bookan and tripartite plan, and two Bookan plans, are strictly contemporary. But the cairn dug by Calder on Calf of Eday (*8*) had a stalled four-compartment chamber and, behind it on a different axis, a small low two-compartment chamber which is best classified with the Bookan chambers. The excavator considered the small chamber was secondary to the large chamber, but the excavation report provides no proof of this assumption and it seems to the writer that the reverse is more likely. On the other hand at Bigland (*1*) on Rousay an unexcavated site gives every appearance of a tripartite chamber being secondary to a long stalled chamber. The close connection of the three varieties of chamber plan so far discussed cannot be in doubt, nor the derivation of the stalled and Bookan plans from the tripartite plan, but the typology suggested by the plans should not be used to construct a chronological sequence, except to note a strong likelihood that at least some small tripartite chambers were the earliest to be built in Orkney.

There are sixty sites which can be identified as certainly or probably tombs of the Orkney-Cromarty group. Of these, fifteen certainly or very probably have tripartite chambers, eighteen have stalled chambers, at fourteen chambers the number of compartments is not known, and seven chambers are of Bookan type (in three cases the cairn covers two chambers). The overall distribution is curious (map 1, p.116), with a concentration on Rousay and the adjacent coast of Mainland, on Eday and Calf of Eday, and a somewhat less intense concentration on Westray with Holm of Papa Westray. Apart from these islands there are a few tombs on Stronsay, Shapinsay, and on South Ronaldsay with Burray and Swona. Otherwise there is only a scattering of sites on the rest of Mainland, and one each on Sanday and Hoy. The gaps on Mainland and Sanday are filled to some extent by tombs of the Maes Howe group (described below), but there remain some areas where occupation by tomb-builders would have been expected, around Scapa Flow, in other parts of Mainland, and on others of the smaller islands, where no sites have been identified. Within this distribution, the occurrence of tripartite and stalled cairns is, in general terms, similar and widespread except that the longest stalled chambers are all on Rousay, but half of the small number of Bookan chambers are on Calf of Eday and north Eday, with a pair under one cairn on Rousay, and single examples on Mainland and Hoy.

There may be a hint of some difference of function for the Bookan chambers, as the similarity between their compartments and the shelved end-sections of some of the stalled chambers is striking; at Isbister in particular there is the marked structural contrast between the central part of the chamber and the terminal compartments. It may be that this difference led to the building of such terminal compartments as separate tombs, but it must be admitted that evidence from the contents of the tombs is too scanty to demonstrate a functional difference, though at Isbister and Knowe of Yarso (32) the end areas had been particularly intensively used for bone storage.

Long cairns and short horned cairns. Besides the forms of cairns already described, there are also five, possibly seven, long cairns of the type in which the chamber occupies only a small part of the whole structure, the cairn being wider and higher at the end containing the chamber. Long cairns are well represented in Scotland, and have been discussed in some detail (Henshall 1972, 207–40). Their origins were separate from passage-graves, and it is now generally accepted that in northern Scotland they were often (indeed, possibly always) additions to existing passage-graves. In Caithness the forecourt at the wider end was faced with dry-walling, and was sometimes extended by building out long 'horns' from each corner, and this feature may be repeated on a smaller scale at the rear. Only one long cairn in northern Scotland has been excavated this century (CAT 58; Corcoran 1966, 5–22), and another (CAT 12) is presently under excavation. Corcoran showed that, at one site at least, the long cairn post-dated by some time the simple early passage-grave it covered, and in fact masked the tomb entrance so that it could not be used. It is clear that a similar situation existed at other sites in the north mainland, but alternatively the secondary long cairn was sometimes arranged so that the tomb was still accessible, and it is possible that in a few cases the two funerary building traditions merged to produce a chambered long cairn built as an entity. It is worth noting that whereas about a quarter of the chambers in Caithness were covered by long cairns, the proportion in Orkney is only about ten per cent, and it is doubtful if the long cairn tradition ever reached Shetland.

The Orcadian long cairns are similar in size to those in the north mainland, ranging from about 47 to 70 m in length including the horns. All cover, or seem to have covered, OC passage-graves, one being the unusual tripartite chamber already referred to at Knowe of Lairo (*28*), and one a stalled chamber at Point of Cott (*41*). At the former certainly, and at the latter probably, the chamber was accessible from the forecourt. The forecourts vary from a gently concave plan at Knowe of Lairo to a deeper curved plan to front and rear at Head of Work (*18*) and an angled plan at Point of Cott, in each case the cairn being faced by dry-walling. Parallels for all can be found in Caithness. The skew axis of the Knowe of Lairo chamber, and the markedly humped profile at Head of Work, almost certainly indicate a two-period structure. The distribution of these sites is scattered, on Mainland, Papa Stronsay, Westray, and a probable site on Shapinsay.

A more modest embellishment of the exterior of passage-graves is sometimes found in northern Scotland, where round cairns may have forecourts similar to those at long cairns, formed by two pairs of horns projecting at the front and back. Cairns of this plan were first recognised by Joseph Anderson excavating in Caithness in the 1860s (1868, 489–93) who named them 'short horned cairns'. Subsequently another version of the plan was found with a forecourt at the front only, the 'heel-shaped cairns'. Both plans are common amongst Shetland cairns so examples are to be expected in Orkney. It was formerly thought that three such cairns could be identified, but on recent visits to two of them it seemed to the writer preferable to interpret the horns as part of the later structures which certainly exist beside each site. This leaves Burray (*7*) as the only Orcadian short horned cairn, a site destroyed in 1863 and only known from brief descriptions.

A curious addition was made to the oval cairn at Isbister (*25*), for a straight wall abuts its N side, and behind the wall is a deposit of earth and rubble in which were animal and occasional human bones as well as human bones buried deliberately. This structural feature, referred to as a hornwork, has only been partly excavated and both its extent and purpose are obscure (J. W. Hedges 1983a, 23–31, 208–9, 301–2).

THE MAES HOWE GROUP

The second group of chambered cairns on Orkney, the Maes Howe group, contrast both in their design and their contents with the OC group. Whereas the latter are relatively easily recognised when seen in a ruinous state, the former are much more difficult to identify. At present the total of certain MH cairns is only ten, with three probable sites, but there are many cairns with no diagnostic features visible, some of which are likely to cover MH chambers. This relatively high proportion of probable and possible sites would, if verified and excavated, profoundly alter the picture.

In his recent re-assessment of the group following his excavations at Quanterness (43) (figure 5.2) Renfrew has argued persuasively for a revision of the typological arrangement put forward by Piggott and followed by the writer (Renfrew 1979, 201–3; Piggott 1954, 243–6; Henshall 1963, 123–4). If Maes Howe is left aside for the moment, the structures can be described as entirely dry-built with no vertical slabs, the chambers being rectangular (though rather irregular at Vinquoy Hill (53)), roomy and lofty, the walls gently oversailing from a metre or so above the floor. At the ground level there are low inconspicuous openings arranged more or less symmetrically, leading to cells which are roofed at almost the same height as the chamber. The roofing of the chamber, cells, and passage was by flat lintels, or more often by slabs set on edge. The masonry is of excellent quality, most walls in the chamber being bonded at the angles, having massive slabs for the lintels to the cell entries, and frequently one long slab spanning the whole length of the shorter walls.

With the exception of the Holm of Papa Westray (22), the cairns are round but sometimes large, carefully built, with an inner casing of minimum diameter to enclose chamber and cells, and one or two outer casings, all revetted with dry walling. The cairns at Quoyness and Wideford Hill (44, 54) have, since excavation, been left with these walls partly exposed resulting in a curious stepped profile, but there is little doubt that when finished the cairns were either domed in profile with all the revetment walls hidden as at Quanterness (Renfrew 1979, 48), or domed within an exposed outer revetment wall as at Wideford Hill (Kilbride-Jones 1973, 92, 95). At Quanterness a covering mantle of rubble was found, and where best preserved the outermost slabs were deliberately inclined with the slope of the cairn probably to keep the chamber dry (Renfrew 1979, 48). The passages are relatively long, but low, entering the chamber at right angles to its axis. In two cases the outer section of the passage, beyond the inner casing, does not seem to have been roofed but left as an open trench with the side walls rising with the slope of the mound, though in another case the passage was entirely roofed.

Three of the MH cairns, Cuween Hill, Vinquoy Hill and Wideford Hill

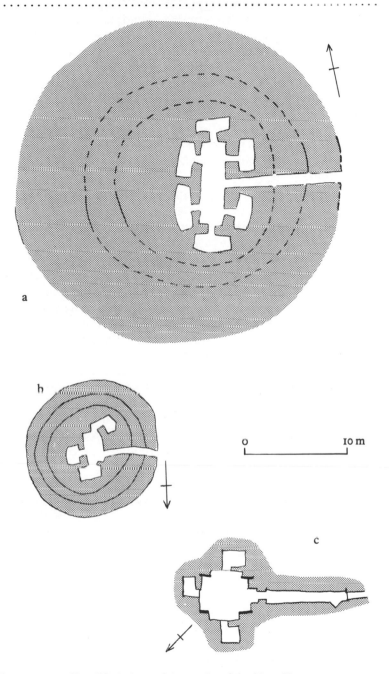

FIGURE 5.2. Simplified plans of the tombs of the Maes Howe group:
(a) Quanterness; (b) Wideford Hill; (c) Maes Howe.

(*12, 53, 54*) (figure 5.2), are similar in points of detail. A sloping site was chosen and the chambers were built level, entered from the lower sde, which necessitated some rock-cutting for the inner part of the structure. The number of cells varies from three to four, and one of them gives access to a subsidiary cell. The cells themselves are irregular in ground plan and, at the first two sites particularly, have been arranged to minimise the amount of excavation into the hillside. Two other cairns, Quanterness and Quoyness (*43, 44*) are on nearly flat sites, and cover larger chambers which are remarkably alike, both having two cells entered from the long sides and one from each end. Those at Quoyness are irregular in plan, but at Quanterness they are rectangular except for bowed outer walls conforming to the curve of the cairn casing. The chamber at this site measures no less than 6.35 m by 1.83 m, by 3.5 m high, somewhat larger than Quoyness. The procedure for constructing one of these remarkable monuments has been analysed by an architect (Renfrew 1979, 66–8).

The tomb on the Holm of Papa Westray (*22*) is an extraordinary structure by any standard. The excessively long chamber measuring in all 20.5 m, has the two ends divided off by cross-walls reaching to roof height, and through these walls are low openings: the remaining central area is 13.5 by 1.5 m. Around the chamber are twelve openings leading to fourteen cells, for two are double. A round cairn to cover this structure would be immense, so the same solution as for the stalled chambers was adopted, an elongated cairn casing.

Maes Howe (figure 5.2) is one of the supreme achievements of neolithic Europe, and stands apart because of its very excellence, but now seems on architectural grounds to be the last and most sophisticated product of the MH tradition of tomb-building. Most of the skills and ideas developed in its design can be found in the chambers already described. The layout of the very spacious chamber is strictly symmetrical, it being square in plan, the passage entering on one side and a cell entry being placed centrally on each of the others. The elevation of these entries together with the cells which lie behind them well above ground level is unique, but a small step up into a cell is found twice at Cuween Hill. The blocking of the entries at Maes Howe by masonry also seems unique, but may reflect a desire to distract attention from them; at other sites the entries were very small and at ground level, here they were disguised. Cells of rectangular plan are found at Quanterness, but at Maes Howe they differ in having low flat roofs. The quality of stonework at the other sites is notable, including bonding of walls, the use of slabs stretching the whole length of a wall, the use of an oblique natural fracture to construct smooth oversailing of the walling below the stepped corbelling (Renfrew 1979, 67), and at two sites there has been restricted use of dressing on the stonework (Childe 1952, 126; Renfrew 1979, 65). But the excellence of the masonry at Maes Howe goes far

5. Isbister chambered tomb, S. Ronaldsay. One of the round side-cells is clearly seen, with the entrance passage immediately to the left, and the rectangular chamber behind.

6. Taversoe Tuick chambered tomb, Rousay. The plate shows one of the stone benches in the lower of the two chambers (see page 90).

7. Maes Howe. The mound is shown during an investigation, in the 1970s, of the shallow encircling ditch.

8. Maes Howe, the chamber. 'The excellence of the masonry goes far beyond that of any other tomb' (page 96).

PLATE 5.2. The passage at Maes Howe, looking towards the entrance.

beyond that of any other tomb, for the blocks fit extremely closely with occasional fine pinning to bring them into position, occasional rebating to take the corner of an adjacent block, and considerable areas of dressing by pecking and chiselling to achieve a flat surface or to round the edge of the corbelling or the sharp edge of the innermost passage lintel. The way that

97

PLATE 5.3. The chamber, Maes Howe.

massive rectangular slabs have been used is also unique to this site, for some are 5.6 m long and estimated to weigh three tons, and they form the walls, roof and floor of most of the passage, fitting together with unbelievable precision. Vertical slabs, accurately plumbed, are used in the chamber to face one side of each of the four buttresses which fill the corners and support the potential points of weakness, the corners of the oversailing roof. As at two other MH cairns, the outer passage has been an open masonry-lined trench, but only Maes Howe is provided with a recess just within the roofed passage, which contains a block intended to close the entrance when drawn forward against the door-checks (plates 5.2, 5.3, and colour plates 7, 8).

The great domed mound which covers the chamber contains an inner stone casing, but the outer parts of the mound are largely clay and turf with angular stones (Childe 1956, 162–4). The cairns of the three first tombs described were probably partly built from the rock dug to allow construction of the chamber. Limited recent investigation (Renfrew 1979, 31–8) has shown that the shallow Maes Howe ditch encircles only part of the site, for on the NW side it is largely an illusion between the edge of the platform on which the tomb is built and the low bank which encircles the monument. This bank is of two or more periods of construction, the later being modern, an earlier probably being Norse, and a still earlier bank probably being contemporary with the ditch digging. The Ring of Bookan, an enigmatic site which certainly has a wide deep ditch and a ruined cairn within, was formerly considered a parallel to Maes Howe, but this now seems unlikely (see chapter 6).

At Holm of Papa Westray (22) several slabs built into the chamber wall have enigmatic pecked markings and one has 'eyebrow and eye' motifs. A slab with linked spirals and concentric circles was recovered from a destroyed site, probably an MH tomb, on Eday (16), but Pickaquoy (40) which produced a slab with pecked concentric circles is now known to be a burnt mound, not a chambered tomb. A most remarkable discovery in 1981 was the two parts of a decorated stone at a greatly disturbed mound, almost certainly an MH cairn, at Pierowall, Westray (Neil 1981). The intricate all-over design of pecked spirals and concentric circles is of superb quality (plate 5.4).

PLATE 5.4. Carved stone found in the wrecked mound at Pierowall, Westray, almost certainly a Maes-Howe-type cairn.

The Maes Howe tombs, as known at present, are concentrated on Mainland where five are strung across the centre of the island. On Sanday there are two certain tombs, and probably another. There is a tomb each on Holm of Papa Westray, Egilsay and Eday, probably a second on Eday, and probably a site on Westray (map 2, p.117). No sites are known in the southern part of Orkney.

CONTENTS AND RITUAL

When the contents of both groups of tombs are considered, and deductions regarding the builders and users of the tombs are attempted, it is clear that interpretation of the data is beset by the problems common to most groups of tombs. One of the most striking features is the variation in the quantity of material recovered, of durable artefacts and of human and animal bone. Lack of finds may be due to earlier interference with the site, or to indifferent standards of excavation. With bones and other organic deposits there is also the problem of decay, and it is likely that at some sites a large quantity of material has totally disappeared. Finally, there is the possibility of the removal of the contents of tombs for cult purposes during the period of their use. On the other hand, the range and detail of information from the two latest excavations, Quanterness (*43*) and Isbister (*25*), reflects the achievement of modern recovery techniques, such as wet sieving, and of detailed scientific study of every aspect of the material recovered.

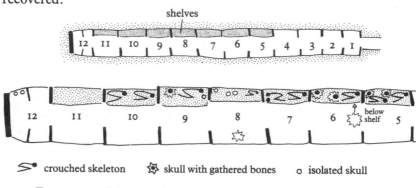

S• crouched skeleton   ☼ skull with gathered bones   o isolated skull

FIGURE 5.3. Diagram of the burials at Midhowe.

As far as the burials go, there is no firm evidence of cremation, for the scorching of bones noted at a number of sites is almost certainly due to the use of fire or embers in the burial rituals in the chambers. All six excavated tripartite chambers, and four stalled chambers, have produced minimal information, whether because of true absence of burials or through other causes is unknown. Bone was reasonably well preserved at Midhowe (*37*), and the description and photographs make possible a diagram of the burials (figure 5.3, plate 5.5). On the low shelves which had been constructed along more than half of one side of this long chamber were nine articulated crouched skeletons, their backs to the wall, laid on their right or left sides to face the corridor with their heads generally in the corner beside a stall-slab. These burials were more or less complete and undisturbed except that in three cases the skull had been placed upright. In addition, there were remains of fifteen more individuals, incomplete, the bones generally arranged in heaps. Some were represented by 'scanty remains', some by more of the skeleton, but six only by their skulls. Some of the bones were stowed under the shelves. In all there were remains of twenty-five individuals, men, women, adolescents and children. A similar pattern seems to have been found in the smaller chamber at Holm of Papa Westray (*21*) where at least seven individuals were present, three crouched lying against

PLATE 5.5. The burials at Midhowe, photographed during the excavation in 1932–33.

the wall, two of them with the skulls detached but nearby, also four detached skulls and other miscellaneous bones.

The brief account of the Unstan chamber indicates that there was a considerable amount of bone in all parts of the chamber, the interesting points being several crouched skeletons in the compartment entered by the passage and two in the side cell which was still roofed. But at Burray (7) there were twenty-two or twenty-three skulls and other bones, ten of them in a part of the structure that was probably a side cell (Petrie n.d., 76, 82, 83). The brief description of Korkquoy (34) implies sixty or seventy bodies, some crouched. All that can be said about burials in Bookan-type chambers is that remains of three bodies lay on the benches in the lower chamber at Taversoe Tuick, one of them crouched.

An interest in skulls was obvious at Knowe of Yarso. There were no articulated skeletons, but the bones lay in confusion and almost all were broken. Yet the confusion was not total, for groups of bones in the passage and in the first two compartments were each identified as the scanty remains of an individual, four in total. Thirty adult skulls were counted. All but four were gathered into the end compartment and mainly arranged along the base of the walls, seventeen in its inner section all without lower jaws, eight in the outer section. Other bones were also concentrated in the end compartment, seemingly piled to a depth of 0.5 m; indeed four-fifths of all human bone was in this compartment. A few bones had rested on the shelf which had divided the innermost section horizontally.

Isbister, classified for convenience as a stalled chamber, is an exceptional tomb not least for the extraordinary quantity of human bone it contained and which has been very fully studied (Chesterman 1983; J.W. Hedges 1983a, 20–2, 213–26). Here again there was interest in skulls, many of which were intact and stored in two side cells (the original contents of the third cell are not known), whilst others had been placed against the sides of the chamber along with other bones, some arranged in piles (colour plate 9). Under the shelf in one end-compartment was a jumble of bones but only a few fragments of skulls, and pieces of bone were strewn on the floor throughout the chamber. All the bones were disarticulated, and all the skeletons were incomplete, indeed often only a small part was present. One distinct pile of bones was analysed and found to contain fragments of six individuals ranging in age from adult to infant. J.T.Chesterman estimated that whilst the chamber was in use parts of at least 312 individuals had been deposited there. A quantity of bones which had been placed on the ground before the chamber had been built came from 15 more individuals. Chesterman and Hedges, following the 'excarnation theory' already propounded for the Quanterness material, were of the opinion that very incomplete skeletons had been brought to the chamber which had functioned as an ossuary.

The excavations in the Maes-Howe-type chamber at Quanterness had also produced a large quantity of human bone which was studied in detail by Chesterman and Renfrew and published four years before the Isbister report (Chesterman 1979; Renfrew 1979, 156–72). Twenty per cent of the chamber including five of the six cells was left unexcavated. The total of

12,600 bones or bone fragments were estimated to represent 157 individuals, from which it was calculated that if conditions were constant through the chamber the remains of some 394 individuals had been buried. These figures rest on several assumptions (Renfrew 1979, 158, 162) but if only approximately correct it is evident that the number of bodies involved was as great and probably greater than at Isbister. The age range at both tombs was similar including many infants, children, and adolescents as well as adults, the main difference being that no infants under eight months old were identified at Quanterness whereas newborn babies were present at Isbister. Only slightly more than half the communities survived into adulthood (i.e. reached the age of twenty), few lived beyond thirty and none beyond fifty. The proportion of deaths from infancy to twenty-five years was fairly normal for a neolithic population, but the small number of older individuals, only seven per cent over the age of thirty at Quanterness, is surprising. The bones at Isbister, which were in particularly good condition, showed a high incidence of degenerative disease of the spine, and other abnormalities probably caused by carrying heavy weights, all indications of a very hard life. The ratio of males to females at Quanterness was 32:27, at Isbister 93:38. It appears that all, or nearly all, members of the community were eligible for burial in the tombs.

At Quanterness the floor of the main chamber, cell, and linking short passage was covered by a fairly thin layer of soil with burnt matter, in which were the relatively sparse scattered bones of the first burials. Next, three pits had been dug through this layer and into the bedrock; one pit contained a crouched inhumation with bones from two other bodies, one contained a cist with a crouched inhumation, and the third a cist was not excavated, all three being covered by capstones. Following this the filling of soil, stones and bones continued to accumulate, the stone slabs sometimes laid quite compactly, and the density of the bones increasing nearer the top of the deposit. The upper level was disturbed, and had had a shallow pit dug into it to receive an extended inhumation. The total depth of the bone deposits was about 30 cm. The disarray and fragmentation of the bones suggested that the tomb had been disturbed often during its use, and the sporadic layers of slabs in the bone spreads suggested gradual accumulation, as was indeed confirmed by the radiocarbon dates. The bones lay in total confusion and most were broken into very small pieces (plate 5.6). In a few cases bones of a limb, hand or spine were still in articulation. Most bodies were represented by only a few bones. Observation in the chamber and study of the condition of the bones led the excavator and anatomist to the conclusion that the bones had been in a skeletal, or near-skeletal, condition before they were brought to the chamber, the bodies having been kept elsewhere for a time (perhaps buried in sand as the bones show little gnawing), then exhumed, the missing bones being extracted and the residue of mainly small bones

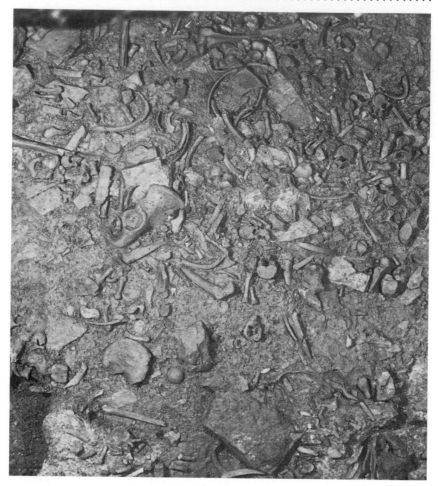

PLATE 5.6. The main bone spread in one of the cells at Quanterness.

brought to the chamber and scattered on the floor. It was found that some selection of bones had been in operation, for instance relatively few skulls were represented and these were broken with most of the pieces missing, and a relatively large number of neck vertebrae and bones from hands and feet were present. It is difficult to explain the reasons for this selection. At Isbister also there was selection of bones, for instance there were few bones from hands but plenty from feet, relatively few vertebrae and these mostly from the neck, and as mentioned there were stores of whole skulls.

Although there were similarities between the Quanterness and Isbister burials, there were also important differences. At the former site the bones were in very small pieces without any sorting or grouping, and they were embedded in a continuous filling of earth and stones. In the OC chambers, by contrast, the bones were always accessible until the final sealing of the chamber, and in a number of chambers the bones were sorted or heaped together, and there was especial care for the skulls. At some OC chambers complete crouched bodies were present, sometimes placed on benches which suggests the idea of sleeping on beds. The fact that the benches were original features and occur in all three varieties of OC chamber, taken with the complete burials on benches which presumably belong to the final phase of the use of the tomb (as at Midhowe), suggests that the rites for which the chambers were built did not change radically. The evidence seems to indicate that complete bodies were laid in the tomb, and at a later stage after decomposition the bones were re-arranged and some removed for cult purposes. At Midhowe and Isbister we may be observing the same rite at different stages. Possibly the sparsity of bones in some tombs is complementary to the abundance in other tombs, the bones being moved from one to another: the bones which predated the Isbister chamber must have come from elsewhere.

But the Quanterness rites were not used in other MH tombs. Quoyness (44), architecturally so like Quanterness, had a circular shallow cist sunk through the clay floor to the rock below and covered by a capstone, reminiscent of the cists at Quanterness. It contained not a crouched burial, but was full of bones which were fairly intact though lacking skulls. Bones and skulls found in the cells and inner part of the passage represented ten adults of both sexes, and four or five children. At Cuween Hill (12) eight skulls and other bones were found. Maes Howe produced only a fragment of skull in one of the cells. In the brief reports of operations at these chambers there is no hint of a bone spread similar to that found at Quanterness, but it may be noted that without wet sieving only a dozen or so bodies would have been reported from that chamber (Renfrew *in litt*).

The situation is further complicated if the seven OC chambers dug by Anderson in east Caithness in 1865–6 are considered (CAT 12, 13, 26, 31, 42, 54, 55), together with two dug earlier by Rhind (CAT 64, 65). There were two distinct layers of burials, of which the upper tallies in general with the Orcadian OC rite, at two chambers there being incomplete articulated skeletons and at two special treatment of the skulls. At other Caithness chambers, as far as can be seen, the rite conforms, and particularly the circumstances found by Corcoran at Tulloch of Assery (CAT 69) where the solid stone benches should be noted. The rite may also be detected as far away as North Uist if the curious 'cist' found in the Unival chamber is in fact a collapsed bench (L. Scott 1948, 12). The lower strata of burials at Anderson's sites were quite different, of compacted earth and stone (the stone sometimes like a partial paving) with bones mixed throughout, the depth being 0.15 to 0.5 m. At three sites it is recorded that the quantity of bone was very great, and mostly it was in small fragments. The descriptions sound like the Quanterness bone layer except that in Caithness fire played a greater part in the rites.

Besides the human bone found in the chambers, the inclusion of animal bone is a widespread practice in Scottish tombs. The relatively moderate amount of such bone at Quanterness was thoroughly studied and it was established that a wide range of animals, many immature or newborn, of birds and of fish, were deliberately introduced at the same time as the burials (Renfrew 1979, 112–49, 153–62). Generally each animal was represented by only one or a few bones, and in the case of a more complete skeleton it could be shown that the remains were widely scattered horizontally in the chamber. Remains of sheep far outnumbered the other species, cattle, red deer, pig, horse, domestic dog, otter and fox, also a very wide range of birds from large to small, and seven species of fish. Studies of the faunal remains from the Isbister chamber showed sheep again to be the main species, with cattle, red deer, otter, dog and pig subsidiary, mainly from immature animals; also thirteen species of fish, two of shellfish, and ten species of birds. Among the last, the most remarkable discovery was at least ten white-tailed eagles, probably introduced as carcases (J. W. Hedges 1983a, 164). A similar range of mammals was identified at some of the stalled cairns though with different species of the larger mammals predominating, as at Knowe of Yarso (32) with parts of thirty-six deer but only a few bones of sheep and one of cattle, or at Midhowe (37) where immature cattle were most numerous. Dog occurred at several sites, as many as twenty-four skulls being found at Cuween Hill (12) and seven at Burray (7). At both OC and MH chambers the animal bones were mixed with the human bones, but they were also in the deliberate filling of the chambers where this existed, notably in quantity at Wideford Hill (54). It is generally assumed that the animal bones represent either the remains of ritual funeral feasts for the living, for there are instances of bones showing cuts or splitting to obtain marrow, or of offerings for the dead as at Isbister where the meat seems to have been introduced as joints but not further butchered. In some cases the extremities of animals, the skulls, antlers and horn-cores, were included; and some of the smaller mammals and birds seem undesirable food. The extraordinary high proportion of white-tailed eagles at Isbister suggests a totemic significance. The dogs may also be a special case, especially where the skulls have been carefully preserved, perhaps explained as the hunters' and herdsmen's best friend.

Like the human and animal bones, the artefacts in the tombs, and particularly the pottery, occur in unpredictable quantity and all stages of incompleteness, and though objects made of perishable materials may have disappeared through decay, this is not the case with stone and pottery. Three OC chambers which have not been disturbed since they were sealed can be compared: Knowe of Yarso (*32*) with at least twenty-nine burials and no neolithic pottery; Unstan (*51*) with an unknown number of burials above five and sherds of at least thirty-five pots; Isbister (*25*) with a very large number of burials and sherds of at least forty-five pots (J. W. Hedges 1983a, 33–43). In the MH group, Wideford Hill with no recognisable burials also had no pottery, Quanterness with a very large number of burials had sherds of at least thirty-four pots. It is generally assumed that the pots came to the tombs as containers, many having been used previously for cooking, and that, having been smashed, sherds were removed haphazardly. At three OC tombs, Calf of Eday, Midhowe and Isbister (*8, 37, 25*), the sherds were in a heap on the floor. At Quanterness the sherds were scattered but their distribution along with other artefacts showed that they had not arrived with the human bones, for no artefacts were found in the cell where the bone was most densely scattered, but the pottery in particular tended to be concentrated in the chamber opposite the end of the passage.

Closure and Sealing

All chambers, when there were no ceremonies in progress, must have been closed by some temporary but substantial means, and in Orkney this was commonly walling, found in place at one or other end of the passage at five OC sites and one MH site (Henshall 1963, 98, 128). At Maes Howe (*36*) there was the unique arrangement of a block of stone which could be pushed back into a recess in the wall.

A different matter is the deliberate infilling of the chamber and/or passage with earth and rubble as the final ritual act, sealing in the contents of the tomb. At some sites the filling was near total, almost to the roof, at some partial, and at some there was no filling at all. As early as 1849 Petrie found the completely roofed MH chamber at Wideford Hill two-thirds full of debris, above the level of the passage roof. He recognised that the filling, which contained animal bones, must have been deliberately introduced through the roof, and observed a chimney-like construction on the top of the mound which seemed to have been built for this purpose. Petrie was present at the opening of Maes Howe (*36*) and observed that the floor of the passage was covered with rubble to a depth of 0.45 m. The entries into the cells are assumed to have been walled up, using the large blocks of stone found on the chamber floor (Petrie 1861, 355–6). At Quanterness (*43*), on the other hand, it is clear that there was no infilling of either the chamber or passage after the last burials, but at Quoyness and Cuween Hill (*44, 12*) the passage was completely filled. With the OC chambers, because they have lost their roofs, there is often uncertainty in interpreting their fillings, but at three chambers certainly, and probably at others, a deliberate filling was present, containing animal remains, occasional artefacts and human bones. At Isbister (*25*), as at Wideford Hill, the cells were not filled though the chamber was: at other OC chambers there was no filling at all (Henshall 1963, 100–1).

DISCUSSION AND CONCLUSIONS

Two distinct groups of chambered cairn have been described, the origins and development of the OC group being fairly clear, but the origins and development of the MH group still being problematic. The writer's suggestion that they derived from the Irish Boyne tombs was never very satisfactory (Henshall 1972, 268) and even less so now that Maes Howe itself is considered to be late within the group. Yet the discovery of the carved slab at Pierowall with its best parallels amongst the Boyne tombs, points clearly to an Irish element in the culture of the tomb builders. A recent suggestion that the MH tombs developed locally as a variant of the shorter of the stalled chambers such as Unstan in response to a desire for a larger rectangular chamber with a more stable roof (Renfrew 1979, 210, fig.55) seems too simple an explanation. It is true there are some striking architectural similarities between the two types of cairn: the basic rect-angularity of the chambers, the rare occurrence of cells in the one and consistently in the other, the cutting back into the hillside for some chambers in each group, the use of an inner and outer casing for the cairn, the adoption of an excessively long chamber plan with rectangular cairn at one MH site in seeming imitation of the long stalled cairns. Yet the differences are even more impressive: in the MH group the lack of vertical slabs in the chamber, the absence of any shelves or benches, the distinctive way the rectangular corbelling is handled, the high roofing of the cells, the use of lintels set on edge, the occasional appearance of pecked decoration, the retention of round mounds even when the size of the chamber required it to be very large, all contrasting with the practices in the OC group. Alone of all the OC tombs Isbister (25) provides a possible link with the MH group, but the radiocarbon dates show this is a hybrid and not a transitional plan.

The individuality of the two groups of cairns is echoed by the pottery they contained, for, as is well known, the OC chambers have consistently produced round-based bowls, local versions of the widespread early neo-lithic ceramic tradition, whilst only two MH chambers have produced pottery, and this is in the flat-based grooved ware tradition (figure 5.4). If the few sherds of beakers and food vessels are omitted, and the possible grooved ware pots from Bookan (4), the pottery from the OC chambers is of two forms, present in roughly equal numbers. The first is a simple deep bowl which is seldom decorated, but exceptionally at Isbister (25) may bear lugs. The other form is a distinctive wide shallow carinated bowl generally decorated on the collar by incision, stab-and-drag or impressions, and is commonly referred to as an Unstan bowl. Both forms have simple rounded or internally bevelled rims. It is convenient to refer to all this pottery as

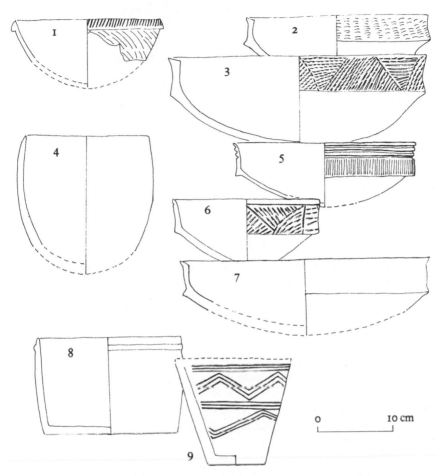

FIGURE 5.4. Pottery from chambered tombs: 1 Sandyhill Smithy;
2 Isbister; 3, 4, 7 Unstan; 5 Midhowe; 6 Taversoe Tuick;
8, 9 Quanterness. Types: 4 simple deep round-based bowl;
2–7 shallow carinated Unstan bowls; 1 open uncarinated bowl;
8–9 grooved ware.

Unstan ware. There is no correlation between either the quantity of pottery,
or variations in its form and decoration, and the varieties of OC chambers,
except in one respect where three unusual uncarinated open bowls (not to
be classed as Unstan ware) were found in three small tripartite chambers, in
two cases in or under the clay floor. The implication is that both the tombs
(2, 27, 47) and the bowls are of early date. In other cases it has to be realised
that most of the pottery is likely to belong to the late use of the chambers,
though a few and probably small sherds might relate to earlier phases; the

difficulty is to recognise them. Little can be said about the affinities of the plain bowls, but the Unstan bowls, generally considered characteristically Orcadian, are known in small numbers from the Western Isles and north-east Scotland as far south as Deeside (Henshall 1972, 177; Reynolds and Ralston 1979). In Orkney, only one habitation site has produced pottery of this type, Knap of Howar, described in chapter 3.

The grooved ware from Quanterness and the less distinctive sherds from Quoyness (44) (Henshall 1979, 75–9) provide a contrast, for their affinities are with the pottery from the habitation sites discussed in chapter 4 and the ritual monuments discussed in chapter 6. The other artefacts from Quanterness fit into this context, and certainly the bone pin and strange stone objects from Quoyness have good parallels at Skara Brae (Henshall 1979, 79–83; 1963, 130). A further link between the tombs and Skara Brae is provided by the designs pecked on stones of three tombs, and the designs on some stones and some sherds at the habitation site.

In the OC chambers, besides the sherds, there was an undiagnostic selection of flints, bone pins, and stone axeheads; also there were some leaf-shaped arrowheads such as might be expected to accompany round-based bowls. A few diverse but interesting objects are likely to have come from a grooved ware source: ground flint knives, a 'fabricator', a macehead, roughly chipped stone objects, bone points, a perforated ox phalange, and bone beads. In most cases the findspots have not been precisely recorded, but twice these objects appear to have been associated with the burials, and at least once, at Isbister, they were in the deliberate filling of the chamber. Immediately outside the cairn at this last site was a cache of objects, some with grooved ware affinities. It is clear that the makers of grooved ware had an interest in OC tombs, sometimes at a late stage in their use or during the sealing of the chamber, or even later.

Following his hypothesis that the MH chambers evolved from OC chambers, Renfrew tentatively suggested that the two pottery styles which correspond with these tomb groups may be explained in the same way, that grooved ware evolved in Orkney from Unstan pottery (1979, 205–8). There seem to be three major difficulties: the great differences in form and decorative techniques, the long chronological overlap of the two styles, and the necessity to account for the grooved ware in the rest of Britain. Regarding the first, recent work on the pottery from Skara Brae and Rinyo has shown that links between the two styles exist, for D. V. Clarke claims that round-based bowls form a small component of the Orcadian grooved ware assemblage at both Skara Brae and Rinyo, and at the latter site the corky fabric familiar from the OC tomb assemblage was used for a flat base (Clarke 1983, 49, 51). Conversely, the pottery from Knap of Howar includes a few sherds with features of grooved ware derivation. Clarke has also shown that the sequence of Unstan ware preceding grooved ware, long thought to have been established at Rinyo, has no firm basis. The relationship of the two pottery styles is not as clear cut as once it seemed, but on the other hand no substantial evidence for a transition of one to the other can be cited. It seems rather that the two styles ran parallel for several centuries, with some contact between them.

A series of radiocarbon dates is now available for neolithic Orkney (appendix), of which those from Quanterness and Isbister (the latter not available to Renfrew for his recent assessment) alone relate to the foundation of tombs (Renfrew 1979, 200–12; J.W. Hedges 1983a, 61–71, 262–66). Although surprisingly early dates for the building of these two tombs are indicated, it must be admitted that, due to the wide latitude involved in one standard deviation and certain inconsistencies in relating some dates to the stratigraphy, the dates can be applied only in very approximate terms. The probability is that the Isbister chamber was built about 3150 BC and was probably not sealed until about 2400 BC giving a period of use of 800 or so years. The dates from Quanterness indicate that it was probably built before Isbister, for the earliest level is dated about 3400 BC, and the main bone deposits span the period about 3000–2400. Satisfactorily, bones from the Quoyness chamber have been dated to about the middle of this period. It is unfortunate that the early foundation date for Quanterness rests on a single determination, perhaps supported by one early date from the chamber deposits, for if correct they confirm that Isbister could not be a link between the OC and MH chamber designs. The dates, spanning the first four centuries or so of the third millennium, which were obtained from animal bone from three stalled cairns on Rousay, do not relate to their foundation, but are likely to belong to the later phases of the use of the chamber or possibly even to the sealing. All that can be said is that a proportion of the tripartite and smaller stalled chambers are likely to be earlier, indeed probably considerably earlier, than Isbister. This is supported to some extent by the radiocarbon dates from The Ord (SUT 49), an OC chamber in Sutherland which is not typologically early but which was in use more than two centuries before Isbister (Sharples 1981, 53). So a date in the early centuries of the fourth millennium seems likely for the earliest Orcadian OC tombs.

The dating of the MH tombs is even less precise. The only chamber directly dated, Quanterness, is unlikely to be amongst the earliest. Wideford Hill (54) which is geographically close and both smaller and simpler in design, may be expected to be earlier. Typologically Vinquoy Hill (53) and Cuween Hill (12) are close to Wideford Hill. Although Maes Howe (36) is thought to be the latest because of its size and sophistication, and the radiocarbon dates from the bottom of the ditch (averaging about 2700 BC) appear to confirm this, yet in design it is nearer to the simpler tombs; also the relationship of the dated material to the tomb, and the true date of the two radiocarbon assays, are uncertain (Renfrew 1979, 36–7, 206).

The pottery found in the tombs presumably mainly dates from the later phases of the use of the tombs. The Unstan pottery from Isbister may date about 3000 BC, the end of the main period of use of the chamber for burials, or possibly later, up to the time it was sealed; the bulk of the pottery from Quanterness can be no more accurately dated than to the first half of the third millennium. The chronological span of Quanterness and Isbister is roughly the same as Skara Brae and all but the earliest centuries of Knap of Howar. The date of the last burial at Quanterness, about 2400 BC, and the sealing of Isbister at about the same time, have been noted. Late closing dates for chambers are indicated at Calf of Eday (8), Knowe of Yarso (32) and Unstan (51), where sherds of beaker and food vessel, and barbed and tanged arrowheads, were found. At Knowe of Yarso the sherds were certainly in the filling (Callander and Grant 1935, 334), and possibly this was the case at the other sites also.

On the present evidence from the Orcadian chambered cairns it seems necessary to accept that through the later fourth and the first half of the third millennium there were two distinct cultural groups occupying Orkney, however difficult it may be to envisage this in operation in such a restricted area. They could not each live in isolation, and some evidence of the give-and-take has been noted, either the acquisition of objects by exchange or otherwise, possibly the adoption of new building techniques, or even perhaps more fundamental changes in attitudes and beliefs. The distribution of the sites attributable to the two cultures emphasises the complexity of the situation (maps 1, 2), with MH tombs dominant on Mainland and Sanday, OC tombs dominant on Rousay, north Mainland, and the southern islands, and a mixture on Eday, Westray and Holm of Papa Westray. It is also surprising to find the habitation site of Rinyo on the OC-dominated island of Rousay, and the same situation obtained on Westray until the recent discoveries at Pierowall. But the distribution map compresses into one picture events spanning a millennium or so, with no allowance for shifts of population or political dominance.

Two burial rites have been detected in northern Scotland, exemplified by Quanterness and Midhowe-Yarso, as suggested above. It may be assumed that the two designs of tombs on Orkney reflect differences in their use and perhaps their symbolism. The construction of benches seems appropriate for crouched inhumations of the Midhowe rite. The nineteenth-century excavations in east Caithness revealed the Quanterness rite below the Midhowe rite, with an indication at one chamber of yet earlier inhumations. There is no helpful information regarding artefacts from five of the nine tombs and most of the finds from the other four are missing. It may be significant that, besides round-based pottery, objects with grooved ware associations have been found at three chambers, and in one case (CAT 13) there is the rare record that one object (a polished knife) was in the lower

9. Isbister chambered tomb, S. Ronaldsay. 'Here again there was interest in skulls' (page 102). The photograph, taken during the recent excavation, vividly captures the 5000-year-old setting.

10. Ring of Brodgar. The great ring ditch, which originally encircled some sixty upright stones, is clearly seen. It is assumed to be about 4000 years old.

stratum. These observations in Caithness seem to indicate interaction between the OC group and representatives (as it were) of a grooved ware/Quanterness rite in an area were MH tombs were not built, with the OC group taking over again in the final phase. The curious chamber at Knowe of Lairo (*28*) may reflect such changes structurally, in the opposite direction, for the chamber in the OC tradition was lined with secondary walling having niches containing parts of burials, reminiscent of a MH tomb.

These observations regarding the interaction detectable between the OC/Unstan ware and the MH/grooved ware groups still leaves the origin of the latter uncertain, for nowhere else in Britain are the makers of grooved ware involved in building chambered cairns. The undoubted connection with the Boyne tombs indicated by the carvings and perfectly acceptable on chronological grounds, cannot be claimed as particularly powerful as far as the structures go, for the building techniques are purely Orcadian and the design of the tombs have no more than a remote resemblance to Irish passage-graves; nor do the artefacts have much in common with their Irish counterparts. It seems probable that the MH tombs are a largely local development. Investigation of the chamber of the Pierowall site would be the most helpful contribution to assessing the contribution from the Boyne.

The importance of chambered cairns to the communities who built them is self-evident when the time, organisation and the economic surplus needed for their construction are considered. The labour estimate for Quanterness is a minimum of 10,000 man hours, and, because of the distance very large stones had to be brought, the estimate for Maes Howe is of the order of 100,000 man hours (Renfrew 1979, 212–4). This continued, and perhaps changing importance of the tombs is revealed by the long time span through which they were in use, and the embellishment of the exterior of a few with long cairns and horned forecourts. It is quite clear that they became much more than just suitable receptacles for the remains of the dead.

Finally, to pass from matters of mystery to matters of imagination, another possible aspect of the significance of the tombs was explored by Lynch (1973) with regard to Irish passage-graves and their possible use as oracles. Her starting point was the 'roof-box' at New Grange which gave access to the passage through a gap in the roof, the gap being too small to allow physical entry. A similar but less elaborate arrangement seems to have existed at some other Irish cairns. This access may have been used for offerings of a perishable kind, but she suggests the design was for

> 'some form of intangible contact with the spirits of the dead inside the chamber . . . that this narrow slot in a complex hollow stone structure could have been used as some form of oracle. People might seek the advice of their ancestors by asking their questions through the slot and their distorted words would come back to them as an answer, of which they could make what they liked.' (Lynch 1973, 152)

We may just consider whether something similar may have been done in Orkney, for instance at Maes Howe where the block designed to close the passage left an 0.5 m gap below the roof, which at such a sophisticated structure was likely to be a deliberate feature. Again, at Wideford Hill (*54*), the chimney-like opening into the chamber roof has been mentioned already: although it was evidently used to infill the chamber, it is tempting to think it had an earlier purpose and was part of the original design of the chamber.

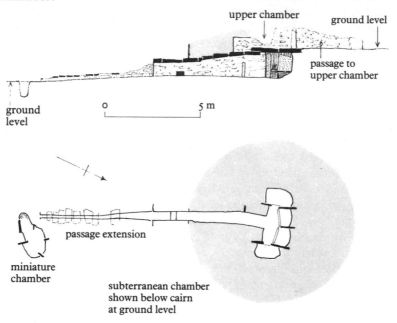

FIGURE 5.5. Simplified plan and section of Taversoe Tuick, a two-storey cairn of the Orkney–Cromarty group.

There are curious arrangements outside the lower chamber at Taversoe Tuick (*49*) (figure 5.5). The lintelled passage projects outwards beyond the revetment of the cairn through a low platform of slabs, the entrance being 1.6 m forward of the cairn edge. Beyond this point the passage walls continue for another 5.8 m, gradually narrowing to only 0.06 m apart at the outer end, with the height of the lintels diminishing from 0.22 to 0.05 m above the floor. The outer end of the passage extension ends at the entry into a subterranean miniature chamber. The entry is a vertical drop, leading to a chamber only 1.5 m across, roofed at a height of 0.9 m, lined with fine masonry, with projecting slabs echoing the Bookan plan. The effect is a half-scale model of a burial chamber. It was intact when found, and contained three complete bowls. Perhaps it was intended for offerings, but it would be possible to crouch in it and speak into the tiny opening of the passage extension. However it was used, it seems obvious the intention was communication with the lower burial chamber, and the miniature chamber was sited in relationship with its outer end. A passage extension once existed at Calf of Eday (9) also, and it could well be that other examples await discovery.

The classification of Orcadian chambered cairns
according to chamber plans (maps 1 and 2)

ORKNEY–CROMARTY GROUP

Tripartite chambers: ORK 1, 2, 5, 6, 11, 23, 26, 27, 28, 42, 47, 56, 62, 67, 70

Stalled chambers: ORK 1, 3, 8, 17, 19, 21, 25, 29, 30, 31, 32, 33, 37, 41, 50, 51, 68, 73

Chambers either tripartite or stalled: ORK 7, 14, 15, 18, 24, 35, 52, 57, 59, 60, 61, 63, 69, 74, 76

Bookan chambers: ORK 4, 8, 9, 10, 13, 23, 49

Sites probably but not certainly Orkney–Cromarty cairns: ORK 34, 39, 46, 58, 64, 65, 78, 79

MAES HOWE GROUP

Certain: ORK 12, 22, 36, 38, 43, 44, 53, 54, 66, 71

Probable: ORK 16, 72, 77

LONG CAIRNS (mapped according to chamber type)
ORK 14, 18, 28, 34, ?41, ?62, 74

Two sites listed in Henshall 1963 are not now considered to be chambered cairns: ORK 40, see comment p.99; ORK 45 is a burnt mound. Four other sites, ORK 20, 48, 55, 75, are unclassifiable and have been omitted from the discussion and the maps.

Sites listed here as ORK 58–79 are additions to the list in Henshall 1963 and 1972 and will be published in Davidson and Henshall *An Inventory of the Chambered Cairns of Orkney* (forthcoming). ORK 58, 59, 61, 62, 64, 67, 69, 70, 75, 77, 78, 79 are included in RCAMS 1946 on the following pages, the inventory number in brackets: 204 (564), 204 (564), 330 (952), 279 (797), 190 (546), 287 (824), 334 (984), 287–8 (827), 332 (967), 172–3 (474), 351–2 (1038), 259 (687). ORK 60, 63, 68, 71, 76 were found by the Archaeology Division, Ordnance Survey, their records are now in the National Monuments Record for Scotland. For the remaining sites the references are: ORK 65, *New Statistical Account 15*, (1845) 54; 66, Bell and Haigh 1981; 72, Neil 1981; 73, Fraser 1980b, 25; 74, Davidson and Henshall 1982.

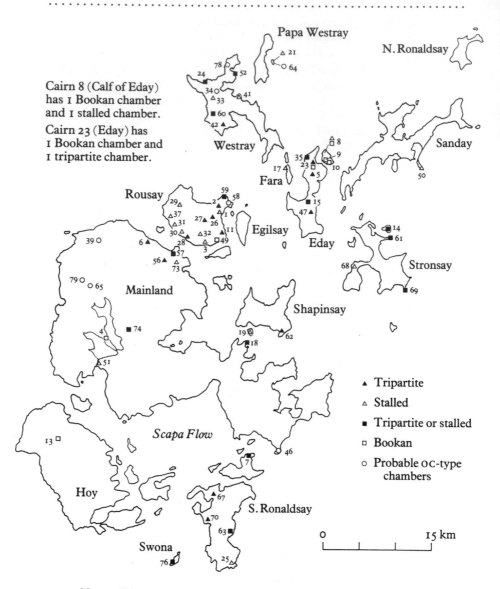

MAP 1. Distribution of cairns with chambers of Orkney–Cromarty type.

MAP 2. Distribution of cairns of Maes Howe type.

6 Graham Ritchie **Ritual Monuments**

The largest of Orkney's inland lochs, the Loch of Harray and the Loch of Stenness meet only at the reedy narrows now spanned by the Bridge of Brodgar and they are separated for the most part by two tongues of land; by far the larger is the NW ridge on which there are the impressive earthworks of the Ring of Bookan (ORK 45), the smaller cairn of Bookan (ORK 4) and the henge monument and stone circle known as the Ring of Brodgar, as well as several groups of burial mounds and standing stones. The smaller and lower promontory to the SE is dominated by the henge monument and stone circle known as the Stones of Stenness, but there are also several other standing stones, and the site of the famous Stone of Odin destroyed in 1814. The chambered tomb of Maes Howe (ORK 36) is some 1.2 km to the E. The superb situation of the Ring of Brodgar, the impressive standing stones both here and at the Stones of Stenness, and the folklore that has accumulated around these sites, have ensured that they have been visited and described by all visitors to Orkney with antiquarian interests since the mid-eighteenth century. Indeed the drawings of Brodgar and Stenness by Richard Pococke, Bishop of Ossory, in 1760 and by the illustrators accompanying Sir Joseph Banks in 1772 are among the earliest representations of northern prehistoric antiquities (Lysaght 1974; plates 6.2, 6.2). George Low, minister of the parish of Birsay and Harray, writing in the 1770s also described and illustrated the stones, although his own account was not published until 1879. The stone circles have retained their fascination for visitors; Sir Walter Scott, for example, used the Stones of Stenness as the location for the climax of his novel *The Pirate*, which was published in 1821. More recently Professor A. Thom has suggested that the Ring of Brodgar

PLATE 6.1. The Stones of Stenness, with the Stone of Odin, the
Watch Stone and, in the background, the Ring of Brodgar:
watercolour by John Cleveley, 1772. (British Library, London,
Add. Ms 15511, f.10.)

and the complex of cairns round it form a lunar observatory.

The Stones of Stenness and the Ring of Brodgar are the most northerly
examples of one of the most enigmatic classes of prehistoric sites – 'henge
monuments'; in general these are circular or oval earthworks comprising a
ditch and a bank, with the latter normally to the outside and composed of
material dug from the ditch. The enclosing earthworks are broken by one or
more entrances to allow access to the central area, and the number of
entrances involved has been used to divide the sites into two main classes:
Class I henges have one entrance and Class II have two or more. Their
distribution is widespread from Cornwall to Orkney, with concentrations in
Wessex and Yorkshire, but such sites are not known on the continent, and
thus represent a peculiarly British response within the social and religious
framework of the third millennium BC (Wainwright 1969). Stone circles are
present in some cases within henge monuments (most notably at Stonehenge, which provides the name for the class of a whole), but they are
exceptional, and the presence of rings of upright timbers for example can
only be demonstrated by excavation (colour plate 10).

Although several campaigns of excavation have been undertaken on
the henge monuments of Britain (particularly at Durrington Walls, Wilt-
shire, at Mount Pleasant, Dorset, at Balfarg, Fife, and at Strathallan,

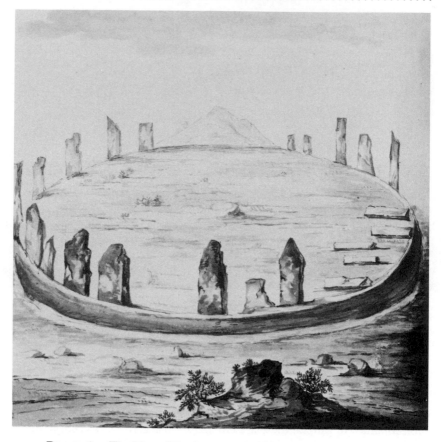

PLATE 6.2. The Ring of Brodgar: pen and ink wash by Richard
Pococke, 1760. (British Library, London, Add. Ms 14257, f.77v.)

Perthshire) our knowledge of the purpose of such sites is still scanty. As will
be seen later, we have rather fuller information about the chronological
range for their use, while the presence of grooved ware at sites both in the
north and in the south has increased interest in the Orcadian henges because
of their proximity to Skara Brae. The excavations at the Stones of Stenness
and at the Ring of Brodgar in 1973 and 1974 were thus designed to set the
Orcadian henges both within a local framework and within a much wider
context.

In their original form the Stones of Stenness seem to have been a classic
Class I henge with the addition of a central stone circle (Ritchie 1976); the
ditch and bank are approximately circular on plan, measuring about 70 m
overall and enclosing an internal area some 44 m in diameter with the single
entrance to the N. Natural erosion and subsequent ploughing have levelled

PLATE 6.3. The Stones of Stenness: ditch terminal cut into
natural bedrock. (Crown copyright: Royal Commission
on Ancient Monuments, Scotland.)

the bank and all but filled the ditch, but the evidence of early plans and
illustrations, air photographs, geophysical survey and limited excavation
combine to confirm this interpretation. The suggestion that the causeway to
the N is the only one is, however, more tentative; no excavation has been
undertaken in the opposing quadrant, but, on the other hand, there is
nothing in the other forms of evidence mentioned above that would make
the presence of an S causeway likely. The bank survived only as a low clayey
band some 6.5 m wide and 0.15 m in thickness, but the ditch was found to
have been at least 7 m across and over 2 m deep the lowest metre or so cut
into the solid bedrock (plate 6.3). Within these features there was a ring of
twelve standing stones laid out on the perimeter of a circle with a diameter of
about 30 m. Four stones stand today, but two of these were re-erected in
1906–7; the stumps of four others are known, the stone holes of a further
three were recovered in the course of excavation and only the position of the
twelfth remains uncertain. Economy of effort suggests that it is likely that
the stones were set up before the ditch and bank were completed, for the

PLATE 6.4. The Stones of Stenness: central stone setting. (Crown copyright: Royal Commission on Ancient Monuments, Scotland.)

existence of the encircling works would have made the manoeuvring and raising of the stones more difficult. At the centre of the site, excavation revealed a setting of four stones set flush with the ground and enclosing an area measuring about 2.1 m by 1.9 m (plate 6.4). From this setting and running in a line towards the entrance causeway in the N, there were the traces first of a pair of standing stones, although only the stone holes and packing remained, secondly the bedding trench of what may have been a small timber construction, and finally another setting of upright stones. This group of uprights was 'restored' in 1907, and was, with the addition of a fourth stone, made into a 'dolmen' or table tomb; it must be stressed that there is no archaeological evidence for such a construction being an original feature, and the additional stone has now been removed.

The finds recovered during the excavations of 1973–4 include a small amount of pottery which may be compared with that from several sites mentioned in earlier chapters: e.g. Skara Brae, Rinyo and Quanterness. Almost a quarter of a grooved ware vessel was found just above the thin initial silt at the bottom of the ditch in the W terminal of the rock cut ditch. Further sherds of grooved ware were found in the complex of deposits, including cremated bone, within the central setting.

Three radiocarbon dates provide further chronological indication of the use of the site. Determinations of 2356 bc ± 65 (SRR-350), from animal

PLATE 6.5. The Stones of Stenness: general view. (Crown copyright:
Royal Commission on Ancient Monuments, Scotland.)

bones at the bottom of the rock-cut ditch, and 2238 bc ± 70 (SRR-351), from
wood charcoal associated with grooved ware sherds in the central setting,
indicate that activity on the site was under way by the early third millennium BC. A date of 1730 bc ± 270 (SRR-592) was obtained from a small
quantity of decomposed wood from what may have been a small timber
structure. Activity on the site in the mid first millennium AD has also been
discovered, for a pit containing carbonised cereal remains and charcoal gave
a date of ad 519 ± 150 (SRR-352) – a reminder of the wonder that the stones
would continue to generate.

It must be remembered that the excavations at Stenness were on a very
small scale and that other features may exist in the interior, though none was
indicated on the geophysical survey (plate 6.5).

At the Ring of Brodgar, 1.5 km to the NW, excavation has been confined to three trenches, two across the henge ditch and one in an attempt to identify the remains of an outer bank; this site has not suffered the vicissitudes of destruction and reconstruction of its sister circle, and the pattern of its layout is reasonably clear. There were originally sixty stones in the circle, which has a diameter of 103.7 m, and these were surrounded by a rock-cut ditch with entrance causeways in the NW and SE quadrants to form a Class II henge; the evidence for the existence of an outer bank is at best inconclusive (Renfrew 1979, 41–3). It may be that the circle was set out using the standard unit of length identified by Alexander Thom as the megalithic yard of 0.829 m and the circle thus has a diameter of 125 megalithic yards. A geophysical survey of buried features in the interior of the circle did not suggest the presence of any pattern of features, although in the absence of excavation it is impossible to be certain. The ditch was originally some 10 m across and as much as 3.4 m in depth (plate 6.6). Radiocarbon determinations from organic mud in the silted ditch at depths of 0.7 m and 0.6 m below the surface respectively provided dates of 255 bc ± 60 and 375 bc ± 45 (SRR-502 and 503). These do little more than indicate that the ditch would still have been a conspicuous feature by the second half of the first millennium BC. The silting of the ditch does not provide helpful evidence of the presence or not of an outer bank; at both Brodgar and Stenness there is a layer including flagstones and boulders within the earliest levels of the ditch fill, but in both cases such a layer is on the inside of the ditch and must represent material introduced from that side rather than slumped bank material (Ritchie 1976, 11, fig.3; Renfrew 1979, 41, fig.15, layer 16). The similarity of the residual remains of the outer bank at Stenness (a clayey band representing material washed down through what must have been a very stony bank) with the dense hump of clayey soil in the appropriate position at Brodgar (Renfrew 1979, 41, fig.15, layer 3) suggests that there was indeed an outer bank at the latter.

The vessel from the west ditch terminal at Stenness is closely comparable to a pot from the chambered tomb of Quanterness (Renfrew 1979, 79, vessel 2); the triple-line incised slack lozenges or triangles and a series of incised lines below the rim show that the vessels belong to a group which includes pottery from Knappers, Dunbartonshire (Mackay 1950; Ritchie and Adamson 1981, 187, vessel 6), Tentsmuir, Fife (Longworth et al. 1967, 75, 90–1) and Balfarg, Fife (Mercer 1981, fig.43, no.8) but here the decoration is confined to the incised lines below the rim. The comparable radiocarbon dates from Stenness, Quanterness and Balfarg (and the pottery here belongs to a period just predating the earliest, and dated, structures) and the similar pottery styles, may suggest wide-ranging contacts outside Orkney – a possibility that has important implications when we come to consider the origins of the henge monument tradition in Orkney.

PLATE 6.6. The Ring of Brodgar: section across the rock-cut ditch.
(Photo Nick Bradford, courtesy Professor A. C. Renfrew.)

It is possible that deposits within the chambered cairn of Bookan (ORK 4) excavated in 1861, may also have been associated with grooved ware; although the pottery is now lost, the small finds within the tomb are quite clearly described (George Petrie quoted by Henshall 1963, 186). 'At the N end of the central chamber a rude flint lance head was found, with fragments of two rudely fashioned fire-baked clay cups or small vessels on its W side, and also fragments of one or more of the same kind of cups on its E side. A rudely formed raised moulding in a waved form encircled the upper part of one or more of the cups.' Whether or not this is indeed a description of grooved ware, the fact that Bookan is the only example of this class of cairn on Mainland serves to underline the rather special nature of the Stenness-Brodgar area.

The interpretation of the Ring of Bookan, the final site of this group lying 1.6 km NW of the Ring of Brodgar, is not at all certain; what survives at present is a broad flat-bottomed ditch, rock-cut in part, enclosing a flat area measuring about 44.5 m by 38 m (RCAMS 1946, ii, 270, no.732). The ditch itself is about 13.5 m across and at least 2 m in depth. The width of the ditch is certainly greater than the two henge monuments already discussed, and its depth, though less than that of the Ring of Brodgar, is comparable to the Stones of Stenness. There is, however, no sign of a causeway across the ditch, although the E side has been obscured by ploughing, nor is there any trace of an outer bank, but the cultivated ground now comes up to the edge of the ditch. Placed eccentrically within the ditch there is an irregular mound and a number of stones, one of which appears to be earth-fast, but it is not altogether clear whether or not these are the remains of a cairn. Certainly on the surviving evidence the interpretation of the site as a Maes-Howe-type tomb finds less favour with the writer than that as a henge monument with a series of internal stone settings or a cairn. The internal area of the Ring of Bookan is closer to that of the Stones of Stenness (44 m in diameter) than that of Maes Howe (76 m by 60 m); clearly only excavation can solve the problem.

INTERPRETATION

One of the most comprehensive interpretations of megalithic remains is the result of the pioneering research of Professor Alexander Thom following his detailed fieldwork and observation in Scotland, Wessex and Brittany; in a series of books and articles Thom has suggested the use of a standardised unit of length in the construction of many megalithic sites, as well as a knowledge of complex geometry in their layout. He has also postulated that the erection and positioning of standing stones and cairns was designed to allow sophisticated observations of the major celestial bodies including the prediction of eclipses (summarised in Heggie 1981). In 1973 Professor Thom and Dr A.S. Thom suggested that the Ring of Brodgar and the burial mounds around it had served as the backsights from which lunar observations could be made, and in 1978 a fourth sight line was put forward (Thom and Thom 1973; 1975; 1978, 122–37). Indeed they suggest that the position of the Ring of Brodgar and the surrounding mounds was determined by the demands of such observations. The four foresights are the high cliffs at Hellia on Hoy, a notch on Mid Hill, two slopes on Kame of Corrigal and a dip on Ravie Hill. Between about 1600 BC and 1400 BC particular phases of the moon's cycle could be detected when it was in such positions, and the burial mounds are used to line up with the distant horizon in order to make the required observation.

It is clear that the evidence of archaeology cannot be used to disprove the possible use of prehistoric monuments in this way; the sight lines as drawn out by Professor Thom and Dr Thom could conceivably have been designed in the way that they envisage. But we lack information about the dates of the construction of the henge monument and stone circle and of the burial mounds. From the evidence of other sites, it seems likely that the Ring of Brodgar itself was constructed within the third millennium BC in terms of calendar years, but the surrounding mounds may well belong to the period postulated by the Thoms.

In other words one's reaction to such interpretation depends on a personal assessment of the mass of statistical evidence in the light of an equally personal evaluation of the archaeological information about the society of the time. The writer's view is that the engineering skills involved in the quarrying and layout of the circles mean that a common unit of length as described earlier is not unlikely, but that the sophistication of astronomical observation required within the contemporary society as we understand it, albeit very imperfectly, makes the detailed niceties of such interpretations most improbable (Heggie 1981). This is not to deny the likely importance of the sun and the moon in the religious calendar of prehistoric Orkney; the illumination of the rear wall of the chamber of Maes Howe (ORK 36) by the setting midwinter sun is a vivid reminder of the way that prehistoric sites may have been constructed with astronomical happenings in mind (e.g. Brown 1975, 95–6). Maes Howe appears to be the only tomb of its type to be so oriented (Henshall 1963, 130); perhaps the unique arrangement at the entrance to the tomb, where a stone found originally in the passage neatly fits a recess on the N side, could be a blocking stone that could readily have been moved out of position and into the recess when required (Henshall 1963, 220). A further midwinter orientation, in this case of sun rise, has been observed at Newgrange, Co. Meath, where the sun shines through the 'roof-box' over the entrance to the tomb, a sort of dormer window, and along the passage to the central chamber. At Newgrange as the sunlight increased 'various details of the side and end chambers could be seen clearly in the light reflected from the floor' (O'Kelly 1973, 142). The observation of the effects of what must be both deliberate orientation and carefully contrived constructional techniques underline the appreciation of such celestial events by prehistoric man.

The radiocarbon dates and the discovery of grooved ware from the Stones of Stenness mean that the use of the henge monument should not be isolated from any consideration of tombs of Maes Howe type and of the settlements of Skara Brae or Rinyo (D. Fraser 1980a, 6). Renfrew has attempted the most detailed assessment of Orcadian society at this time; he sees Maes Howe, the Stones of Stenness and the Ring of Brodgar as the 'three major works of the later neolithic period, reflecting a labour investment of an order of magnitude larger than that embodied in the other neolithic cairns' (1979, 218). Renfrew envisages a shift in the organisation of Orcadian way of life at this time from one based on an egalitarian society, to which belong the vast majority of chambered tombs and presumably the settlement site of Knap of Howar, to a society based on centralised chiefdoms; to this period may be attributed the henge monuments discussed above and the construction of Maes Howe. This attractive and persuasively argued view-point takes on a particular importance because of the similarity of the sequence of events to that postulated for Wessex at broadly the same period (Renfrew 1983). Clearly the three major monuments under discussion, Maes Howe, the Stones of Stenness and the Ring of Brodgar may all have been constructed rather later than the majority of the Orcadian chambered tombs; the existence of the two main categories of tomb outlined earlier by Miss Henshall means, however, that even at an earlier date it might be possible to envisage the sort of larger social grouping that Renfrew sees as being necessary for the organisation of the building of the three central sites.

Approaches to the interpretation of archaeological evidence differ, one school may see the articulation of social frameworks from the mute testimony of fieldwork and excavation, against which an ever increasing body of archaeological data may be gauged and new frameworks created, as providing the one way forward; thus only the demolition of one hypothesis and the formation of another are permissible intellectual attitudes in such archaeological endeavour. Another approach is to admit that the nature of the evidence is such that wide-ranging theorising is not possible nor indeed constructive; thus the inability to build a theoretical edifice amounts to a positive statement that there may be so many imponderables that planning permission should not be sought. This may be a more constructive, and certainly tactful, approach than to attempt to pick out the foundation stones of such a rickety fabrication as that put forward by Hodder for example (1982, 218–28). Thus, although the construction of henge monuments may indeed indicate a change in the social organisation in Orkney, the contemporary use of chambered tombs such as Quanterness may equally suggest a continuing pattern in burial rituals. There are still remarkably few interlocking pieces of our jigsaw puzzle. In his discussion of the Later Neolithic in Orkney based on the excavations at Rinyo, D. V. Clarke has described the current state of knowledge as 'a beginning in understanding the complexities' of the period (1983, 56). Thus to think of the evidence of pottery, tomb

11. Ring of Brodgar. During the 1970s, excavation of the rock-cut ditch exposed the original depth of some 3.4 metres.

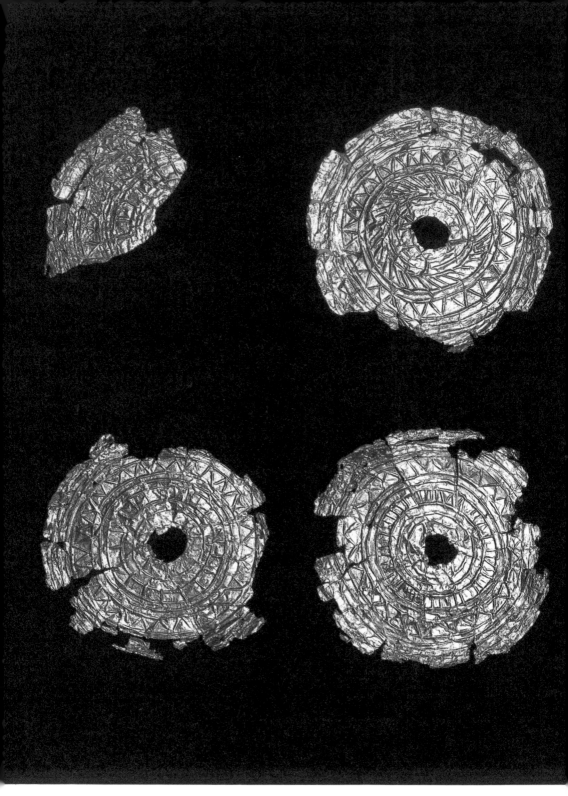

12. Knowes of Trotty. During excavation of this barrow cemetery in 1858, these discs of thin gold foil were discovered. They are thought to be covers for jet buttons, and are probably not of local workmanship.

PLATE 6.7. The Ring of Brodgar: general view.

typology and settlement forms as strands within what may well be a complex society, or succeeding, or parallel societies may well not be far from the mark. Perhaps the work-effort involved in the construction of monuments should not be given more weight in any interpretation of society than the archaeological evidence that implies the contemporary use of the Quanterness and Stenness sites by people using similar pottery. It is wrong to think that the construction of the two henge monuments 'complicates the picture' (Renfrew 1979, 219); the contemporary use of Quanterness and Stenness merely makes it possible to suggest different pictures. In other words the Stones of Stenness must be drawn into 'the pattern of simultaneously functioning sites' outlined by Renfrew (1979, 220), perhaps with a key central location.

Perhaps it is worth re-stating the major questions to which there are as yet no adequate answers – and may well never be! We do not understand the mechanisms by which henge monuments were introduced to Orkney; the absence of any tradition of ditch-digging, partly because of the shallow depth of easily-workable material (and thus the necessity for cutting into the underlying rock), means that the concept of such monuments is indeed likely to have come from the south (plate 6.7; colour plate 11). In his discussion of the monument at Balfarg, Fife, Mercer has, however, raised a chronological problem (1981, 166): the sites at Balfarg and Stenness appear to be earlier in date than those farther south. They are certainly earlier than the large late neolithic enclosures on which recent excavation resources have been concentrated (Durrington Walls, Marden and Mount Pleasant), but early dates have been obtained from henge monuments at Arminghall (2490 bc ± 50; BM-129), Barford (2416 bc ± 64; Birm-7) and Llandegai (2790 bc ± 150; NPL-220) and it may be that imbalance in our knowledge of their date results from excavation preferences. However, the early date for henge monuments, stone circles and indeed grooved ware in North Britain seems assured (Burgess 1980, 41, 48, 339), but what this means in our understanding of Orcadian society is still far from clear. It may well be that henges are a consistent feature of the British Neolithic from at least 3000 BC and that our general picture is unclear because of the small number of radiocarbon windows open to us. Associated with the introduction of the henge-monument tradition from the south is the use of what may just possibly have been a unit of length standard throughout Britain (Thom and Thom 1973; Renfrew 1979, 211). On the other hand, more recent analysis by Heggie has 'found little evidence for a *highly accurate* unit' and 'little justification for the claim that a *highly accurate* unit was in use throughout the area' (1981, 58). Thom's evidence for the possible use of the 'megalithic yard' at Brodgar still seems to this writer at least to be impressive.

Nor do we understand the position of grooved ware pottery, either as far as its floruit in Orkney is concerned, its relationship to Unstan ware in Orkney, or the nature of the relationship between Orkney grooved ware and that from the south. It is worth considering whether the appearance in Orkney of grooved ware need be related at all to the construction there of henge monuments. It is likely, however, that the grooved ware from the settlement sites will provide a more reliable framework for such discussion than will the small number of sherds from ritual or funerary contexts, which may perhaps have been specially selected for such use from a wider ceramic range.

In discussing the Orcadian stone circles in 1814, Sir Walter Scott remarked that the 'idea that such circles were exclusively Druidical is now justly exploded'; in this chapter we have been at pains not to imply that we know more than we do.

7 Sandra Øvrevik **The Second Millennium BC and After**

Social organisation in the Orkney islands in the second millennium and later seems gradually to have evolved along locally autonomous lines, moving away from the centralised organisation which is suggested by the monuments of the Late Neolithic. The burnt mound communities and the barrow cemeteries suggest a dispersed pattern of settlement, with the people represented by these sites having a non-specialist economy based on a combination of hunting, fishing and agricultural activities, perhaps on a semi-nomadic or seasonal transhumance pattern, their few hut circle sites perhaps representing another aspect of this way of life. Evidence of trade is scant, suggesting insular development but not poverty. The artefactual record points to the gradual isolation of the islands. There are few indications of durable wealth, and little evidence of artistic activity. The impression received from the evidence is that the islanders lived in small self-sufficient communities producing little in the way of a surplus to enable the development of a leisured class. Climatic deterioration, and the overuse of the soil in the Late Neolithic, were probably the main reasons for this apparent decline (figure 7.1).

FUNERARY EVIDENCE

Most of our knowledge of Bronze Age society in general comes from studying the funerary monuments which offer most of the site evidence over much of the British Isles. In Orkney, there are over 250 barrows and cairns, alone or in groups (figure 7.2), as well as record of nearly 100 short cists (1946; Ordnance Survey Record Cards), yet our knowledge remains rather patchy. Although a large number of Orcadian barrows or cairns have been

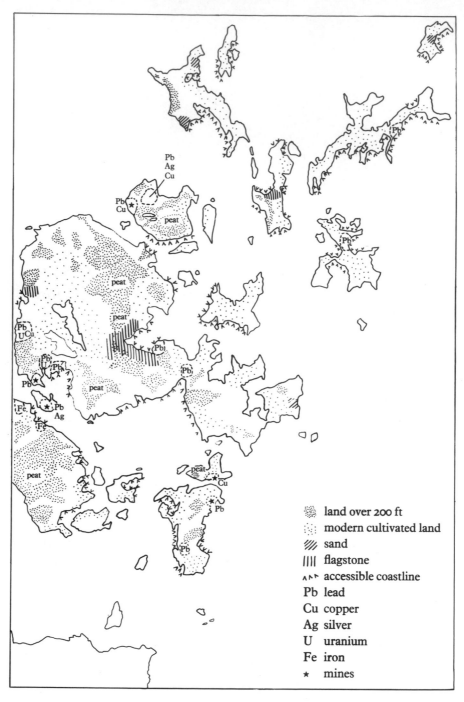

Pb Ag Cu

Pb Cu

peat

Pb

Pb

peat

peat

peat

Pb UCu

Pb

Pb U Pb

Pb

Pb

peat

Fe

Fe Pb Ag

Fe

peat

peat Cu

Pb

Pb

⣿	land over 200 ft
⠿	modern cultivated land
⁄⁄⁄	sand
‖‖‖	flagstone
ʌʌʌ	accessible coastline
Pb	lead
Cu	copper
Ag	silver
U	uranium
Fe	iron
★	mines

FIGURE 7.1. Distribution of the main resources of the Orkney Islands.

N. Ronaldsay
Papa Westray
Westray
Sanday
Rousay
Eday
Egilsay
Wyre
Gairsay
Stronsay
Shapinsay
Mainland
Flotta
Hoy
S. Ronaldsay
Habitation sites
Funerary sites
Ceremonial sites
N. Caithness

FIGURE 7.2. Distribution of Bronze Age sites in the islands.

investigated, few excavations are recent, and there is still only one series of radiocarbon dates for any of the Orcadian barrows (M. E. Hedges 1977). This group, the Knowes of Quoyscottie, is of Middle Bronze Age date. Secondly, burial studies in the islands have been hampered by a lack of dateable associations. In this chapter, chronology is therefore considered in general terms only, except in cases where dates are available: and in a discussion of the bronze artefacts, in the light of John Coles' definitive series of articles on Scottish bronze work (1960, 1964, 1969). Despite a known distribution of about 700 monuments for the period (figure 7.2), based on the records of the Royal Commission and of the Ordnance Survey, absence of recent excavation seriously limits our understanding.

During the Early Bronze Age in the islands, collective burial probably continued in the chambered tombs, and there is certainly evidence of a continuing regard for these monuments. Henshall (1974, 163) concluded her discussion of the Scottish chambered tombs by saying that, although the main period of tomb building was over by the early second millennium BC, they often continued to be used down to the eighteenth and sixteenth centuries BC. There is also Bronze Age evidence of the secondary use of the tombs. For example, Taversoe Tuick (Rousay; ORK 49) had three cists inserted into the infill of the upper chamber (Henshall 1963, 119). The henge monuments, too, became a focal point of burial, as the density of tumuli around the Ring of Brodgar and the Standing Stones of Stenness implies. Graham Ritchie (1976) has demonstrated a continued interest in the Standing Stones of Stenness for 2000 years.

In parallel with the survival of neolithic traditions into the Early Bronze Age, barrow burial and cremation gained in favour. One of the earliest barrow groups in the islands appears to be the Knowes of Trotty, which can be dated on the evidence of the grave goods found in one of the group of twelve. When the largest barrow was excavated (Petrie 1860), it was found to cover a stone cist which contained a cremation deposit together with four gold discs and a number of amber beads (J. J. Taylor 1980, 23, 49) (plate 7.1; colour plate 12). The gold discs may be interpreted as covers for v-bored jet buttons (Coles 1969, 53, 71) and compared to decorated Irish goldwork which is Early Bronze Age. The amber beads included spacer-plate pieces and are comparable with finds from South Britain (Coles 1969, 71). V-bored buttons have beaker associations (D. L. Clarke 1970, 260-5). The only v-bored jet button found in Orkney came from the outside wall of the neolithic tomb at Isbister, where it was discovered with three polished axes, a macehead and a polished flint knife (Henshall 1963, 112, 205, 247), artefacts with both indigenous late neolithic and beaker associations (Roe 1968).

This continuity of late neolithic associations into the Early Bronze Age is also demonstrated by the finding of a beaker in a cist at Birsay close to a disturbed barrow which Hugh Marwick considered may once have covered the cist (1949b, 239–401). It is likely that a number of the short cists which have been uncovered also belong to the Early Bronze Age. About half of these were inserted into natural hillocks or knolls and have been found to contain cremations and inhumations (Ordnance Survey Record Cards). Associated artefacts include polished stone axes, from Dounby and Huan (RCAMS 1946, 38, no.146 and 273, no.770) – a type of artefact not so far associated with barrow burials in the islands.

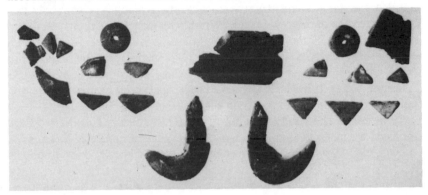

PLATE 7.1. Amber beads and spacer-plate pieces from
Knowes of Trotty, Orkney.

The concentration of large barrows in the vicinity of the henge monuments might indicate that they were the earliest to be erected in the islands, predating the *groups* of barrows; for there is some evidence to suggest that these latter belong, at least in part, to the Middle Bronze Age. There are some notable distinctions between barrow groups and single barrows, with regard to size and location in particular. In a study of barrow diameters based upon measurements given on the Ordnance Survey Record Cards it was apparent that single barrows tend to have a larger diameter than those in groups. It was also clear that in a number of barrow groups, where sufficient details of dimensions permitted such a study, over half of the sample included one or two barrows in a group, which were considerably larger than the rest. This pattern is demonstrated at the Knowes of Trotty (Petrie 1860). If the suggestion is accepted that large barrows represent Early Bronze Age burials, it may be that these groups represent chronological relationships. Equally, the larger barrows might tend to indicate social superiority, and the grave-goods from the Knowes of Trotty would support this view. But this find is exceptional.

The structural composition of barrows and cairns is not well documented. Petrie (1857), in referring to Farrer's excavation of Plumcake Knowe, does not even consider the nature of its composition, though it is probably a stone cairn. Stone kerbs have been recorded from a number of sites. The cairns on Rousay excavated by Grant in the 1930s at the Geord of Nears and Trumland (Grant 1933; Craw 1934) appear to be examples of kerb-cairns, a form of Bronze Age burial noted in Mainland Scotland (Ritchie and Thornber 1975). Radiocarbon dates from a barrow cemetery with small stone kerbs (M. E. Hedges 1977) all fall in the Middle Bronze Age. The Knowes of Quoyscottie is a group of at least 7 mounds, all apparently small scrape-barrows with diameters less than 9 m, and surrounded by roughly-constructed stone kerbs which were probably not visible when the barrows were completed, a feature noted elsewhere in the islands by Petrie. This barrow group shared a number of features with several other excavated sites in the islands, Queenafjold (Ritchie and Ritchie 1974), Quandale (Grant 1937), Corquoy (McCrie 1881) and Summersdale (Ashmore 1974). It has been suggested that this type of barrow cemetery is typical of the Middle Bronze Age in the islands (M. E. Hedges 1977).

The burial rite was cremation, generally in a neatly constructed flagstone cist buttressed (as at Quoyscottie and Quandale) or clay luted (as at Queenafjold). Urn burials occurred at Quandale. Partially beneath one of the barrows at Quoyscottie there was a cremation cemetery of over thirty small pits containing cremated bone and pottery sherds. The cremations were not deposited in urns. Slight evidence from Summersdale (Ashmore 1974) and a site on Fair Isle (J. Anderson 1883, 66–7) and another in Shetland (Barron 1895) suggests this was not an unusual pattern in the Northern Isles.

MATERIAL CULTURE

Artefacts from funerary contexts are fairly undistinguished, and ceramics are almost entirely confined to simple urn forms. Petrological analysis of the pottery from Quoyscottie (Williams 1977, 147–8) showed the vessels had been locally manufactured. Steatite vessels have been recovered from cists and barrows on numerous occasions and were probably as popular as clay vessels, although their rate of survival is higher than that of clay. The nearest source of this soft stone is the Shetland Isles. Originally, steatite vessels were considered to be of Viking date (J. Anderson 1874), but in a series of articles on funerary ceramics manufactured from clay, published in the 1930s, Callander (1934 and 1936) suggested the steatite vessels were of Bronze Age date, and of course the contexts in which they have been found now puts the issue beyond dispute, although steatite was also used later by the Vikings. The decoration on steatite vessels is almost exclusively confined to parallel incised lines beneath the rim, and the occurrence in funerary contexts of similar decoration on pottery urns from the islands suggests that it was copied from the stone vessels. This seems to support the idea of indigenous development in funerary ceramics in the islands, and

PLATE 7.2. Incense cup from South Ronaldsay, Orkney.

perhaps indicates a growing insularity in the Bronze Age, even though developments continued along the lines of a wider tradition.

A rather exceptional find from South Ronaldsay was a yellow clay incense cup (plate 7.2); its discovery is not well recorded, but it appears to have come from a barrow (J.A. Smith 1872). D. L. Clarke (1970, 272) suggests north or west Ireland/west Scotland as the probable place of origin of such vessels. In its total isolation among the funerary ceramics from the islands it should probably be regarded as an import and it may represent a further link between Ireland and Orkney in the Early Bronze Age.

Because of poor conditions of preservation, textiles are rarely recovered from Bronze Age contexts. Portions of woollen cloth of different textures were recovered from a short stone cist at Greenigoe, Orphir, in the 1880s. No traces of bone were apparent, but an amber bead and another of opaque vitreous paste were said to have been found with the cloth (PSAS 23, 1888–9, 123–4). A famous fringed hood of twilled fabric from St Andrews Parish was originally regarded as of Viking date (J. Anderson 1883, 103–5), but is also possible that it may belong to the Bronze Age. It was not recovered from a funerary context, however, but was found unassociated in peat moss. In a cist at Arion found in 1966 a skeleton wrapped in woven material was discovered (Ordnance Survey Record Card no.HY21SE23).

A variety of stone artefacts, typical representatives from prehistoric sites throughout the Northern Isles, has been recovered from barrows and cists. They include pounders, hammerstones and rubbers. Agricultural implements have been recently recovered from the Middle Bronze Age cemetery of the Knowes of Quoyscottie (M.E. Hedges 1977), and it is probable that at least some of the crude stone implements referred to by Petrie (1868) as coming from barrows and cists were also agricultural implements. Stone ard shares have come from a variety of domestic contexts in the Northern Isles, including Tougs, Shetland (S.E. and J.W. Hedges forthcoming), and the burnt mounds of Liddle and Beaquoy, Orkney (J.W. Hedges 1975). The stone ard share distribution is so far confined to the Northern Isles (Rees 1977, 145).

Ritual. The ritual associations of Middle Bronze Age barrow cemeteries are indicated in a few different ways. The presence of charcoal and fragments of cremated bone in the mound material at Quoyscottie (M.E. Hedges 1977) and Queenafjold (Ritchie and Ritchie 1975) indicated that cremation was carried out on or very close to the site of the barrows. Animal bones were found together with the primary burial at Queenafjold and one of those at Quoyscottie. The inclusion of animals as burial deposits seems to have its origins in the Neolithic. Henshall (1963, 72) records numerous instances of animal bones from tombs. The bone analysis at Quoyscottie (Young and Lunt 1977, 146–7) reveals a high occurrence of burials of infants and youths. One of the primary burials was that of a small child and another was of a young person. A double cremation pit on the site contained discrete burials, that of a child and of an adult. Multiple burials in cists are fairly common in the islands (Traill 1876; Petrie 1866) and there is slight evidence to suggest that these multiple burials are more often inhumations in flat cists than cremations (though in the past it would have been more difficult to recognise multiple cremation deposits). In a barrow in the parish of Evie and Rendall, described by Petrie (1866), there were two central cists sharing the same basal flag but divided by a central flagstone beneath which was another cist containing two contracted skeletons. These double and treble cists which appear to have been erected simultaneously may represent a family or tribal catastrophe. They are rarely found outside of Orkney. The deposition of agricultural implements in Bronze Age funerary contexts indicates the significance of agriculture to the Bronze Age communities in the islands.

The distribution of Bronze Age burial monuments must be regarded with reserve. J.B. Stevenson (1975, 104–8) has emphasised the problems which hinder any attempts to understand prehistoric settlement patterns. Cultivation has clearly affected the distribution of barrows in the Orkney Islands. Even in the nineteenth century F.W.L. Thomas (1852, 100) was lamenting the adverse effects of agricultural practices on archaeological monuments in the islands. The fact that the larger single barrows and cairns are often situated on flat cultivated land whilst the smaller barrows in

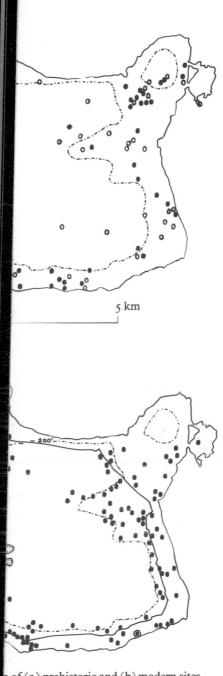

5 km

n of (a) prehistoric and (b) modern sites

groups tend to be in marginal areas is probably as much a result of destruction by cultivation as anything else. Nevertheless it is tempting to suggest that the location of the barrow groups which are probably of Middle Bronze Age date indicates a growing awareness of the value of cultivable land. The close association between agricultural complexes and funerary monuments and the dual purposes attributed to some cairns in the Bronze Age period, particularly in Highland Zone regions, has been demonstrated in Yorkshire (Fleming 1971), and Shetland (Calder 1956). There is certainly some evidence to suggest a close geographical relationship between hut circles and barrows, and the site to the south of Mid Howe (RCAMS 1946, 263, no. 706) and recent excavations at Spurdagrove (S. E. Hedges forthcoming) suggest that the hut circles and field systems may be contemporary with at least some of the barrows in the islands.

A study of a selection of barrow groups similar to Quoyscottie by Parry (1977, 151–2) has shown that their distribution may relate to that of the burnt mounds. The tendency of the cemeteries to occupy the junction of arable and uncultivated ground might be taken as an indication that these cemeteries were positioned on the boundaries of territorial zones occupied by the users of the burnt mounds (figure 7.3).

TECHNOLOGY AND TRADE

The number of bronze objects from the Orkney islands is small, but still provides evidence of some trading contacts, and links the Orcadian Bronze Age to the rest of Britain. Because most of the artefacts have been found unassociated, and a good number unprovenanced (Ordnance Survey Record Cards), they do not give us much help in clarifying the chronological relationships of Bronze Age monuments in the islands. Any review such as this is greatly indebted to John Coles' study of Scottish metalwork and its accompanying corpus of Scottish material (Coles 1960, 1964, 1969).

There are a few copper deposits in Orkney (figure 7.1; based on Mykura 1976, 121) and although they are comparatively small, attempts have been made in the past to mine them. Mykura (1976, 119) notes one site in Burray, and another on Rousay, worked in the past. But there is no evidence to date, either in the form of site evidence, or derived from the objects themselves, to suggest that copper ore was mined in the islands in the Bronze Age.

Throughout the Early and Middle Bronze Age periods the Orkneys stand in contrast to neighbouring Caithness in the paucity of metal artefacts. Only two flat axes have been found in Orkney, but Caithness has eight. The reasons for this difference must lie in the growing isolation of the islands, which is evidenced in other aspects of the archaeological record. A flat axe (type Bc), possibly from Orkney (Coles 1969, 84; plate 7.3) may well represent the earliest bronze artefact in the islands. Another Early

PLATE 7.3. Early Bronze Age flat axe, unprovenanced, Orkney.

Bronze Age artefact, found in a peat cutting in Rousay in 1905, is a rather fine dagger with double ribs and rivets and the remains of a horn hilt (Cursiter 1908; plate 7.4). No other metal artefacts which typify the Early Bronze Age are represented in the islands; spearheads, flanged axes and halberds are all lacking, and there is a similar narrowness of range in the types of metal artefacts from Caithness. The paucity of bronze objects in the islands in the Early Bronze Age is particularly characteristic of the north of Scotland generally. Coles (1969, 69) suggests that the first real phase of industrial activity in Scotland commences around the seventeenth century BC.

PLATE 7.4. Bronze dagger with handle of horn, Rousay, Orkney.

A similar situation is seen for the Middle Bronze Age and suggests that Orkney failed to establish itself within the mainstream of developments at this time. The idea of regional insularity is favoured by Coles (1969), though Burgess (1974, 199) disputes the notion. Climatic factors began to affect the British Isles unfavourably in the late second millennium (Burgess 1969, 167), and it is reasonable to assume that areas in the extreme north of

Britain felt the effects earlier and more strongly. Communication routes could have been affected, and this could account for the apparent isolation of the islands during the Middle Bronze Age.

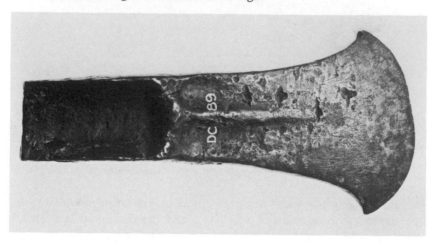

PLATE 7.5. Flanged axe, unprovenanced, Orkney.

Nevertheless, the metal artefacts in the islands reflect sporadic links with other areas of Scotland. A flanged axe (Class II) (Coles 1964, 140; plate 7.5), attributed to Orkney, represents a series of axes which appear to be late on typological grounds; Coles classified it as of the 'Haddington' Group, which is regarded as a local industry probably based in the Forth Valley (Coles 1964, 92). The presence of this axe in the islands indicates contact, possibly conducted along east coast sea routes. A type D spearhead (Coles 1964, 143) found in a peat cutting near Nether House, Firth (H. Marwick 1949b) could have reached Orkney from neighbouring Caithness, for, although this type of spearhead has a fairly general distribution in Scotland and south Britain, a number of moulds have been found in north Scotland (Coles 1964).

A sandstone mould for a flanged axe (PSAS 43, 1908–9, 10) represents half the total for that particular type of axe in Scotland; both moulds were broken. Moulds have generally been taken to indicate manufacture within the vicinity of the find (Coles 1964), but usually only when there is more than one, and, as there is no other evidence to suggest metal-working in the islands at this time, the mould fragment must be regarded as something of an anomaly.

The only associated metalwork for the Middle Bronze Age in the islands is a small double-edged razor with an oval blade and partial midrib on one surface, which was found in a cist inserted into Laughton's Knowe (C. M. Piggott 1947; plate 7.6). It has a tang and appears to have been cast in one piece (Coles 1964). A late second millennium BC date is preferred for this type of razor which compares with radiocarbon dates for burnt mounds and small barrow cemeteries.

PLATE 7.6. Bronze Age razor from Laughton's Knowe, Orkney.

By the Late Bronze Age, however, metal artefacts were clearly more commonly in use in the islands. This is in accord with the increase in production of metal objects which occurs in Scotland at this time (Coles 1964, 129). The relative numbers of metal artefacts in Orkney and Caithness is now reversed, with Orkney having eight, twice as many as Caithness (Coles 1960). The range of bronzes is also greater in the islands, with socketed axes, socketed knives, and razors all represented in Orkney and absent from Caithness. On the other hand, Caithness has two native, Ewart-Park type, swords; a wooden version of this type was found in a peat cutting in St Andrews and Deerness Parish (R. B. K. Stevenson 1958; plate 7.7). During the final stages of the Late Bronze Age a settlement producing locally manufactured artefacts was established at Jarlshof in Shetland. The artefacts produced at this site are consistent with native developments and represent the Adabrock phase of the Scottish Late Bronze Age (Coles 1960). The wooden sword already mentioned is made of yew, a type of tree represented in the pollen from prehistoric sites in the islands. It has been dated to 900–700 BC and is a fairly early copy of the British Hallstatt series of leaf-shaped swords and indicates how rapidly this new type penetrated the British Isles.

Some rather unusual metal artefacts now appear in the islands, unusual because of their distributions. Two socketed knives, one representing part of a personal hoard, have been found at different times in peat in St Andrew's and Deerness parish. They are classified by Coles (1960) as of Thorndon type and their distribution in Scotland is extremely sparse. The one that formed part of a hoard was found together with a bifid, notched, and perforated razor (plate 7.8). Coles (1960) compares the hoard with one from Thorndon, Suffolk, which is dated at around the eighth century BC

and which gives its name to the Thorndon class of socketed knives. The presence of two of this type in Orkney is of some interest in view of their predominantly southern distribution. It is also interesting that they were found in close proximity (C. M. Piggott 1947).

Socketed axes make their appearance in the Late Bronze Age and two have been found in the islands. One, which is now lost, and unclassified, was apparently discovered under a cist (Cursiter 1887). The other axe is described as a facet-type (Coles 1960, 71) and can probably be related to the ribbed axes which have an east Scottish distribution and are attributed to a fairly late phase in the Late Bronze Age (Coles 1960). Other finds from the islands include three spearheads, two of which have rather unusual associations and perhaps indicate the value of these objects to later cultures. A 'pair' of spearheads (Cursiter 1887) were recovered from sites in Birsay. The first, listed by Coles, was found in the top of Saevar Howe, a large sandy knoll known to contain a Viking settlement. The second, according to Cursiter, came from a location a mile or so away from the first and this is presumably the one referred to on the Ordnance Survey card as coming from the Bishop's palace, Kirkwall or Birsay. It was apparently found sticking in a skull. The contexts of both of these are clearly uncertain. The third, a Class IV leaf-shaped spearhead, is comparable to two from Caithness, and Coles assigns them all to the Late Bronze Age although they are of a type which has been found in Middle Bronze Age contexts elsewhere (Coles 1964).

Where associations are known, in three instances they are with funerary monuments. Five artefacts have been discovered in peat cuttings. The reason for this is probably one related to factors of preservation. However, the fact that three of the finds, including the Late Bronze Age hoard, all came from the same peat moss in St Andrews and Deerness deserves consideration. Both of the Thorndon socketed knives and the wooden sword came from this peat moss. It is possible that they represent deliberate depositions, at a time of increasingly hard conditions due to climatic deterioration.

Deductions. When the metal artefacts are compared with the ceramics from the islands they seem to indicate an

PLATE 7.7. Late Bronze Age model, in yew, of a Ewart-Park-type sword, St Andrews and Deerness, Orkney.

13. Liddle 'burnt mound'. The plate, taken during 1970s excavation, shows the typical stone cooking-trough. Filled with water, and heated by dropping in hot stones, it was then used, it is thought, to cook large joints of meat. Burnt mounds were much in use about 1000 BC.

14. Spurdagrove farmstead. Bronze Age Orkney reveals, as yet, 'few indications of durable wealth'. A paved area, and part of the wall of a Bronze Age hut, are shown during excavation in 1978.

15. Midhowe Broch, Rousay, was excavated in 1930-33.

16. Broch of Gurness. Part of the interior, showing hearth and flagged compartments. Compare plate 8.5.

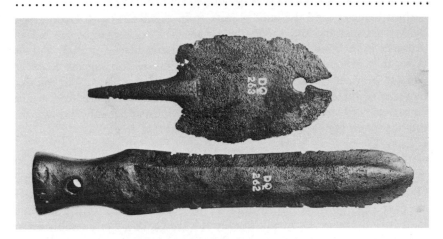

PLATE 7.8. A razor and a socketed knife from a Late Bronze Age hoard,
St Andrews and Deerness, Orkney.

absence of any sustained, substantial, contact with the rest of Britain, with the exception of Shetland.

The context and association of funerary ceramics for the Bronze Age in Orkney have already been discussed and apart from a few rather unusual finds, such as the incense cup from South Ronaldsay (Smith 1872), funerary ceramics appear to be the result of local manufacture developed in response to an imported funerary tradition, but displaying little of the variety of form, decoration and fabric found elsewhere in Britain. Funerary ceramics are very simple and there is little display of skill. One of the most interesting features of this pottery is the incised line decoration which appears to have been adopted from that used on steatite vessels. This form of decoration is almost exclusive to vessels from the Northern Isles, both steatite and ceramic. It is interesting to note that steatite has not so far been found in domestic contexts in the Orkney Islands although it does occur on such sites in Shetland. This shows that steatite vessels at least were produced specifically to meet the demands of the funerary traditions. The same cannot really be said for the pottery, although incised line decoration has not been found on domestic ceramics. There does seem to be evidence, largely from the form of decoration, to suggest that funerary ceramics and domestic ware, whilst basically similar in fabric and form, were separate industries.

The presence of metal artefacts and steatite vessels in the islands is a result of outside contacts. The steatite indicates a steady trade, probably with Shetland, and the form of decoration using incised lines is common to both groups of islands. The metal artefacts, particularly in the Early and Middle Bronze Age, indicate sporadic import, rather than trade. The earliest bronzes, and the gold objects from the Knowes of Trotty, have beaker associations and should be regarded as an aspect of the beaker presence in the islands. The differences in the numbers of artefacts and the types they represent in Orkney and Caithness seem to suggest a lack of contact between the northeast Mainland and the islands. The sudden increase of metal objects in the islands in the Late Bronze Age, whilst consistent with trends in the Scottish metal industry, might indicate the establishment of new contacts with Shetland at this time.

DOMESTIC EVIDENCE

Burnt mounds. The best documented and most easily identified group of domestic sites in the Orkney Islands is the burnt mounds, of which there are over 200 known: a similar number has been recorded for the Shetland Isles (RCAMS 1946; Ordnance Survey Record Cards). Considerably fewer have been noted in Caithness and Sutherland (Ordnance Survey Record Cards) but dense distributions are recorded for Wales and southern Ireland (O'Riordain 1953). This general distribution, implying peripheral locations, is belied by the distribution of the sites within the Orkney Islands themselves – where they have been found to occupy the best agricultural land (J.W.Hedges 1975, fig.22). J.B.Stevenson (1975, 104–8) has emphasised the factors of discovery and survival as they affect archaeological site distributions in Britain, and in particular the effect on the proportions of sites in the Highland and Lowland Zones. It is therefore merely speculation to try to reconstruct a meaningful general distribution for these sites at the present time.

The dating of two burnt mounds in Orkney, Liddle and Beaquoy, suggests a range in the Middle and Late Bronze Ages (J.W.Hedges 1975). A series of thermoluminescence dates for a group of burnt mounds in the islands provides a date range of 1000–400 BC (OxTL 189 b–i) (Huxtable 1975, 82–4). However, dating evidence from Ireland, where a number of excavations have been carried out by O'Kelly (1954), indicates a more diverse date range with dates covering the Neolithic and Iron Age (J.W. Hedges 1975, 78, fig.23). Theories as to the purpose of these sites are equally varied. They are connected with a domestic function, and O'Kelly (1954) has suggested that they were temporary hunting camps used for cooking huge joints of meat. Evidence from the excavated sites in Orkney suggest they were used by agriculturalists. A typical burnt mound is characterised by a huge heap of burnt stone and domestic midden. Evidence from the records of the Royal Commission and the Ordnance Survey show that at least forty, or one-fifth of the total, were associated with structures usually in the form of a large, watertight container; walling has also been noted (colour plate 13). Cooking with burnt stones was practised at prehistoric sites throughout Britain but what distinguishes the burnt mounds is the huge size of the mounds and the dominating presence of the cooking trough. It is clear that the sites had a specific function.

The plans of the buildings at Liddle and Beaquoy (J. W. Hedges 1975, 44, 55, figs 5 and 16) (figure 7.4) resemble other domestic site plans in the Northern Isles, particularly Calder's prehistoric houses in Shetland (fig.74).

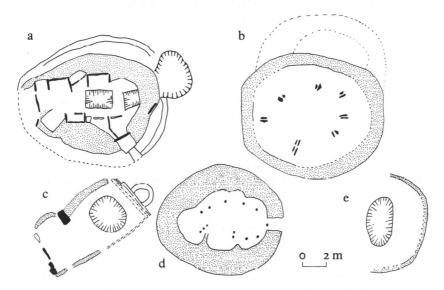

FIGURE 7.4. Some prehistoric house plans from the Northern Isles:
(a) Liddle burnt mound; (b) Spurdagrove farmstead; (c) Beaquoy burnt mound; (d) Ness of Gruting, Shetland; (e) Spurdagrove farmstead.

Some of the domestic pottery from the burnt mound sites, Liddle and Beaquoy (J. W. Hedges 1975) appeared to be gritted with burnt stone. This indicates local manufacture and suggests that pottery was produced, at least for domestic purposes, on the lines of a cottage industry.

Ard shares were found at both Beaquoy and Liddle: and bones of sheep or goat, fragments of a quern and the presence of cereal pollen in the records from Liddle all connect the sites to agricultural activities. Shetland has provided more direct evidence. Recent excavations at an agricultural complex at Tougs showed that a burnt mound was contemporary with the other structures. Skeletal remains at Beaquoy, however, included bones of seal or whale and red deer providing evidence of other activities besides agriculture and more readily comparable with O'Kelly's ideas for the Irish burnt mounds.

The problems of function and period of occupation are interrelated. Arguments in favour of permanent occupation can be found in J. W. Hedges

(1975). It is also possible that they were a focal point for small communities and not actually dwellings themselves. The small available floor space in the buildings, suggests that they were not dwellings. Quite possibly a burnt mound served as a cook-house for a small community (figure 7.4). There is no very good evidence to indicate whether or not the communities using the burnt mounds were sedentary or mobile. Higgs and Jarman (1972) suggest that houses and even villages need not necessarily be regarded as indications of a sedentary society.

Field systems. The few known hut circle and field system complexes in the islands provide some further evidence of developments in agriculture. Recent excavations at Spurdagrove (S. E. Hedges forthcoming) showed that, although the visible field system was confined to uncultivated land, there were indications that it had originally extended downhill on to present-day cultivated land. The occupation of a lower slope is repeated at other field-system sites in the islands, notably one on Auskerry, Stronsay. Due to the poor state of preservation at Spurdagrove little environmental material was available for study, but artefactual evidence included a number of implements similar to those found at the burnt mounds and at Quoyscottie. In particular, stone ard shares and other agricultural implements were well represented. Flint was notably absent at Spurdagrove as it was at the burnt mounds and Quoyscottie; a few flints from Beaquoy appear to predate the site. An interesting feature of the 'huts' at Spurdagrove was the use of small field stones in the construction of the walls (colour plate 14). A similar use of small stones was noted at Tougs, Shetland, and seems to have been a good way of using field-cleared stones. The field walls at Spurdagrove had obviously been adopted by later agriculturalists and it was felt that the remaining field shapes were not representative of the original farm. Perhaps the most interesting feature at Spurdagrove was the likelihood that one of the 'huts' was in fact a byre. A series of stone-lined oblong post-holes, 2–3 m apart, formed a radial pattern about 1 m in from the inner wall face; the resulting divisions could have been used as animal stalls (figure 7.4). The pattern is similar to that recorded at the Iron Age site of Alnham, Northumberland (Jobey and Tait 1966). The absence of domestic refuse and of a hearth are also consistent with the interpretation of the building as a byre. The other 'hut' at Spurdagrove had been refloored. The primary floor had contained a large, clay-lined pit of similar size and shape to that at Beaquoy burnt mound. Again there was no evidence of a hearth. At some stage this pit had been filled in, and a new floor laid using stones to produce a cobbling effect. This floor level showed signs of heavy disturbance consistent with it having been trampled by large animals: Bradley's remarks on the devolutionary cycle of uses of buildings may be relevant here (1978, 49).

The disproportionately low number of hut circle sites in comparison with burnt mounds makes difficult any comparison of their relative distributions within the islands. The hut circles appear to favour the lower hill slopes now relegated to pasture, whereas burnt mounds are usually found on agricultural land or in marshy places. Of course, burnt mounds would have a better chance of surviving the onslaughts of agriculture than field systems and hut circles. The field systems survive in so fragmentary and altered a condition that it is not possible to make any calculations about crop sizes or population. The pollen evidence from the burnt mound sites (R. L. Jones 1975) and Quoyscottie (R. L. Jones 1977) suggests an open landscape dominated by *Calluna* heath and small shrubs with indications of cereal production at Liddle and slight indications at Quoyscottie.

CONCLUSION

By the middle of the first millennium BC the Scottish Highland Zone and the Northern Isles appear already to have begun to develop the special character they have today. Population declined as cultivation became impossible at higher altitudes and on poor soils. Encroaching peat and heath resulted in pressure on the best land (Burgess 1974, 167). Apart from the metalwork there is, as yet, no direct evidence for the Late Bronze Age in the islands. The Orcadian earth-houses may, however, provide a missing clue. There are 30 in all in the islands and they form a remarkably uniform group quite distinct in some important aspects from those found in the rest of Scotland. So far they have been regarded as Iron Age largely on the basis of evidence from mainland Scotland and despite the fact that one in Shetland at Jarlshof is of Late Bronze Age date (Hamilton 1956, 38). They are fairly consistent in architectural design, being around about 3–4 m long and extremely low, usually about 1 m in height. They have been sunk into clay or hewn out of rock, and generally lack stone built walls. They were roofed with huge slabs of stone supported on free-standing pillars of stone. The means of entering the chamber was by a short (usually) narrow and low passage. At Upper Cairn on Hoy there were door checks at the inner end of the passage.

Most have been robbed in the past, but half have produced a few finds, usually in the form of domestic midden, animal bones, simple unclassified pottery and simple stone implements: querns were found at a couple of sites. The domestic nature of these sites seems to be attested by the nature of the finds from them (excluding Rennibister which must be given special consideration). Quite possibly they were storage houses (Hamilton 1956, 39). Earth-houses have been interpreted as possible storage rooms for dairy products (Bradley 1978, 51). The apparent desire for concealment has led to the suggestion that they were hiding places used in times of adversity. It is, however, quite possible that some of these buildings were food stores of semi-nomadic groups who occupied the islands towards the end of the Bronze Age.

8 John W. Hedges **The Broch Period**

HISTORY OF RESEARCH

Norsemen in the ninth century evidently knew what brochs were for, since they called them *borg,* a defence (from which broch comes), and they may even have been quite familiar with them, since Mousa on Shetland, at least, was still usable at that time (J. Anderson 1873, cxi). There then seems to follow a period in which the knowledge was lost; Wallace (1700, 57) confused them with burial mounds. Barry, who considered them Pictish, gave a passable account of a broch tower in 1805, but stated it to be based on excavation further south, as the inhabitants of the Northern Isles had more respect for their ancestors than to carry out such investigations (Barry 1805, 96–8).

In spite of Barry's sentiments, there can be no doubt that casual enquiries did continue. The first actual account of an excavation was in 1825, when the son of the parish clergyman dug into the Broch of Burgar (Evie). He found a comb, a deer's horn and a skeleton. In the 1840s the proprietor conducted considerable excavations there, and found a great treasure which he reputedly threw into the sea lest the Crown should seize it (Petrie 1890, 89). In the mid-nineteenth century, Captain F.W.L. Thomas' visit to Orkney resulted in his important and original article on the antiquities, but he was able to illustrate only two plans of brochs: Burgar and Hoxa, neither of which was in any way satisfactory (figures 8.1 and 2). He made a plea for further excavation (F.W.L. Thomas 1852, 119, 210, pl. 17): 'though nearly all the Pictish Broughs in Orkney are greatly dilapidated, good service may yet be done by clearing away the rubbish which surrounds the original tower'.

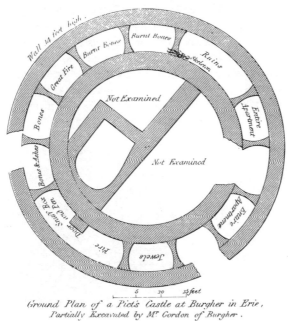

Ground Plan of a Pict's Castle at Burgher in Erie,
Partially Excavated by M.r Gordon of Burgher.

FIGURE 8.1. Broch of Burgar, Evie. A cryptic plan exemplifying the
state of knowledge in the early 1840s. (Thomas 1852, pl.17.)

The age of intelligent *antiquarian* enquiry in Orkney is very clearly
defined, only spreading slightly either side of the date bracket 1850–80.
Many individuals were involved, but there are three main characters. Of
these, George Petrie is by far the most important. He was a local man who
worked as factor for an estate. His station in life meant that he was directly
responsible for the exploration of only two brochs; for the most part he just
made rough sketches, with annotations and measurements, of what others
had done.

James Farrer, the second of the trio, was Member of Parliament for
Durham and was on good terms with the Earl of Zetland, the owner of large
tracts of land. During his summer visits Farrer hired labour to dig into a
number of brochs (and other sites). In most instances his work was of the
lowest quality and were it not for Petrie we would have hardly any record of
it. Finally, there is Sir Henry Dryden, the famous architectural illustrator.
His name was connected with the recording of several of the monuments at
the time of their opening or soon after. A large number of his extant
drawings are however based solely on Petrie's sketches which he obtained
after the latter's death.

Up to his death in 1875 Petrie was involved in the recording of some
twenty or more broch sites. Most of these were investigated only in a minor

and uninformative way. We see him first of all in 1847, at Oxtro in Birsay, making notes on the quarrying away of a mound by workmen (Petrie 1890, 76–8, 86–7); here, supposedly 'Bronze Age' cists overlay the broch, relegating it, as he erroneously inferred, to the Stone Age. In 1848 at the Howe of Hoxa (South Ronaldsay), came one of the two widely separated occasions when he was actually in charge of operations; he positively scoured the inside, preparatory to it being turned into an ornamental garden by the owner (figure 8.2) (F. W. L. Thomas 1852, 119–22).

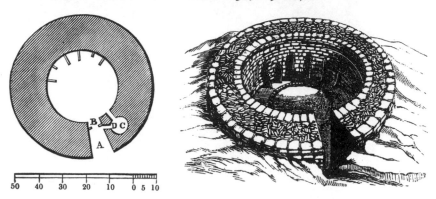

FIGURE 8.2. Howe of Hoxa, S. Ronaldsay. Excavated by Petrie in 1848 when his knowledge of brochs was rudimentary. The interior was scoured; the wall, as shown, is rebuilt; and the entrance plan has been fabricated. (Thomas 1852, 120.)

In 1862 at Burrowston (Shapinsay) Petrie was invited to see the works undertaken by the landowner, and recorded by Sir Henry Dryden. Not only was the broch tower emptied out with some care so that internal structures were preserved, but it was trenched around and a narrow run made out to the sea (figure 8.3) (Petrie 1890, 81–4, 87). In 1865 and 1866 a precisely similar undertaking was carried out by the Reverend Dr Traill at Netlater, Harray (plate 8.1) (Petrie 1890, 78–81, 88). In 1866, perhaps catching the spirit of the times, Farrer worked more systematically in emptying out the Broch of Burrian (Russland), Harray (plate 8.2) (Farrer 1868, 103–5).

The year 1866 is a key reference point, for Petrie then addressed the Society of Antiquaries of Scotland on the subject of Orkney brochs. His paper was not printed until 1874 and was not published for a further sixteen years (1890). It was perhaps as a result of reflections on this summary of work-to-date that Petrie commenced his own large-scale work at the Broch of Lingro (St Ola) in 1870; he was funded both privately and by the Society of Antiquaries of Scotland. Here he had the opportunity of investigating as he wanted to; surprisingly there is no increase in the precision either of the

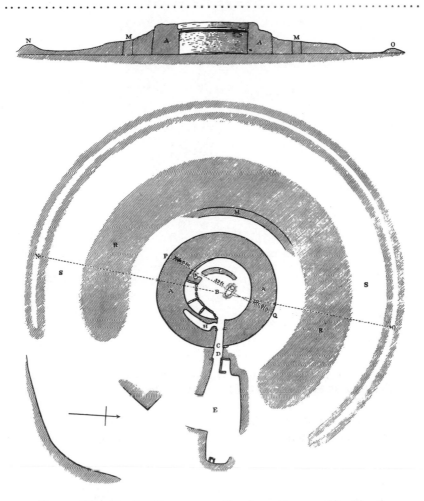

FIGURE 8.3. Broch of Burrowston, Shapinsay. Excavated in 1862; the interior was carefully cleared, the tower trenched around and a barrow run made through outbuildings. (Petrie 1890, fig. 10.)

digging or the recording but Petrie not only emptied the interior with care but had an extensive area of outbuildings around the broch cleared out (plate 8.3) (largely unpublished; J. W. Hedges forthcoming a). The possibility of such outbuildings had already often been suggested by the appearance of structures during trenching operations around broch towers, and in digging out barrow runs.

The impetus continued for a short time after Petrie's death. The Broch of Burrian in North Ronaldsay was investigated by the proprietor of the island in 1870 and 1871 with some help in recording from Dryden (Traill

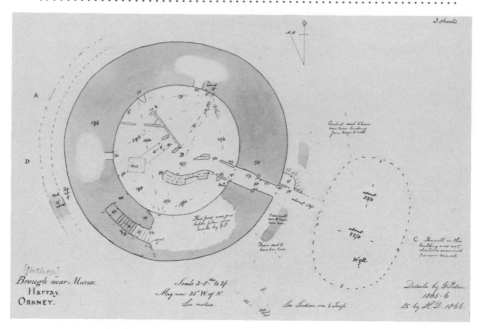

PLATE 8.1. Netlater, Harray. Excavated in 1865 and 1866. (Dryden nd.)

1890, 341–64). The approach taken was unimaginative in the sense that only the interior was cleared, but here two occupations were found and the finds were rigidly separated. This is the first instance of such stratigraphic excavation. In 1881 W. G. T. Watt of Skaill House, Sandwick, commenced operations at the Broch of Borthwick. His work was unsystematic and his publication incomprehensible (Watt 1882), but he did notice two phases of occupation and he not only uncovered some outbuildings but, for the first time, investigated part of the rampart and ditch beyond them. By the end of the main period of antiquarian enquiry a firm outline of what constituted a broch had been drawn. Petrie's paper has already been mentioned; the other major work, which took in Scotland as a whole, was Joseph Anderson's third series of Rhind lectures presented in 1881 and published two years later (1883).

The concept of a broch embodied in Anderson's work has, by and large, stayed with us. A broch is a hollow tower some 17 m in diameter with walls *c.* 4.5 m thick and an enclosed courtyard *c.* 8 m across. Mousa (Shetland) and other less-well-preserved examples indicate that originally the towers may have been up to 14 m high. In order to achieve this and to permit access to the top, the walls were built in two tied skins, between which went a staircase. Sometimes the base of the wall was solid and this was occasionally used to house cells which could be entered from the courtyard.

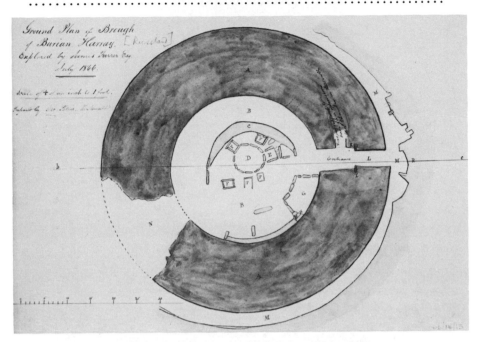

PLATE 8.2. Burrian (Russland), Harray. Excavated in 1866.
(Petrie nd (a) opposite p.8.)

The only opening to the exterior was the entrance, which was highly
defended by having a recessed doorway often with guard cells behind it.
These towers were thought of as places of refuge standing in isolation; all
the internal furnishings and external buildings were simply dismissed as
secondary usage.

In picking out seemingly broad architectural similarities from a mass of
data of varying worth, the antiquaries defined a type of monument which
has retained its broadly homogenous image. Dating was a problem; they
had been called Danish, Pictish and Stone Age, and their Norse origin was
still being cogently argued (Ferguson 1877). In the Rhind lectures, however, Anderson had them firmly dated to the first and second centuries AD,
on the basis of Roman finds, of which plenty had come from Orkney. After
this the towers were thought to have been dismantled as being of no further
use, and the internal and external features considered to have been created
as shanty dwellings. Ramparts and ditches were even further from the
minds of the excavator and theoretician and attracted little attention. Petrie
in his list of 1872 gives 70 brochs for Orkney (1890, 93–6) a figure later
increased by Graham (1947, 51) to 102 out of a total of some 500 for
Scotland. Close scrutiny of all available documentation suggests there is
evidence for 52 brochs or similar structures in Orkney.

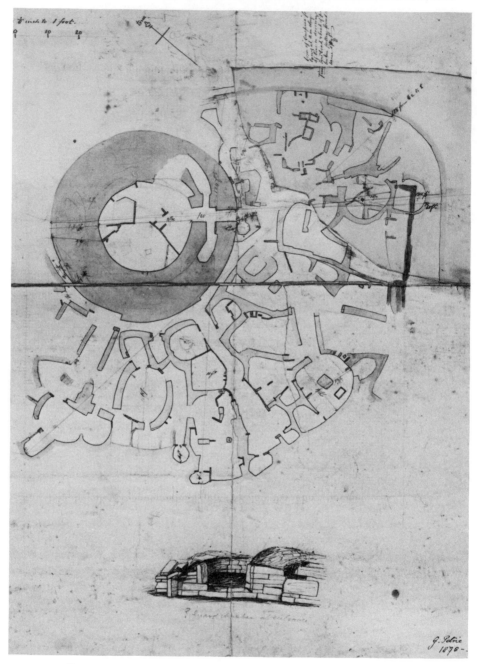

PLATE 8.3. Lingro, St Ola. Excavated by Petrie in 1870 and 1871, the outbuildings being extensively cleared. (Dryden and Petrie nd.)

In the half century after Petrie and his contemporaries very little happened. One James Cursiter was party to the clearing of the wall top of Eves Howe (Deerness) in 1883, and in 1887 was involved in emptying the contents of the halved interior of Green Hill (Hoy) into the sea (1923, 51–2). Cursiter was a little out of the main stream of thought and when he summarised his own views (1898, 10; 1923, 51) he attempted to demonstrate that the brochs came with the Phoenicians *via* a land bridge from Atlantis prior to the last glaciation. After him the only spark of archaeological activity was in 1901 and 1909 when the Loch of Ayre (Holm) was amateurishly trenched into (Graeme 1914). The interior was cleared out badly, but completely, and a few of the outbuildings and parts of the passage between them and the broch revealed. Certainly a few sites may have been damaged or investigated but, by and large, there was a striking gap between 1880 and 1930 when practically no excavation was undertaken and little appeared in print about Orkney brochs except in gazetteer articles (J. Fraser 1923; 1924; 1925; 1927).

Archaeology in general developed markedly in Orkney in the pre-war years when, among other sites, the Brochs of Gurness (Evie) and Midhowe (Rousay) were opened to the public (figures 8.4 and 5; plates 8.4 and 5). Gurness was 'rediscovered' in 1929 and a whole decade of summer seasons embarked upon (largely unpublished; J. W. Hedges forthcoming a); public finance took over from private when the latter ran out. Even after a gap of half a century the approach made and the techniques used had changed little and there is no need to speak separately of this excavation or that at Midhowe. At both, the centre of the broch was emptied, then all the outbuildings and, finally, the ditches and ramparts beyond were excavated. The idea of digging the ramparts and ditches may have come from Midhowe which was smaller, and privately financed, and was finished by 1933 (Callander and Grant 1934; colour plate 15). With the outbreak of the Second World War in 1939 came the end of broch studies in Orkney for another forty years.

So ended a century of fairly intensive work but, by present-day standards, the results of it were very limited. We know little of many of the structures and much only about a few; there are some with many finds, but none is well stratified; there is no reliable dating evidence or evidence relating to environment.

TYPOLOGY

Starting with Graham (1947) or even Petrie (1890), there has been a tendency to analyse attributes of broch towers by simple statistics. This goes to show that they have certain shared traits; granted that, there is wide variability resisting any classification that actually aids understanding. The average broch tower in Orkney has an overall diameter of *c.* 18 m (this and

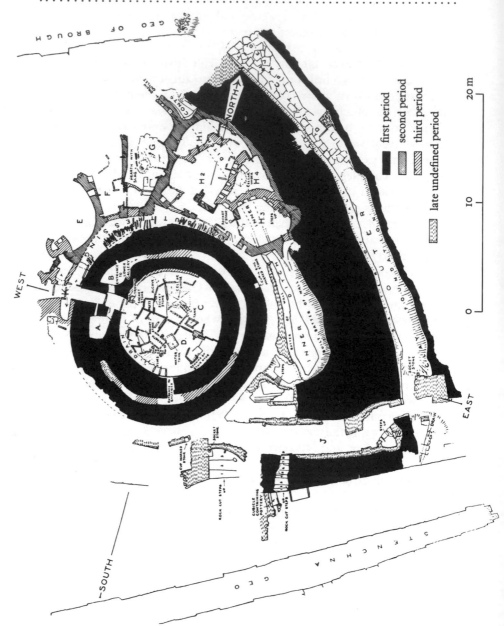

FIGURE 8.4. Midhowe, Rousay. Complete excavation 1930–33
included the outer defences. (RCAMS 1946, fig.273.)

Fig. 7. Midhowe Broch: Interior from south-west. 1. Entrance. 2. Scarcement. 3. Facing wall. 4. Alcove. 5. Stair entrance. 6. Fireplace at high level. 7. Divisional wall. 8. Entrance to compartment D. 9. Socket stone *in situ*. 10. Hearth. 11. Tank. 12. Remains of stair. 13. Cubicle. 14. Modern buttresses.

PLATE 8.4. Midhowe, Rousay. View of the internal furnishings from the south-west. (Callander and Grant 1934, fig.7.)

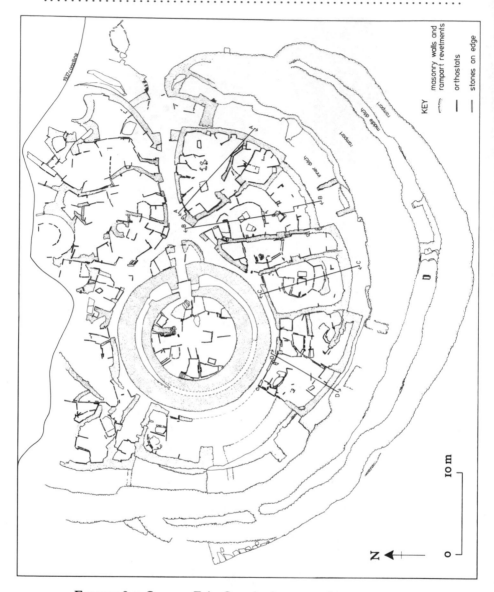

FIGURE 8.5. Gurness, Evie. Completely excavated 1930–39.
(NOSAS, based on original unpublished plans.)

subsequent figures are for a maximum sample of 51 brochs which includes
Bu but excludes Howe), has walls *c.* 4 m thick and a courtyard *c.* 9.5 m
across; the walls occupy 46 per cent of any whole diameter and the floor area
is *c.* 75 m². Around these averages is a great deal of variability. Diameters

PLATE 8.5. Gurness, Evie. View of the internal furnishings taken at the time of excavation. (Thomas Kent collection, Kirkwall Library.)

vary from 12 to 22.5 m, wall thicknesses from 2.75 to 5.2 m and the diameter of the courtyard from 7.3 to 13.7 m. On any of these counts the figure for one broch may be double that for another and this applies to the proportional wall thickness and to the internal area which varies from 28 m^2 to 148 m^2. These variables show little obvious and definite correlation. There are all sizes of dwelling with most of the range of thicknesses of wall; large courtyards with similarly thick walls are not easy to document however and may not have existed. Some of the brochs have had their height preserved quite well; in fact 26 of the 51 are known to have been over 1.5 m high and seven of these were over 4 m high. There is a tendency for these to have a below-average floor area, or an above-average wall thickness, or both.

Both ground-galleried and solid-based brochs are found in Orkney and the latter sometimes house intra-mural cells. In both types the wall is found to be used as an access to a higher floor; the stairway usually starts c. 1.8 m from the floor and winds round to c. 3.6 m where one can re-enter the courtyard area by a doorway above the scarcement. There are also two examples where the stair starts at ground level but neither of these has much height preserved.

The entrances are very variable. The two ground-galleried brochs,

Midhowe and Gurness, have fully fledged ones with jambs halfway along and two guard chambers behind. Some of the solid-based brochs have two guard chambers, some have one and others none at all; several brochs have their guard cells outside the door jambs. In the eight instances where the height of the entrance has been preserved it is *c*. 1.8 m high and over this, where preserved again, there is a cell. The height of the entrance and the floor of the cell above it is that of the access to the intra-mural stairway. At Midhowe the cell itself had the remains of a roof at the height of the scarcement.

Of the 51 Orkney brochs, we have evidence for internal furnishings made of flagstone in 27; of these only 8 have revealed a true floor plan. These internal furnishings, as mentioned, have been dismissed as secondary usage of the towers. They have, however, so many points in common with the structural features of the towers themselves that this is an unfounded assertion. Those floor plans which are clear fall into two types; one-unit dwellings, and those which have been divided. Both would obviously have been installed after the tower had been built and the latter may represent remodelling. In a sense therefore there is no evidence that they are secondary: and it is now suggested they were used by the original broch occupants.

At Burrian (Russland) in Harray, Farrer revealed a beautiful single-unit floor plan (plate 8.2). More or less central to it was a circular hearth, defined by a kerb of flagstones on edge, and around this was a service area approximately 5.5 m in diameter in which at least five tanks were set in the floor. Around the north part of this hearth and service area a wall was built, and the area between this and the broch wall formed a large bent hall accessible from just inside the broch entrance. Across the other side of the courtyard around the inner wall face were three compartments accessible from the service area. At 5 o'clock in relation to the entrance there is supposed to have been the entrance to an intramural staircase *c*. 1.8 m above the floor but this may have been spurious.

Burrowston (Shapinsay) was similar (figure 8.3) and perhaps more exciting, though the central area was less well preserved; all that remained was the entrance to a well. From 6 o'clock to 9 o'clock the circuit was taken up with three flagged compartments and from there to 2 o'clock by a large bent room which, when found, was actually roofed. On top of this roofed room was an entrance to a stairway which continued up to the height of the scarcement at *c*. 3.5 m where there was another entrance. Bu, which falls within this group of single unit floor plans, is discussed below.

The other five floor plans are examples of the divided type. Midhowe and Gurness are the best of these and demonstrate clearly the relationship between the furnishings and the wall fittings; the others are Lingro (St Ola) (plate 8.3), Loch of Ayre (Holm) and Netlater (Harray) (plate 8.1).

At Midhowe, it is almost as though the single plan were reproduced by binary fission (figure 8.4; plate 8.4). The courtyard was divided east/west into two compartments by a row of large slabs standing over 2 m high and in line with the entrance passage. At the inner end of the entrance passage was a vestibule and on both sides of this a doorway leading into a short lobby from which access could be had to the north and south apartments. Around the peripheral arc formed by their share of the broch wall each had compartments made of orthostats, and centrally placed in each area were rectangular hearths and a cooking tank.

The correspondence between the internal furnishings and the wall fittings was such at Midhowe that it is worth detailing. A floor at the height of c. 3.5 m together with a mezzanine one at the height of c. 1.8 m is suggested by features at other brochs but here, in particular, there is strong evidence. It will be remembered that these measurements were the heights of the floor of the cell above the entrance and the floor of the cell above that; they are also the heights of the beginning of the stair to the scarcement and of the scarcement itself and the entrance over it as well as the intra-mural galleries at both these levels. The furnishings fit very well with this. The entrance to the northern apartment had on its left-hand side an alcove which oversailed the broch wall and on its right a stone press. The alcove was the height of the scarcement; the press was the height of the landing and its roof was fire-cracked and had burnt material on it. Between the press and the alcove was a fitting for a lintel to the entrance to the northern apartment, at a height of 1.88 m. The compartments around the walls were badly preserved but seem to have been roofed at a height of between 1.5 and 1.8 m. In the southern apartment there was an internal stair which went from the top of a compartment to the height of the scarcement.

Gurness, which has so many other features in common with Midhowe, also latterly had a divided floor plan (figure 8.5; plate 8.5), though it is nowhere near as neat and regular. The larger apartment occupies the southern part of the courtyard and contains a hearth, cooking tank and various flagged compartments as well as the access to a landing at 1.8 m (colour plate 16); the well here was actually sealed when the courtyard was divided. The other living area occupied the north-west third of the courtyard and was divided from the larger by an east/west partition. This too had a hearth and peripheral compartments; from it there was an internal flight of steps to the scarcement where it oversailed the interior. The courtyard is complicated at Gurness at the entrance; access to the ground floor is gained by going to the right of this through what must have been a covered passage and over a threshold which has a door jamb c. 1.8 m high *in situ*.

Wells are a common feature of brochs, having been found inside ten of them. One well, at the East Broch of Burray, was on the outside but accessible from the interior. In using a broch well one did not lower a bucket, but instead went down a flight of steps to the water. The well was built by digging a large hole and then facing it with masonry and roofing it.

Outbuildings were found at many brochs during their excavation in the nineteenth century, as the tower was trenched round and a path cleared for spoil. They too were dismissed as secondary and have only been investigated fully at Lingro (St Ola), Midhowe and Gurness, where this stigma has continued to be applied. It seems clear to the author – because of their layout and level with respect to the tower – that they are contemporary with the main broch occupation and they should not be thought separate from it.

Of the three examples, Gurness is the clearest (figure 8.5). There is a passage through the external defences and aligned with the broch entrance itself; at the latter the passage bifurcates and forms a corridor about 1 m wide round the base of the tower. This naturally results in the wall surrounding the broch found in so many old excavations. From it and the main passage to the entrance there are passages to the outbuildings which have rubble-built walls and tend to be wedge-shaped. They share their longitudinal walls and their back ones form a continuous, if irregular, curtain round the settlement. Like the broch interior, these buildings were often subdivided and have in them furnishings made of flagstone; there are fires, cooking troughs, box beds, aumbries, and even a recognisable privy. After subdivision, perhaps 30 or 40 families may have lived at Gurness.

The design at Lingro is very similar (plate 8.3) though Petrie's plan does not show the limits or contents of the buildings; some access to the broch entrance can be seen, as can a corridor 0.7 m wide round the tower from which the buildings were entered. The whole settlement here must have been slightly larger than at Gurness while at Midhowe (figure 8.4) it was smaller. The smaller site is an interesting example of a plan constrained by topographical restrictions.

Because of the method of study, the outer defences have been the least-examined features. They are not uncommon – there are fourteen where identifications have been made – and in almost all the cases outbuildings are known. Purely on typological grounds one may distinguish defences which encircle a broch tower and those which cut off a promontory on which it is situated. Gurness is one of the former type, though coastal, and here the outer defences are entered from the east where the ramparts and ditches incurve on each side (figure 8.5). The outbuildings have a continuous wall round them which goes to the bottom of a surrounding ditch. Beyond this were two ramparts with putative ditches. Midhowe (figure 8.4) and Borthwick (Sandwick) are examples of brochs on promontories, and both are defended by a stout, ditched, wall across with a gate at one end. Some defences are perhaps worthy of note on rather negative grounds; Burrian (North Ronaldsay) for instance, has four ramparts on the landward side and is totally undefended along the low coast.

BU AND HOWE

The century of work on Orkney brochs, which I have summarised, created an unparalleled corpus of information on the subject. Unparalleled though it might be in the context of broch studies it must still be seen as the product of its time and its limitations recognised. One may continually sift through the old material looking for answers to new questions but ultimately the only real way forward is to excavate. It is unfortunate that the very factor that attracted the antiquaries, size, accounts for a lack of recent work due to the limitations of funding. In the last few years, however, there have been two exceptional opportunities to advance our knowledge, both undertaken by the North of Scotland Archaeological Services.

Bu Broch (Stromness) was a salvage excavation carried out during five hectic weeks in 1978 (J. W. Hedges forthcoming, a). During a rescue investigation, a mound of low elevation and unknown content was mechanically trenched prior to destruction. The discovery that it was a broch rather than a cairn meant that, with the time available, a series of objectives had to be defined and rigidly adhered to. If earlier authorities were to be believed, no primary floor plan for a broch in Orkney was known; clearly one should be sought. Secondly, dating for the Orkney brochs had hitherto been on the basis of imported Roman finds with the consequence that brochs could only be dated to the timespan when such imports were feasible; an independent series of radiocarbon dates was desired. Thirdly, the relationship between the broch and any outbuildings and fortification should be sought. Finally, almost unbelievably, there had never been any stratified small finds or environmental material from any Orkney broch and this was a situation that ought to be remedied.

Bu had an overall diameter of 19.5 m with walls 5.2 m thick and a courtyard 9.1 m across; it therefore fits well in the size range for Orkney brochs. Unfortunately, excavation showed the inherent unreliability of such statistics, since the outer 1.6 m of the wall turned out to be an added cladding. Originally the wall had been 3.6 m thick and the whole monument 16.3 m in diameter. The proportion of wall to total thickness thus changed from 44 to 53 per cent. The entrance had been obscured by later re-use but it appears to have been simple, having door jambs halfway along and no guard cells. The wall was only preserved to a height of 1.5 m, depriving us of the opportunity of seeing what, if anything, happened higher up. If the amount of rubble is any indication – and the broch may well have been robbed – then Bu was never very high.

The courtyard bore incontrovertible testimony to the originality of the furnishings found in other brochs and previously described and dismissed as secondary (figure 8.6; plate 8.6; colour plate 17). The floor plan was of the single undivided type, showing great similarity to those at Burrowston

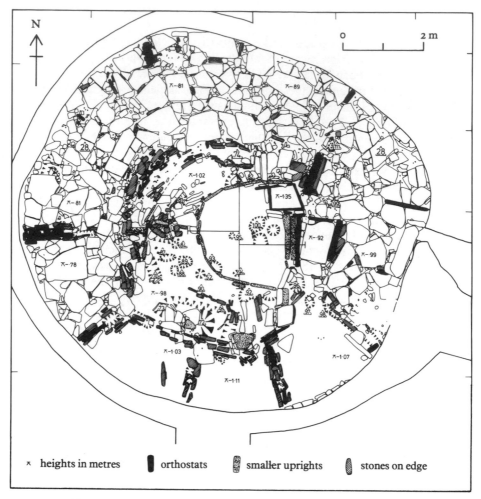

FIGURE 8.6. Bu, Stromness. The original floor revealed in 1978. (NOSAS.)

(Shapinsay) (figure 8.3) and Burrian, Harray (plate 8.2). Centrally placed, and accessible directly from the entrance via a vestibule, was a service area with a massive semi-circular hearth and a cooking tank. This service area had present, *in situ*, a number of kitchen implements, and was covered with carbonaceous material including spent granite pot-boilers. Turning right on entering the broch one would enter a series of three flagged rooms set end-to-end round the inner circumference of the broch wall. The middle one of these was much larger than the outer two and, from the last one, access could be gained to the central area. To the left on entering were the sockets for radial partitions from the wall, suggesting three compartments floored with a mixture of mud and midden. The centre was excavated by means of one trench, while outbuildings and defences were sought by four radial ones. The result was entirely negative; Bu had neither outbuildings nor outer defences; it stood alone. The finds from the broch phase of the site were neither numerous nor exotic but they fitted within what we would call a broch assemblage. Real food for thought came with the radiocarbon dates, three of which put the occupation of the site at *c*. 600 BC: half a millennium earlier than the conventional date.

PLATE 8.6. Bu, Stromness. The original floor revealed in 1978.
(NOSAS.)

Old assumptions must now be rethought in the light of Bu. Bu shows clearly, and in spite of theories to the contrary (MacKie 1974, 96–104), that broch-type structures have a long tradition in Orkney and were not brought there either by specialist builders or by dominant incomers during the first century AD. This is corroborated by the finding of the round house at Quanterness, near Kirkwall, which was datable to *c*. 700 BC (plate 8.7) (Renfrew 1979, 194). Bu raises serious doubts about the assumed uniformity of the 52 identified brochs in Orkney (and the many more supposed ones). Hitherto, a broch, once identified, has been tacitly credited with all the attributes of the Anderson stereotype: some may in reality have been as unsophisticated as Bu or even the earlier round house at Quanterness. Bu is

PLATE 8.7. Quanterness, Kirkwall. A round-house belonging to
c. 700 BC in the course of excavation. (Renfrew 1979, pl.22b.)

an example of one type of 'broch' which stood alone and without outbuildings and external defences; it was probably occupied by one family.

The other end of the spectrum is exemplified by Howe (Stromness), a broch whose excavation by the North of Scotland Archaeological Services began in 1978. The interior of the tower has been examined together with a large area outside its entrance. The tower has very Mousa-like proportions, having walls 5.5 m thick and a courtyard only 7 m across; this gives an overall diameter of 18 m and a ratio of wall width to total diameter of 61 per cent. Again, it is clear from excavation that the wall had been widened by 2 m after the collapse of an original thinner one. Originally the broch would have had an overall diameter of 14 m and a ratio of wall width to total diameter of 50 per cent. The wall appears to have a clay core up to the height of 1.5 m and to be solid from there to its maximum preserved height of *c.* 3 m. At a height of *c.* 1.5 m at 12 o'clock there is the entrance to the remains of a cell in the wall. The scarcement is not preserved but is suggested by a landing *c.* 1.5 m from the floor from which steps lead clockwise to the preserved height of the wall. The entrance was not preserved well enough for the lintels to be found *in situ*; it widened halfway along its length and had no guard cells.

The original floor was destroyed by the laying of a second one after the partial collapse of the wall, and can only be reconstructed from the sockets for its furnishings. This was, however, a typical single-unit layout with a central area, interconnecting flagged rooms to the right from the entrance and unflagged compartments to the left of the service area. The second floor, some furnishings of which reached almost the full height of the wall (plates 8.8 and 9), was very similar. The interconnecting rooms to the right of the entrance were floored with clay and were reduced to two in number; the partition was moved making their width only 1.8 m as opposed to 2.4 m. The central area was proportionally larger and a fragment of its hearth was preserved. The compartments were in particularly good condition, two of them having their lids in place. During the use of both broch floors a souterrain was accessible from a vertical shaft against the wall at *c.* 12 o'clock.

Excavations outside the broch entrance at Howe have revealed a complex of contemporary outbuildings (plate 8.10). There is a recessed gateway in the external defences from which a passage leads to the broch and around it, giving access to the individual outbuildings. On the outside of these buildings there is a rampart which, at one point where it has been examined, was widened from 1 m in width to 2.7 m and then 3.5 m. Beyond this is very likely to be a ditch and perhaps another rampart and ditch.

Howe has reinforced the conclusion made at Bu that the internal furnishings are original, although they may have been altered and replaced during the use of the tower. Their survival in Orkney is presumably

PLATE 8.8. Howe, Stromness. The replacement floor plan
revealed in 1980. (NOSAS.)

explained by the use of stone there, while wood was used elsewhere. It is
because of this that we can demonstrate the presence of a floor at the height
of *c*. 3.6 m and a partial mezzanine level at *c*. 1.8 m. This discovery adds
greatly to our understanding of broch interiors and should assist in the
interpretation of the slighter traces found in other parts of Scotland. Unlike
Bu, Howe also shows that some broch towers were in effect keeps within a
heavily fortified village which probably accommodated some 250 people.
This major breakthrough in our understanding of what has been found
previously adds a second type of 'broch' which does not fit the stereotype at
all well. Finds from Howe, including Roman ones, suggest that this phase,
at that site, belongs to the first and second centuries AD. This type of
broch-with-settlement is indicative of the development of a form of social
organisation which fits well with the record we have of the Romans making a
treaty with the Orkney chieftains in 43 AD (Laing 1974, 113). It is to be
hoped that this discovery made among the better preserved monuments of
Orkney will lead to the systematic investigation of the immediate surround-
ings of broch towers elsewhere.

REFLECTIONS

In this chapter no mention has been made of the exploitation of the
environment by the people of the broch period, or of the artefact assem-

PLATE 8.9. Howe, Stromness. Elevation showing the replacement
furnishings in the west half of the courtyard. (NOSAS/Richard
Prideaux.)

blage, while social organisation has only been lightly touched on. Environmental evidence was not sought or kept (in any systematic manner) prior to
the Bu excavation of 1978, and the early date of this site together with the
very small size of the samples analysed do not form a satisfactory basis for a
general statement. The same may be said of the finds, for although an
enormous number have been retrieved from Orkney brochs, they have not
been from stratified contexts. At Howe occupation continued up to the
eighth century and beyond (Hedges and Bell 1980) and this may be the
general case with broch sites rather than an exception; the Pictish structures
are so poorly built that previous excavators would not have noticed them.
The inevitable conclusion is that assemblages, such as that from Gurness
(J. W. Hedges forthcoming, b) are likely to represent several phases of
occupation, spanning centuries if not a millennium. This situation is aggra-
vated by the lack of change in the basic material culture over the whole Iron
Age, so that datable artefacts are the exception rather than the rule. As yet
we are ignorant of many aspects of Orkney brochs; only with the conclusion
of the large-scale excavation at Howe and its publication will this situation
be remedied.

The brochs of Orkney have had so much attention lavished upon them

PLATE 8.10. Howe, Stromness. A sector of the outbuildings
excavated in 1980. (NOSAS.)

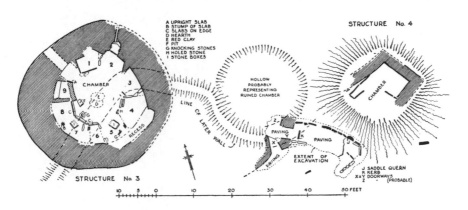

FIGURE 8.7. 'The Potter's Workshop', Calf of Eday.
(RCAMS 1946, fig. 124.)

that our view of the Iron Age is very biased in their favour. Conversely the
small sites have neither attracted attention nor, when come upon, have they
readily been identifiable as belonging to a particular era. It is obvious that
there must be Iron Age burials, yet we know nothing about them. There
may have been other buildings contemporary with the brochs. The state of
our knowledge is poor and the only solution to the dilemma is excavation.
Already Quanterness and Bu have given us an insight into the origins of the
brochs and their attendant social organisation, while Howe with its continued occupation should help with what follows. Three old excavations
should perhaps be mentioned in this context, since they seem to belong to
some part of the Iron Age and may indicate the kinds of sites that will be
encountered. Calder excavated several buildings on the Calf of Eday in the
1930s (1937; 1939). One of these, the so-called 'potter's workshop', was
circular, 12 m in diameter, had a wall 2.25 m thick and a courtyard 7.5 m
across; it was entered by a narrow passage with a door jamb near the interior
(figure 8.7). Around the perimeter were compartments and in the centre
hearths and a cooking trough. The Little Howe of Hoxa (South Ronaldsay)
is a truly enigmatic site excavated in 1871 by Petrie (Turner 1872). This was
not classified as a broch but was about 13 m in overall diameter and had a
wall about 4 m across leaving an inner courtyard only some 5 m in diameter
(plate 8.11). The building had a very long protruding entrance and from its
sides an intra-mural gallery ran right round the wall at ground level and
could be entered from the courtyard at 12 o'clock. Finally, there was a
whole complex of buildings excavated at Howmae (North Ronaldsay) by
Dr William Traill in 1884 and 1889; one of these was shaped like a
wheelhouse (figure 8.8) and the assemblage of artefacts appears to be Iron
Age (Traill 1885, 23–32).

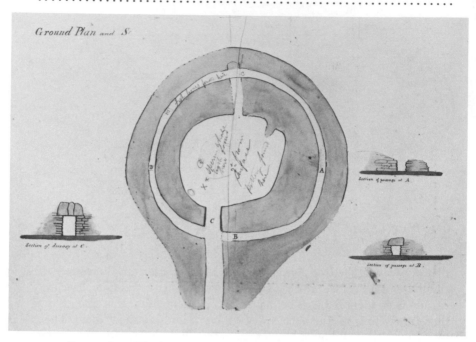

PLATE 8.11. The Little Howe of Hoxa, S. Ronaldsay.
(Petrie nd (b) opposite p.2.)

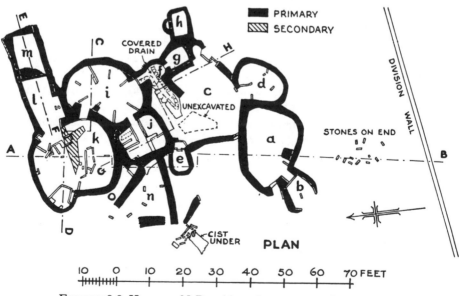

FIGURE 8.8. Howmae, N. Ronaldsay. (RCAMS 1946, fig.93.)

. . . .

In conclusion, it is hoped that this outline sufficiently indicates the nature and limitations of most of our evidence. Recent excavations have brought some advance in our understanding of the Orkney brochs. Much remains to be learnt, and the broch towers will only be understood adequately when we have a much clearer picture of the Iron Age landscape as a whole.

Acknowledgements. The work briefly reported here has been undertaken in connection with projects carried out for the Scottish Development Department. Patrick Ashmore, the Inspector of Ancient Monuments responsible, is to be thanked for his help and encouragement. The work has been conducted under the aegis of the North of Scotland Archaeological Services; practically all the members, present and past, have made some contribution: a list of individuals would be unduly long. I have been much helped by the staff of the Society of Antiquaries of Scotland Library and of the National Monuments Record of Scotland.

I am grateful to the Royal Commission on Ancient Monuments, Scotland, for providing and giving permission to reproduce figures 8.4, 7 and 8, and plates 8.1, 2, 3 and 11. The Society of Antiquaries of London furnished me with copies of figures 8.1, 2 and 3, and plate 8.4. The North of Scotland Archaeological Services, in collaboration with the Scottish Development Department, provided figures 8.5 and 6, and plates 8.6, 8, 9 and 10, of which plate 8.9 is the graphic work of Richard Prideaux. Professor Colin Renfrew provided plate 8.7 and Kirkwall Library plate 8.5.

Peter Gelling **Excavations at Skaill, Deerness**

Excavations have taken place at Skaill, on the east coast of Deerness, every year since 1963, with the exception of 1966. Three principal sites have been excavated: one Iron Age, another Iron Age/Early Christian, and a third Early Christian, Norse, and later.

Somewhere in the neighbourhood there must be an earlier site than any of these, as underlying ploughmarks were a regular feature. Plate 1 shows some of those found under the Iron Age/Early Christian site. There was a fainter grid of ploughmarks diagonal to the one which shows on the photograph, suggesting that there was no clearly defined field. When sectioned, the marks frequently showed that the plough had been tilted to the left. Stone ard-tips were very common, more so in the earlier than in the later pre-Norse levels, which may reflect an increasing use of iron rather than a decline in cultivation.

The oldest settlement so far found consisted of two sub-circular areas separated by a paved passage (plate 2). The ranging pole lies between the opposed entrances to the two areas. Both were probably roofed, but no evidence for roof-supports was found. The photograph shows the final stage of a fairly complicated structural history. The pottery from this level was exclusively of a plain 'flat-rimmed' variety. Two radiocarbon dates are available: 260 ± 120 bc, and 150 ± 100 bc.

While 'flat-rimmed' ware was still in use, but just about to be superseded, occupation began on a site 160 yards to the north. This may have begun as a ritual site. At one point there was a rough horseshoe of stones enclosing a raised clay floor on which there was a hearth, which appeared to be associated with a pit which had upright stones set just below its lip (plate 3). Nearby, to the left, a second pit, approached by a paved path, and eventually covered by large slabs, contained ard-tips and grain-rubbers.

Subsequently a circular house some 30 feet in diameter was built on this site, with an adjacent enclosure opposite one of its entrances which recalled the figure-of-eight layout of the earlier site. Plate 4 shows this entrance (right foreground) with the wall curving away under the left-hand ranging pole. An enclosing wall can be seen on the left, and it appears again on the left of plate 5, with the house wall well preserved near the opposite

17. Bu Broch was excavated in a rescue operation in 1978. The plate shows the original floor (see pages 166 and 167).

PLATE I. Skaill: ploughmarks found under the
Iron Age/Early Christian site.

section, but otherwise very fragmentary. The line of both walls had been
marked out in advance by deep ploughmarks. A second entrance to the
house can be seen in the far right-hand corner of the excavated area. A
radiocarbon date of 70 ± 100 bc related to a very early phase of this site. The
house appears to have been occupied for a lengthy period, with many
reconstructions and alterations, and its exact form at any one time was very
hard to determine.

Eventually this house was abandoned and much of its area paved over.
The paving can be seen in the section on plate 4. The earliest radiocarbon
date so far from this upper level is 530 ± 100 ad, and it may, if only in a
chronological sense, be called Pictish. A sample from a deposit which

177

PLATE 2. Skaill: the oldest (Iron Age) settlement.

PLATE 3. Skaill: Iron Age pit with upright stones below the lip,
on the north part of the site.

immediately preceded the paving gave a date of 600 + 100 ad. At first the
paving covered much the same area as the round house, but later it was
extended some way to the south, where the occupation belonged exclusively
to the Pictish phase.

Quite an extensive building was erected on the paving, consisting of a
group of perhaps six oblong rooms, with generally rectilinear walls. The
room of which a part is shown on plate 6 measured approximately 13 feet by
11 feet. The pottery from this level was very much finer than anything
which had been used previously on the site, with small globular bowls of the
characteristic shape. Neither the potting tradition, nor the relatively sophisticated type of building, survived the beginning of the Viking settlement.

PLATE 4. Skaill: entrance (right foreground) to a circular house of
Iron Age date on the north part of the site. The later (Pictish)
paving is seen at the rear in the section.

PLATE 5. Skaill: Iron Age circular house on north part of site. The enclosing wall is seen on the left. One of the entrances is seen in plate 4.

PLATE 6. Skaill, 'Pictish' phase: part of paved floor of room.

9 Anna Ritchie **Orkney in the Pictish Kingdom**

At one time the very title of this chapter would have been considered contentious, for there was doubt not only whether there ever were Picts in Orkney but also whether the islands were inhabited at all when the Norsemen arrived. These doubts arose from lack of positive information and were strengthened by the testimony of the Icelandic historian, Snorri Sturluson, that the Northern Isles were uninhabited (Egil's Saga, IV). This saga was rightly considered to be a more reliable source than the sensational approach of the *Historia Norvegiae* (A. D. Anderson 1922, 330–1), with its notion of pygmies living underground. Pictish studies have, however, advanced rapidly in recent years, both in history and in archaeology, and it can no longer be doubted that Orkney was indeed a flourishing province of the Pictish kingdom throughout its existence. In strict terms, the Pictish period begins with the first mention of the name *Picti*, the Painted Ones, in the surviving historical record, in AD 297, in a Latin panegyric; and it ends with the union of the Picts and Scots under the Scottish king Kenneth mac Alpin, about AD 843. The geographical area of Pictland, determined both from historical sources and from the archaeological record, included all the lands north of the Forth-Clyde line, with the exception (after about AD 500) of Argyll, which had become Scottish *Dalriada*. In practical terms, however, the history of the Picts properly begins with the reign of Bridei, son of Maelchon, in the mid-sixth century. In the archaeological record, the Picts are not incontrovertibly identifiable before the seventh century.

Few artefacts can be attributed specifically to the Picts, rather than to a common cultural tradition shared with contemporary peoples in northern and western Britain, and their identification depends upon the

183

coincidence of their distribution with the geographical and chronological span provided for the Picts by the historical record. Foremost are the carved symbol stones, without which the Picts would barely exist as an archaeological reality. The symbols on the stones can then be used to identify, as Pictish, silverwork and other objects on which they also occur; most notably, heavy silver chains with symbol-decorated terminal rings. Few would date the stones or the related portable objects before the seventh century. The use, for inscriptions, of the *ogam* alphabet must have been acquired by the Picts from the Scots and, to judge by the style of the letters, most of the surviving Pictish ogam inscriptions ought not to be dated before the eighth century (K. H. Jackson 1955, 139). They are identifiable as Pictish rather than Scottish, because they are not written in Gaelic but in the aboriginal non-Indo-European tongue that the Picts used as an alternative to their Celtic language.

Symbol stones and ogam inscriptions are numerically the most important Pictish artefacts, and they show that in archaeological terms the main Pictish period was the seventh and eighth centuries. To this period also belong specifically Pictish house-types and metalwork traditions. Only painted pebbles and nailed timber-laced forts take Pictish archaeology back into the earlier part of the historical Pictish period, for painted pebbles have been found in post-broch contexts (A. Ritchie 1972) and radiocarbon dates from Burghead in Morayshire suggest that that fort may have been built as early as the fourth century AD (Edwards and Ralston 1978).

Though the archaeological reality of the Picts in Orkney is thus well documented by symbol stones, ogam inscriptions, settlements and portable artefacts, confirmation in the contemporary historical record has until recently been lacking. The gap has now been filled, for Dumville (1976) has drawn attention to the relevance for Orkney of the newly discovered *Bern Chronicle*, the text of which is largely a copy of the early part of Bede's *Historia Ecclesiastica*, with some additions and alterations. The entry for AD 46 concerning Claudius and the Orkneys has been recast to include a reference to the Picts: '. . . Orcadas quoque insulas Pictorum romano adiecit imperio, atque inde Romam rediit' [he also annexed the Orkney Islands of the Picts to the Empire, and from there he returned to Rome]. The basic information in Bede's entry about the annexation of the Orkneys by Claudius was presumably derived ultimately from the fourth-century writer Eutropius, and Maxwell has cast serious doubt on the whole episode (1975, 31–5). Nevertheless the Bern addition is of some importance for it shows, as Dumville pointed out, that an Englishman writing in mid-eighth–mid-ninth century considered the Orkneys to be Pictish.

The Picts were not a new ethnic element in the population of Orkney or elsewhere, despite the legends that would have them come from Scythia.

They were simply the descendants of earlier tribesmen who had lived in nucleated villages such as that surrounding the broch at Gurness, or in independent farmsteads such as the wheelhouse on Calf of Eday. According to the *Ravenna Cosmography* (7th/8th c.), the various tribes in the Orkneys had different names for the same island, and Maxwell suggested that this information implies the survival of the aboriginal tongue alongside the Celtic language (1975, 35). It may well be that the older, non-Celtic, element in the population was stronger in the Northern Isles than further south, for Jackson has argued, on place-name evidence, that the main area of Celtic linguistic influence lay in eastern Scotland between the Firth of Forth and the Dornoch Firth (K. H. Jackson 1955, 146–53). The density of ogam inscriptions in the Northern Isles would support the idea of a predominantly non-Celtic population in that area, for more than half the surviving total of inscriptions has been found there, nine in Shetland and six in Orkney. Orcadian place-names are of no help in trying to identify the ethnic make-up of the pre-Norse population (F. T. Wainwright 1962a, 101–7).

Not one Pict from Orkney is known to us by name, unless the reading of an ogam inscription on a bone handle from the Broch of Gurness is correct to take MATS to be a personal name. An Orcadian chieftain appears in Adomnan's account of St Columba's visit, in AD 565, to the Pictish king, Bridei son of Maelchon, but there is no mention of his name. Adomnan uses the term *regulus* to describe this Orcadian ruler, and mentions that Bridei held his hostages; *regulus* is usually translated as 'subject-king' (Anderson and Anderson 1961, 441) or minor king (M. O. Anderson 1973, 144fn). Campbell has emphasised the ambiguity surrounding the use of various terms for minor potentates, in which *rex*, *subregulus*, *princeps* and so on were at least in the eighth century interchangeable (1979, 7). The title *subregulus* would appear to be far more commonly used than *regulus*, however, and Adomnan's use of the latter may have been deliberate. If A. Jackson is correct (1971, 128) in identifying the Pictish kinship system as avunculocal, their society would have consisted of several matrilineages, all more or less equal in status. Alternatively, Miller has argued that there were several king-producing patrilineages interlinked by matrilines maintained by the marriages of the royal sisters (M. Miller 1978, 51). In either case, the Orcadian *regulus* may not have been greatly inferior in status to king Bridei. Even though Bede was later to describe Bridei as *rex potentissimus*, a most powerful king, he may not have had direct rule over the whole of Pictland.

In the sixth and seventh centuries AD, Orkney was literally closer to the political and cultural heart of Pictland than in later times. Not only was Bridei's royal residence somewhere near the River Ness, according to Adomnan (both Castle Urquhart and Craig Phadraig are major contenders for the title of Bridei's *munitio* (Alcock 1980, 78–9)), but Isabel Henderson has argued that the practice of carving and erecting symbol-stones originated in the Moray Firth area (1958). Even closer to Orkney, the Golspie area on the coast of Sutherland was an important focus of Pictish settlement (Close-Brooks 1975, 209–10). Alcock has proposed the terms 'Heartland Picts' to describe those living in the eastern lowlands from the Forth to Caithness where symbol stones and *pit*-names are concentrated, and 'Peripheral Picts' to describe those living in the west and north who 'are likely to have borne a diluted Pictish or Proto-Pictish culture' (1980, 62). If it is accepted that the historical and archaeological evidence points to the power centre of sixth- and early seventh-century Pictland being in the Moray Firth area, Orkney was no more peripheral than Angus, although the sea crossing may have made it less convenient. Of the distinctive portable artefacts that constitute Pictish material culture, the Northern Isles lack only the massive silver chain – and seven of the ten surviving chains were in any case found outside Pictland. The mere presence of a great Pictish treasure on St Ninian's Isle need not imply that Shetland was in the mainstream of Pictish cultural life in the eighth century, but moulds from the Brough of Birsay prove that the St Ninian's Isle type of brooch was being manufactured in the Northern Isles (Curle 1974, 302) as well as further south; and sculptured stones from Bressay and Papil demonstrate the strength of late Pictish culture in Shetland.

Regional differences detectable in the archaeological record, and perhaps reflected in the historical record, fit better into the old framework, inherited from Bede, of northern and southern Pictland, in which the Northern Isles are not divorced from the northern Scottish mainland. The distribution of the symbol known as the circular disc and rectangle with square indentation is concentrated in Orkney, Caithness and Sutherland; whatever its meaning, its restricted occurrence would seem to imply that it was special to this area. Painted pebbles have been found only in Caithness, Orkney and Shetland. Burials under kerbed cairns appear to have been a northern Pictish tradition, but Alcock has suggested that their equivalent in stone-free areas of southern Pictland may be the square and circular ditched barrows seen on air-photographs (1980, 65).

SYMBOL STONES

Orkney has yielded eight symbol stones, of which one from Oxtro in Birsay is now lost, four are incomplete, and one from Gurness is so lightly incised on a squat boulder that it is perhaps more likely to be a trial piece than a formal monument. In view of the regularity with which new symbol stones are found on mainland Scotland, it is perhaps surprising that a fragment discovered in 1967 on the Sands of Evie is the only symbol stone to have turned up in Orkney in the last 45 years. It may reflect a measure of the difference in agricultural activity, as most mainland discoveries are made

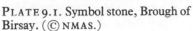

PLATE 9.1. Symbol stone, Brough of
Birsay. (© NMAS.)

PLATE 9.2. Symbol stone, St Peter's
Church, S. Ronaldsay. (© NMAS.)

during ploughing. None of the Orcadian stones appears to be later than the
eighth century AD and most are likely to belong to the seventh century.
Stevenson has demonstrated by typological analysis that the earliest
examples of the common symbol known as the crescent and v-rod are those
in Sutherland and Orkney (R. B. K. Stevenson 1955, 101–6). It is probable
that the stone found in the graveyard on the Brough of Birsay was originally
a cross-slab, for its sides appear to be shaped and one face, on which the
cross may have been carved, is missing. The cross-slab from the Broch of
Burrian bears an ogam inscription and the remains of an incised design
which may represent a fish (MacGregor 1974, 96, fig.21); if so, there are

two symbol-bearing cross-slabs in Orkney, and they should both be dated to the eighth century AD. The Brough of Birsay stone (plate 9.1) was found in scattered fragments and was not, as previously believed, associated with a triple grave (Curle 1982, 91–2). The surviving face bears four symbols (circular disc and rectangle, crescent and v-rod, 'elephant', eagle) and, executed in shallow relief at the foot of the stone, three warriors in long tunics bearing swords, spears and square decorated shields (colour plate 18).

A stone from St Peter's Church on South Ronaldsay (plate 9.2), where it had been re-used as a window sill, is incomplete and bears a rectangle and a crescent and v-rod on one face and another crescent and v-rod together with a circular disc and rectangle with square indentation on the other face. This last symbol appears to have been of special importance in Orkney, for it occurs on three stones and on a bone phalange from the Broch of Burrian on North Ronaldsay, and it is used only rarely elsewhere. It appears on a stone from Greens on mainland Orkney, in conjunction with a crescent and v-rod and a mirror symbol, and on the Gurness boulder together with two rectangles. A rectangle and a crescent and v-rod are incised on a fragment from Redland, Firth, and a mirror symbol is pecked on the sandstone fragment from the Sands of Evie. The lost stone from Oxtro in Birsay bore an eagle, and another exceptionally fine eagle occurs in combination with a crescent and v-rod and a mirror on the stone from the Knowe of Burrian (detailed catalogue of these stones in J.N.G.Ritchie 1969). The ox phalange from the Broch of Burrian, North Ronaldsay, is incised with a crescent and v-rod on one side and a circular disc and indented rectangle on the other and may have been used as a playing piece (MacGregor 1974, 88, fig.16, no.210). This is the only portable artefact from Orkney bearing Pictish symbols, although a pebble incised with a hexagram and a pentagram from the same site may be related (MacGregor 1974, 96, fig.20, no.278). Symbols occur on portable artefacts outside Orkney, particularly on fine silverwork, as well as on the walls of caves at Covesea, Morayshire, and East Wemyss, Fife, demonstrating that they could be used less formally than on stone monuments.

Few of the Orcadian symbol stones are securely provenanced and none sheds any light on the function of the stones or the meaning of the symbols. Jackson has drawn attention to the similarities between the Picts and certain tribes in British Columbia who, like the Picts, had a matrilineal society; they were divided into clans each with its own crest, such as an eagle or a fish, which was tattooed on the body and carved on totem-poles to act as house frontal poles, memorial poles and several other functions (A. Jackson 1971, 136–7). It seems very likely that Pictish symbol stones were similarly used in a variety of ways (the interpretations that have been offered are summarised in I.Henderson 1971; A.Jackson 1971). It is clear that, to a passing Pict, the message conveyed by the symbols on a stone monument was clear and intelligible, and the uniformity of symbols throughout Pictland emphasises the political and cultural cohesion of an organised and complex society.

BURIAL AND RITUAL

Very little is known about the pagan religion of the Picts, although some continuity of Celtic ideas and practices may reasonably be expected. A story recorded by Adomnan in which Columba blesses a well sacred to the Picts implies that water spirits were part of the folklore of Pictland as they were among earlier people (Anderson and Anderson 1961, 61b–62a). There are several references in Adomnan to *magi*, a class of pagan priests or magicians the most powerful of whom lived at the royal court, and the 'gods' of the *magi* are contrasted with the one God of the Christians (Anderson and Anderson 1961, 78a–b). Henderson has suggested that some of the figure scenes on symbol stones may represent incidents in Pictish folk-lore (I. Henderson 1967, 67). There are hints in the archaeological record of pagan practices among the Picts. At the Udal on North Uist, deliberate deposits of animal bones, usually lambs, have been found beneath houses of the sixth–eighth centuries and beneath an earlier wheelhouse (I.A. Crawford 1972, 7), recalling a bizarre deposit of 32 ox teeth at À Cheardach Mhor (Young and Richardson 1960, 141) and of red deer jawbones set in an arc round the hearth at À Cheardach Bheag (Fairhurst 1971, 80), both sites being wheelhouses on South Uist. In Orkney, in the central area of the henge at the Stones of Stenness, a group of four pits was found (J.N.G. Ritchie 1976, 15, 22); one of the pits contained charcoal from which a radiocarbon date of ad 519 ± 150 (SRR-352) was obtained, indicating activity, perhaps of a ritual nature, on the site in the mid-first millennium AD.

From about 1000 BC until the Viking Age in Scotland, it is notoriously difficult to identify the burials of a particular people or of a particular period of time, because there was no strong tradition of placing gravegoods along side the dead. Without gravegoods, or a recognisable type of grave structure, an isolated burial can be dated only by radiocarbon analysis of the surviving bones; and many burials were found and the bones subsequently lost before the development of scientific dating methods. Extended inhumations in stone-built long cists were certainly one favoured mode of burial in later prehistoric times in Orkney and some, such as that found close to the seventh–eighth century farmstead (plate 9.3) at Buckquoy (A. Ritchie 1977, 183–4), may contain Picts. The great mound known as Saevar Howe at Birsay was utilised for a cemetery of long cists, perhaps of Viking-age date; it was also the hiding-place, in a small cist, of an ecclesiastical iron bell (RCAMS 1946, 23, no.40; Farrer 1864). It is perhaps

PLATE 9.3. Long cist burial, Buckquoy. (Crown copyright, SDD.)

significant that the pebble incised with a hexagram and a pentacle from the Broch of Burrian, North Ronaldsay, was similarly found in a small stone cist (MacGregor 1974, 70). With the coming of Christianity, long cists became the norm in ecclesiastical cemeteries, and the lower stratum of graves in the churchyard on the Brough of Birsay is thought to belong to the pre-Norse community (Radford 1959, 17).

It is possible that burial in short cists was also practised by pagan Picts (Close-Brooks 1975, 210); symbol stones have been found re-used as cover slabs for such cists, and this mode of burial is unlikely to belong to Viking or later times. The mound covering the ruins of the broch of Oxtro at Birsay was used for a cemetery of cremation burials in short cists, and one of the cist-covers bore the carving of an eagle; the stone is now lost (it is thought to have been incorporated into the wall of one of the farm buildings at nearby Boardhouse), but it was almost certainly a Pictish symbol stone (RCAMS 1946, 11–12, no.11). The symbol stone covering a short cist at Golspie in Sutherland was interpreted as secondary to the burial on the grounds that the cist was empty and the stone too big to have been the original cover-slab (J.M.Davidson 1943), but it is equally possible that this was a cenotaph, and that the symbol stone was over-large as a cover-slab because this was not its primary function. Both here and at Oxtro, the cist-builders are likely to have been re-using symbol stones which had originally been carved for another purpose, perhaps as house-posts displaying the clan crest of the dead. Another possibility is that the 'statement' made by the symbols had been of a temporary nature and the stones had become irrelevant building material.

Recent studies have identified a Pictish type of grave-structure (A.Ritchie 1974, 31–2; Ashmore 1980), in which a long cist is set centrally beneath a low circular or rectilinear cairn with a slab-built kerb. The type-site is Ackergill in Caithness, where a linear cemetery consisted of one circular and seven rectilinear cairns, together with two unenclosed long cists (A.J.H.Edwards 1926; 1927). Examples have been excavated in recent years in Shetland, Orkney, Caithness and Sutherland, underlining the essentially northern Pictish distribution of this type of grave. The cairn at Sandwick, Unst, Shetland most closely resembles the classic rectilinear form at Ackergill, characterised by taller pillar-stones set at each corner and set half-way along the two long sides of the rectangle and by a white quartzite capping to the mound (Bigelow 1978). A radiocarbon date of ad 445 ± 75 (GU 1291) for a sample of bone from the skeleton indicates that the burial is likely to have taken place within the period AD 300–600 (Bigelow forthcoming). The dead person is likely therefore to have been a pagan Pict. Both at Dunrobin, Sutherland (Close-Brooks 1980) and at Ackergill, a symbol stone was found nearby and some form of association between stones and graves is likely though unproven. Radiocarbon dates from the Dunrobin skeleton suggest burial within the period AD 600–900. These dates lend support to the argument that the rectilinear form of kerbed cairn remained in use later than the circular form, enabling Norsemen to adopt this form of burial (A.Ritchie 1974, 31; Ritchie and Ritchie 1981, 175). It is, however, the circular form that has been found in Orkney, on the Point of Buckquoy at Birsay (Brough Road, Area 1, Morris 1979b, 13–14).

PICTISH BIRSAY

The Birsay area was clearly an important focus of settlement in Pictish times. Apart from the symbol stones and burials already mentioned, all but two of Orkney's ogam inscriptions were found in Birsay: one in the domestic settlement at Buckquoy and three on the Brough of Birsay. One of the latter group was found during recent excavations (Morris 1981a, 36), but there appears to be some doubt about the provenance of the two found in earlier excavations. Radford mentions one from the early churchyard (1959, 5) and one from the beach (1962, 174), while Cruden mentions that one was found re-used as a building stone in the complex known as 'Thorfinn's palace' (1965, 25). This re-used stone is the inscription Birsay I in Padel's catalogue of Pictish inscriptions, where he makes the point about both inscriptions from the old excavations that they have a casual, carelessly incised appearance and are unlikely to have been designed as formal, long-lasting monuments (1972, 2, 10–11, 16, 55). He suggests that they are comparable as casual inscriptions with the runic inscriptions in Maes Howe and implies that they should perhaps belong to a ninth-century Viking Age context. None of the Orkney examples is typical of Pictish ogam inscriptions, and none can be given an early date. A cross-slab from the Broch of Burrian, North Ronaldsay, bears an inscription in the letter-form known as bind-ogam, where the strokes representing each letter are joined together (a device that makes reading the inscription infinitely easier); like Birsay I and II, the ogams are incised rather than pocked in the manner of most Pictish inscriptions (Padel 1972, 75–9). There are possible traces of a fish symbol on this stone (MacGregor 1974, 96, fig.21) which, if accepted, make Burrian the sole example in Orkney of association between ogams and Pictish symbols.

The inscriptions from Buckquoy and Gurness are incised on portable objects, a stone spindle-whorl and a bone handle respectively, and Padel has suggested that such chattel inscriptions imply a widespread knowledge of ogams at some point in Pictish history (1972, 3). There are, however, only two other surviving chattel inscriptions, both on bone handles (Bac Mhic Connain, North Uist and Weeting, Norfolk), and it is equally possible that the ogams bestowed a magical or talismanic dimension on these personal belongings and that the cutting of the ogams was done by a special person such as a *magus* or the local midwife. The ogams on the Buckquy whorl are incised in a circle round the central perforation and have been dated to the early eighth century (K.H.Jackson 1977; A.Ritchie 1977, 181–2, 197, fig.8, no.84, 199). The Gurness inscription extends lengthwise down the handle and is likely also to belong to the eighth century (Padel 1972, 98–100). In common with other Pictish ogams outside Orkney, all these inscriptions are characteristically and tantalisingly incomprehensible. If there were a magical connotation to the cutting of ogams, it might help to explain why they were used to convey the older Pictish tongue rather than Celtic, although, by the eighth century, such practices can hardly have found approval in the Pictish church.

18. Brough of Birsay, symbol stone. For a reconstruction see plate 9.1.
The original stone is now in the National Museum of Antiquities of Scotland.

19. Buckquoy, Birsay. General view of the excavation in progress at Point of Buckquoy. Compare plate 9.5.

20. Buckquoy. A spindle whorl, with ogam inscription, and a painted pebble (possibly a charm stone) from the Pictish farm at Buckquoy. The whorl diameter is about 30 mm and the pebble length about 50 mm.

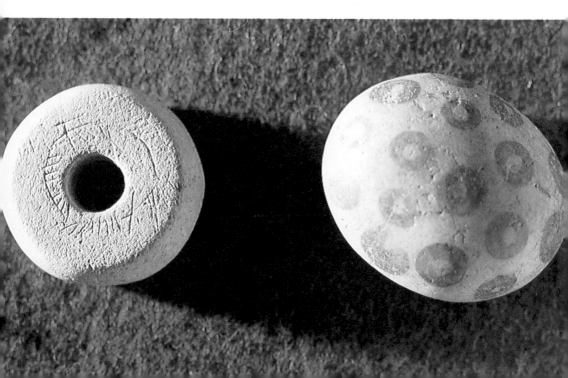

To some extent, the importance of Birsay in Pictish times is a reflection of archaeological activity in the area, which has been particularly intensive in the 1970s and 1980s. Nevertheless, the attraction of the Bay of Birsay for boats and fishing and the outstanding fertility of Birsay soils are likely to have made the area a natural focus for settlement in the Pictish period as in later times. The status of the Brough of Birsay is difficult to determine. There was an early Christian cemetery enclosed by a curvilinear wall, and remains of walling beneath the later church may belong to a contemporary chapel (Radford 1962, 167–9); the cemetery included a square kerbed cairn which might belong to the Pictish type of grave-setting identified elsewhere, but the structural evidence from the early excavations has yet to be published. There are traces of earlier domestic occupation beneath the Viking-age buildings, but the extent of the settlement and its nature, whether monastic or secular, are unknown. Radiocarbon dates in the eighth century AD have been obtained from pre-Norse occupation levels (Morris 1981a, 40), and continuing excavations may clarify further the structural sequence. Pre-Norse artefacts include bone combs and pins, the symbol stone and ogam inscriptions already described, and an important assemblage of metalworking material (Curle 1982). The latter includes a lead disc decorated with a trumpet-spiral design which is a pattern for making cast bronze plaques, possibly intended as escutcheons for hanging-bowls (Curle 1974; plate 9.4). The spirals match those on silver hand-pins from the hoards from Gaulcross, Morayshire and Norries' Law, Fife, and the overall design has been described as 'Durrowesque' (R.B.K. Stevenson 1976, 248, 251). There are also clay moulds used in the manufacture of penannular brooches (Curle 1974), including the special form identified as Pictish by Wilson in the hoard from St Ninian's Isle in Shetland (Small *et al.* 1973, 81–105), characterised by stylistic features such as the presence of a panel with curved ends on the hoop of the brooch. This type of brooch belongs to the eighth century, and other examples have been found in Orkney at Pierowall on Westray and from Stromness (Small *et al.* 1973, 89). Whatever the nature of the Pictish settlement on the Brough of Birsay, it included, temporarily at least, the services of a skilled metalworking craftsman.

Rescue excavation in the early 1970s of a low elongated mound on the Point of Buckquoy, truncated by coastal erosion of the Bay of Birsay, revealed the remains of a farmstead spanning the Pictish and Norse periods, though without direct continuity between the two (A. Ritchie 1977). The erosion meant that the site was incomplete in all periods except perhaps the last, which was a casual Viking-age burial of the later tenth century, inserted into the mound formed by the ruins of the earlier domestic buildings. Nevertheless, sufficient traces survived to allow the identification of Norse and pre-Norse house-plans and to enable some estimate to be made of the respective life-styles involved. The Pictish phases seem likely to have spanned the seventh and early eighth centuries AD, after which there was a brief interval, perhaps of half a century, before Norsemen began to establish a new farmstead on the site around AD 800 (figure 9.1; colour plate 19).

PLATE 9.4. Lead disc, Brough of Birsay, 58 mm in diameter. (Crown copyright, SDD.)

The earliest surviving structures were two successive houses of cellular type, in which small cells open off a central area; less than half of house 6 remained intact, with a central slab-lined hearth and three rectilinear cells along one side of the axis of the house. The other side had been destroyed when first house 5 and then house 4 were built. House 5 was very small and its plan-form virtually intact: three rectilinear cells surrounding a central hearth, the entire internal area measuring only 2.75 m by 3.60 m, although the individual cells were not markedly smaller than those in the earlier house 6.

When the Broch of Gurness (or Aikerness) and its surrounding structures were excavated, two separate and distinct buildings were recognised in the uppermost occupation levels, overlying the earlier 'village' surrounding the broch itself (RCAMS 1946, fig. 132). One of these buildings was a

PLATE 9.5. Figure-of-eight house, Buckquoy. (Crown copyright, SDD.)

simple oblong structure sometimes assumed to be a Viking-age hall-house, and the other was a cellular house closely similar to those found at Buckquoy. The Gurness example had four cells and was comparable in overall size to house 6 at Buckquoy. This type of house seems not to have been found elsewhere, but the Gurness evidence, together with the seventh-century dating likely for those at Buckquoy, suggests that such houses would be late in any post-broch structural sequence and thus vulnerable to destruction.

Although the interiors of these houses were compartmented, their external appearance was probably a rounded oval; the walls were stone-faced, either by horizontal masonry or by a combination of upright slabs and horizontal walling only on the inside, and an earth and turf backing seems likely. The internal divisions were probably as much a device to alleviate roofing problems as they were a means of separating different areas of the house. In this respect they resemble wheelhouses, where the radial piers not only divided up the interior but also helped to support the roof. The resemblance to the wheelhouse tradition is even more marked in house 4, where the rooms were subdivided by piers of masonry (plate 9.5).

The late Pictish house at Buckquoy, no.4, was larger and more sophisticated in design than its predecessors, but it represents a related type of plan-form, the figure-of-eight house. Here the basic form consists of a large oblong or oval living-hall containing a central hearth and a smaller circular chamber opening off one end. At Buckquoy there was an additional rectilinear room at the opposite end of the living-hall, and beyond it a small entrance vestibule, the whole house forming a linear unit of interconnecting rooms, almost 14 m in overall internal length. A second entrance led straight into the living-hall, and the remains of low stone kerbing along either side of the hall was interpreted as evidence for flanking wooden benches or platforms. The hearth was well-designed: paved and kerbed with stone, one end was left open to allow easy removal of the ash, and there was a pit at the other end in which embers could be kept alight during the night. Post-holes on either side would have held the wooden supports for a spit across the fire. Elaborate hearths are a feature of this period, a reflection perhaps of the stability of Pictish society. The hearth in house 5 was not only open-ended but furnished with a removable slab, notched to fit the side-kerbing of the hearth, which could be used for baking or as a rest for pots. Contemporary and similarly elaborate hearths have been found at the Howe, Stromness (Hedges and Bell 1980, 50–1) and at Calf of Eday (Calder 1939, 175, fig.1, pl.LXVII, 2).

The main part of house 4 was built with walls of horizontal drystone masonry, but the circular chamber was walled with a basal revetment of upright slabs and horizontal masonry above. The chamber was in fact partially underground, and the upright slabs were set against the ruins of the earlier house 6 and against the underlying natural boulder clay. The horizontal walling began only at ground-level. This same labour-saving device was used in Orkney in more recent times, for houses were built partially underground in the seventeenth and eighteenth centuries, and even in the late nineteenth century farm workers would choose to build

PLATE 9.6. Figure-of-eight house, Brough Road Area 3, Birsay.
(C. D. Morris. Crown copyright, SDD.)

against a hillside so that one wall was only a stone facing against the earth
(Fenton 1979, 13).

At present there are no very close parallels to the plan-form of house 4
in Orkney. A little to the south of this site on the Point of Buckquoy, a house
of related form has been excavated by Christopher Morris (Brough Road,
Area 3, in the Birsay Bay Project, Morris 1979b, 16–18, and a possible
second house in Area 5, Morris 1980, 27–8). Here the house consisted of
two circular rooms of almost the same size, one about 4.50 m in diameter
and the other slightly smaller, separated by a central drystone pier. The
larger chamber contained a slab-lined hearth and a possible oven. The walls
were built of horizontal drystone masonry with a neatly finished inner face
and an irregular outer face and an earth and stone core; externally the house
was of oval shape (plate 9.6).

Closer in shape and internal layout to Buckquoy house 4 are the
buildings belonging to pre-Norse levels at the Udal on North Uist (I.A.
Crawford 1973; 1974; Crawford and Switsur 1977). They belong to Crawford's 'Scotto-Pictish' levels, dated to the fourth to ninth centuries AD, and a

typological sequence has been identified, showing the development of the house-plan for which the obscure term 'ventral' has been put forward (Crawford and Switsur 1977, 130). The sequence begins with a simple oval house, 5 m by 4 m, with small side-cells, a central slab-lined hearth and a low platform along one side. The second stage, which relates to Buckquoy, consists of a large oval chamber about 6 m long with an oval cell opening off one end, a doorway at the other, a central hearth and flanking platforms on both sides. The final stage sees the addition of more side-cells, and the houses now have fenced yards and small square outhouses. The material culture belonging to these levels is markedly different from that of the preceding wheelhouse occupation of the site (Crawford and Switsur 1977, 129), unlike the situation in Orkney where the basic material culture remained the same throughout the post-broch centuries.

A very small version of the figure-of-eight house forms one of the outbuildings at the Broch of Yarrow in Caithness (J. Anderson 1890, 137, fig. 1). An attempt was made in Ritchie 1974, fig. 1 to produce these various house-plans to the same scale, but mistakenly houses 6, 5 and 4 at Buckquoy, Yarrows F and Gurness were in fact reproduced at twice the size of the rest. The true comparison between Buckquoy 4 and the Udal house n may be seen in Alcock (1980, fig. 4.2).

ENVIRONMENT AND MATERIAL CULTURE

The various Birsay sites are currently the major source of information about the environment and economy of Pictish life in Orkney (Donaldson, Morris and Rackham 1981; A. Ritchie 1977). In general the environment is likely to have been little different in terms of natural vegetation from that of today, though the likely presence of more local pockets of shrub woodland has been stressed. It is clear from documentary sources that cereal crops were more commonly grown in later medieval times than today, especially bere and oats, and the recovery of grains of both these crops from the Brough Road Area 3 of the Birsay Bay Project may hint at the importance of arable agriculture in pre-Norse times (Donaldson, Morris and Rackham 1981, 80). Nevertheless, the emphasis of the archaeological material is upon animal husbandry, and it seems likely that the Pictish economy was predominantly pastoral. At Buckquoy, the animal bones represented about 50 per cent cattle, 30 per cent sheep and 20 per cent pig (Noddle 1977), whereas sheep were predominant in the sample from Room 5 on the Brough of Birsay where there were pre-Norse levels beneath the Viking-age structures. It is possible that Buckquoy functioned as the home farm for the community living on the Brough. These domestic animals were bred primarily for their meat, hides and bone for implement manufacture, and hunting wild animals such as deer and wild cat and birds such as gannet and fulmar was of minor importance. The abundance of bone available from domestic carcases perhaps explains the rarity of whale and seal bones: such mammals would have been butchered on the beach for their skins, meat and blubber and the bones mostly left behind if they were not required.

Marine resources must always have been important in the Orcadian economy. At Buckquoy, fishing appears to have been less important in Pictish times than in the Norse period, but this may be an illusion created by the absence of middens on the surviving area of the Pictish settlement. This factor of partial survival limits many of the conclusions about economic life that can be drawn both from Buckquoy and from most of the Birsay sites. The pre-Norse levels at Buckquoy yielded bones of conger eel, saithe or pollack, ling, cod, hake and ballan wrasse (Wheeler 1977), and cod were also found in contemporary contexts on the Brough of Birsay (Donaldson, Morris and Rackham 1981, 77). This evidence suggests line or net fishing from the shore and line-fishing from boats offshore. Some of the shellfish, predominantly limpets and winkles, from Buckquoy may have been used as fish-bait rather than as food; their meat-weight makes them insignificant as part of the human diet (Evans and Spencer 1977), though a decrease in the size of the limpets from Pictish to Norse samples may suggest an over-collection in pre-Norse times that is not detectable from the surviving numbers of shells. It is possible that, like the modern Faroese and other people who live by the sea (A. Jackson 1977, 50), Picts in the Northern Isles might refuse to eat shellfish on principle. In more recent times, limpets and winkles were eaten only as a last resort in times of famine, though other shellfish such as cockles and razorfish were considered delicacies (Fenton 1978, 541–2). Bede describes the whelk (*coclea*) as a great natural asset to Britain, because its shell was used to make a scarlet dye 'a most beautiful red which neither fades through the heat of the sun nor exposure to the rain; indeed the older it is the more beautiful it becomes' (*Historia Ecclesiastica*, I, i). Dog whelks from which such a useful dye could have been made were the third most common shells found at Buckquoy but not, unfortunately, in the vast quantities necessary for practical manufacture (Evans 1969, 479).

Buckquoy is as yet the only fully published Pictish settlement in Orkney and, unfortunately, the site did not produce a large assemblage of artefacts from the early levels. Once the publication of the Brough of Birsay, Gurness and other sites with Pictish occupation is complete, it should be possible to reconstruct a more detailed picture of the range of Pictish domestic equipment. The first phase of Pictish occupation at Buckquoy included both cellular houses, nos 6 and 5, and the associated artefacts included simple bone skewer pins and a needle, part of a bone mount, a bone spoon and a double-sided composite bone comb. A similar bone mount came from the second Pictish phase, associated with house 4, and they have been interpreted as strengthening plates for the mouths of leather knife-sheaths (A. Ritchie 1977, 179). Carefully made small bone pins were in use in this phase, including one with an animal head, perhaps a cat, and an unfinished example which suggests that such bone pins were manufactured on the site. Pottery vessels were used, including plain large jars, as were iron knives and stone spindle whorls. One of the latter bore an ogam inscription and has already been discussed, and its importance for the site is that it is a specifically Pictish artefact. There was also a painted pebble, well stratified in the primary occupation of house 4 and thus providing a firm chronological context for an intriguing class of object which appears to have been peculiar to the Northern Isles and Caithness. It is a white quartzite pebble, 40 mm long, which has been painted overall with small circles in a dye which has left a brown stain though it may once have been a brighter colour. Twenty such pebbles have survived, all, apart from the Buckquoy example, from broch sites and most belonging to the post-broch period. Although it cannot be claimed as a diagnostic Pictish artefact, the painted pebble was clearly a constituent of material culture in northern Pictland. A variety of curvilinear and dot designs has been used on the pebbles and they are very pleasing objects; unwashed they would be difficult to spot during excavation, and the fact that so many were found even during late nineteenth-century excavations in Caithness suggests that they may have been more common than it appears. It has been argued that painted pebbles were charmstones used to treat sick people and animals by dipping the stones into drinking-water, a tradition that was strong in medieval times and survived in Scotland at least into the late nineteenth century using naturally attractive stones (A. Ritchie 1972). There is even a story recorded by Adomnan about Columba using a holy pebble in just this way at the court of the Pictish king Bridei (Anderson and Anderson 1961, 399–405; colour plate 20).

The Pictish settlement at Buckquoy was succeeded around AD 800 by a Norse farmstead. Although the house-types were distinctly different, and the stratigraphy and chronology of the site indicated that the new buildings were contemporary with the Norse colonisation of the Orkneys, the associated artefacts displayed little evidence of cultural change. The bone combs and pins found in the Norse levels are native in origin, and there is not one indisputably Norse artefact among the finds. The interpretation of this evidence is controversial. It has been argued that there must have been a degree of social integration between the Picts and the incoming Norse settlers during the primary stages of colonisation of the Orkneys in the ninth century (A. Ritchie 1974), in contrast to the traditional view of Vikings inflicting extermination and slavery. An alternative interpretation would have the Norse houses built and the artefacts made under duress by Pictish slaves in the manner to which they were accustomed: 'the Pictish population can only have been subjugated by force' (Graham-Campbell 1980, 69). But the houses were not built according to Pictish custom and, although the Norse takeover of Orkney was indubitably complete in the end, enforced subjugation is not the only answer. The Scots took over the Pictish kingdom on mainland Scotland but no modern historian would suggest that there was wholesale slaughter or slavery there. The political circumstances were different of course, but nevertheless the moral of the comparison is that takeover bids need not be bloody.

Excavations at the Broch of Howe near Stromness have yielded considerable evidence of Pictish occupation (see appendix to this chapter; Hedges and Bell 1980), but assessment of the site must await full publication of the results. The buildings appear to form conjoining units rather than freestanding houses of recognisable plan-form, and the individual components are small in floor area (figure 9.2). The Picts utilised and refurbished earlier buildings in preference to building anew as at Gurness, but the complex sequence of modifications and the quantity of finds argues against any impression of squatter occupation. Pre-Norse structures have also been found at Skaill in Deerness (information Peter Gelling, see appendix to chapter 8, p.176) and at Saevar Howe, Birsay (information John Hedges).

Despite the clear architectural links between house 4 at Buckquoy and wheelhouse tradition, examples of true wheelhouses are rare in Orkney. One was excavated at Calf of Eday, together with later structures which presumably take the site into Pictish times (Calder 1939); the latter include a kerbed and paved hearth with a post-hole on either side for the spit which is virtually identical to the hearth in house 4 at Buckquoy. The spit-supports were made of imported Scots pine probably derived from driftwood (Calder 1939, 175). Alcock has postulated the existence of two different building traditions, 'the circular and the axial', among the Picts and their immediate forebears, the circular represented by wheelhouses and the axial by figure-of-eight, rectilinear and cellular houses (1980, 74), although he admits that it is difficult to date wheelhouses within the historical Pictish period (1980, 71). That wheelhouses could themselves possess an axial element is demonstrated by the site at À Cheardach Bheag on South Uist, where a large wheelhouse had a smaller wheelhouse opening off it (Fairhurst 1971, fig.3). It seems likely that these various house-types represent inter-related architectural development rather than separate traditions, and the impression given by the existing dating evidence is that the development is linear and sequential from wheelhouses onwards.

Information about the early Christian church in Orkney is disappointingly limited by lack of excavation, although potentially interesting sites have been located by fieldwork (Lamb 1973; 1976). Apart from the early Christian site on the Brough of Birsay, no surviving church or monastic settlement can with certainty be dated prior to the Viking Age, even though it seems likely that the Orkneys were converted to Christianity in the course of the seventh century AD. Corn Holm in Deerness and Castle of Burwick on

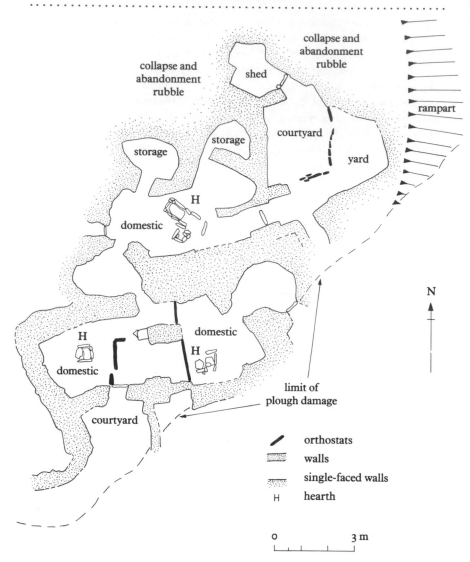

FIGURE 9.2. Howe, Stromness: simplified plan of phase 2
of the Pictish settlement.

South Ronaldsay have been interpreted as eremitic monasteries which may
date from the eighth century through to the tenth and eleventh centuries
(Lamb 1973, 78–82), but there is no evidence for a pre-Norse monastery on
the Brough of Deerness, in fact Morris has suggested that the rectangular
buildings surrounding the chapel may be secular and domestic rather than
ecclesiastical (1977, 70).

Structural evidence for the early Christian church is thus scanty, but there are sculptural and artefactual traces of Christianity from at least the seventh century onwards. The small iron bells from Saevar Howe and the Broch of Burrian mentioned above are normally associated with Irish missionaries and probably date from the eighth or ninth centuries (Bourke 1980), while the 'arm-pit' cross on the Burrian slab is likely to date from the eighth century. The same type of cross appears in considerably more elaborate form on the stone panel from Flotta, which originally formed the front of an altar; the cross is infilled with interlace designs and the piece has been dated to the late eighth century (C. Thomas 1971, 186–8; plate 9.7). The cross-slab from the church of St Boniface on Papa Westray bears an incised cross formed of interlacing segments of circles, and a date in the seventh century has been suggested (Radford 1962, 173).

PLATE 9.7. Altar frontal, Flotta. (Copyright NMAS.)

The Picts were a seafaring nation. They used boats not simply as a means of transport but also as an element of naval power in their armoury. The Pictish threat to late Roman Britain was at least partially sea-borne, and an entry in the Annals of Tigernach for AD 729 mentions the loss at sea of 150 Pictish ships (A. O. Anderson 1922, 226). The great timber-laced fort at Burghead on the coast of Moray must surely have been a Pictish naval base, and Alcock has stressed the coastal distribution of Pictish forts, in two cases coinciding with modern harbours (1980, 80–1). No Pictish forts have yet been identified in Orkney, although they utilised sites defended by the earlier ramparts and ditches associated with brochs, for example at Gurness and probably Borwick on mainland and at Burrian on North Ronaldsay. But there are a few multivallate promontory forts in Orkney, independent of brochs (Lamb 1980, 50–3). There has been virtually no excavation of these forts, and they may belong to the later first millennium BC or to the first millennium AD, but it is possible that some may have been built by the Picts. The Annals of Ulster record that in AD 681 'The Orkneys were destroyed by Brude', and Anderson has interpreted this entry to mean 'the destruction of some fortresses and the taking of hostages' (M. O. Anderson 1973, 175). Certainly something more than the burning of a few farms would seem to be indicated.

There is little evidence to show what sort of boats the Picts used, but Johnstone has concluded that a plank-built rowing-boat is most likely (1980, 152–3). The best documented illustration of a Pictish boat is the carving on the symbol stone at Cossans near Glamis (Johnstone 1980, 152, pl. 11.16), but a possible candidate in Orkney is the lightly incised boat beside a Pictish-looking cloaked figure on the stone from Burness in Firth (RCAMS 1946, 99, no.347, fig.72). This resembles the boat carved on a stone disc from post-broch levels at Jarlshof in Shetland (Johnstone, 1980, 153, pl. 11.18). The fact that the Jarlshof boat has a sail is worthy of note, for sails appear not to have been used as far north in continental Europe until the sixth or seventh centuries AD.

The Picts have left behind them a personal legacy unparalleled by earlier or later peoples in Scotland: their symbols, potentially a key to their ideas, customs and beliefs. These symbols hint at the social complexities commonplace to the anthropologist but mostly hidden from the archaeologist, simply because so many beliefs are barely if at all embodied in the material debris that remains to be examined. For this reason, and because the Picts are, after all, separated from the twentieth century by little more than a thousand years, their legacy deserves to be studied by every means available. More radiocarbon dates will clarify how useful this chronological tool may be for so restricted a period of time; computer analysis of the combinations and geographical distributions of Pictish symbols ought to allow the archaeologist and social anthropologist together to reach some conclusions about their meaning; and, when the financial climate permits, a programme of controlled but exhaustive research excavation on selected sites would solve many outstanding problems of Pictish archaeology. Despite their historical gloss, the basic elucidation of Pictish society depends not on the historian whose tools for that period are unlikely to increase but on the archaeologist, the collection of whose raw material is at yet in its infancy.

Acknowledgements. I should like to thank Professor Leslie Alcock and Dr Joanna Close-Brooks for their kindness in reading and commenting upon the draft of this chapter, and I am grateful to Nigel Neil and the North of Scotland Archaeological Services for providing the following appendix describing recent work at the Howe, Stromness.

Nigel Neil **Excavations at Howe**

Excavations at Howe, Stromness, begun in 1978 in advance of farm-land improvement, have revealed a series of Pictish farmsteads overlying a broch and associated settlement of several phases. A neolithic chambered tomb underlies the broch tower and the rampart of the broch settlement is currently thought to be neolithic in origin. Work up to the end of the 1981 season has concentrated on the excavation of the Pictish and later broch settlements. No abandonment horizon was present between the late broch buildings and those recognisably 'Pictish' in style, but the broch tower soon went out of use. Aspects of the building techniques employed and the generally 'cellular' plan of the house suggest a degree of continuity. Al-though the finds have yet to be studied in detail, it is possible to suggest tentatively that use of the tower finally ended sometime in the fourth century. Although there is ample evidence for metalworking – smelting and smithying – in the later broch period buildings, signs of these activities are noticeably absent from the Pictish phases. Recent plough damage has removed parts of some structures but it is impossible to tell whether or not any have been lost entirely; buildings belonging to the undefended broch phases have been found outside the former defences and thus well beyond the surviving limits of the Pictish settlement. With these provisions, the overall impression is one of a small settlement with no more than three domestic areas in use during any of the eight phases and probably only one by the end of the occupation.

The shapes of the earlier Pictish buildings at Howe are governed partly by the re-use of broch period relict structures and partly by the need for support from the collapsed rubble of earlier buildings. Free-standing walls were frequently thick but unstable, except where larger flags were used, perhaps robbed from the broch tower. 'Single-face' walls were of two types – coursed and orthostatic. The latter, generally surmounted by flags, broad-ly resembles the type encountered at Buckquoy (A. Ritchie 1977, e.g. pl. 10). The 'cellular' plan of the buildings at Howe is also reminiscent of Buckquoy, particularly in later phases where there is a tendency towards greater symmetry. Hearths and flagged floors are generally incompatible, cooking areas being floored with earth and ash spreads. The sw building in

PLATE I. Figure-of-eight house (phase 7), Howe, Stromness.
(NOSAS, Crown copyright.)

figure 9.2 is a relic of an earlier phase, re-used and modified; it contained six stratified hearths and associated earth floors. The building complex illustrated represents the largest expansion in any one phase and all the cells in it continued to be used for several phases. Eventually, an entrance was cut through the w wall of the sw building as access to a group of flagged rooms; these have been illustrated in an earlier report (Hedges and Bell 1980, 51, left fig.). The building illustrated in plate 1 lay to the w of those in that report and is approximately contemporary with them. It typifies the tendency towards more regular shapes and exemplifies the trend of having flagged and earth floored areas under one roof; two other cells of similar size were present to the w at the same time, reached by way of an entrance within the building.

A Pictish-Norse transition is not discernible at Howe, either in the finds evidence or in building style. A possible Norse domestic structure is present in an incomplete state as a result of ploughing, but is not linked stratigraphically to any other structure. A glass linen smoother found during nineteenth-century excavations is considered to be securely of Norse date (Grieg 1940, 80–1). Grieg lists it as a grave find and a late but undatable burial was found in the upper fill of the broch tower.

The finds assemblage from the Pictish levels at Howe includes much pottery – generally undecorated, flat-based and finer than earlier wares. Two flagstone gaming boards have been found, and bone and antler artefacts include double-sided combs with iron-riveted spacer plates, a small knife handle with ring-and-dot decoration, and weaving combs. The small number of bronze finds includes tweezers, spiral rings and two penannular brooches with zoomorphic terminals. The better preserved of the latter has been illustrated previously (Hedges and Bell 1980, 50), when a seventh/eighth-century date was offered; they came from near the middle of the building sequence. The post-excavation work on the Pictish settlement at Howe is in progress, and the finds typology has still to be studied.

Acknowledgements. The writer wishes to thank Beverley Smith for her assistance in compiling this report. The line drawing and photograph are by Frank Moran.

FIGURE 9.1. Buckquoy: plan of the Pictish and Norse phases
(on next two pages).

Buckquoy,
ORKNEY
1970-71
phases I-II

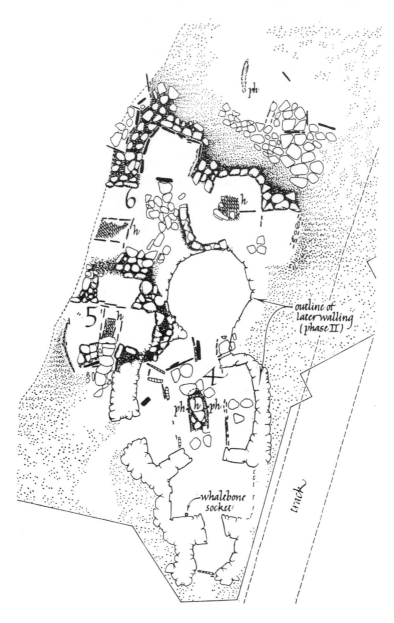

ph

6

h

h

5   h

x

ph h ph

outline of
later walling
(phase II)

whalebone
socket

track

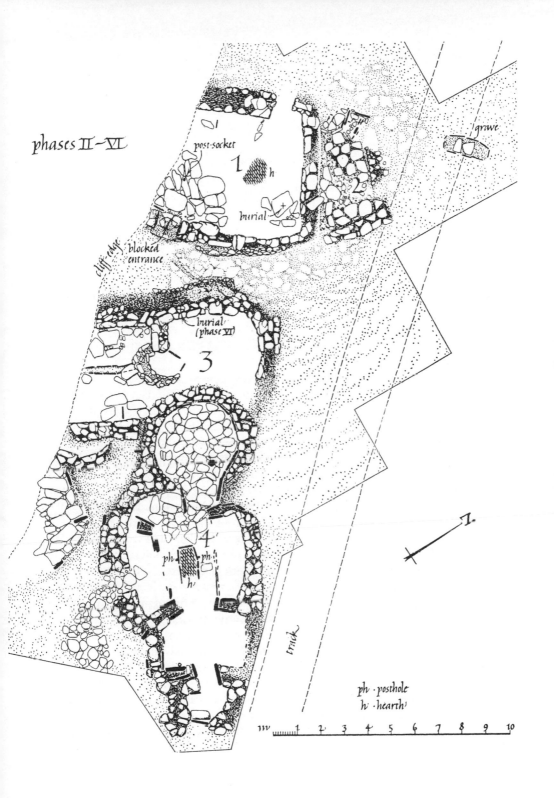

phases II–VI

post-socket

1   h

burial

grave

2

cliff edge

blocked
entrance

burial
(phase VI)

3

4

ph   ph
h

track

ph · posthole
h · hearth

m   1   2   3   4   5   6   7   8   9   10

10 Christopher D. Morris **Viking Orkney: A Survey**

RAIDS AND SETTLEMENT

In Scandinavia, the Viking period is generally seen as the last stage of prehistory: the Late Iron Age, the study of which is fundamentally archaeological. This reflects the lack of contemporary and local historical sources in Scandinavia; although late sagas often refer back to the Viking Age. In Scandinavia this period is generally seen as *c.* 800–*c.* 1050, but the terminal dates are not based on specific events (NAA 1979, Chronological Table, 284). In other parts of Europe it is easier, with fuller written sources, to give a more exact chronology to the period. In England, for instance, the raid on Lindisfarne in 793 is often taken as marking the beginning, and the Battles of Stamford Bridge and Hastings in 1066 the end, of the period. The accounts in Irish annals of raids in western Scotland and Ireland in the last two decades of the eighth century have provided a similar starting point for these areas, but the endings are far from clear. The Norman invasion of Ireland in 1172 effectively ended Scandinavian predominance, although the nationalistic school of historians has tended to prefer a date of 1014, with the Battle of Clontarf. In Scotland, the Battle of Largs in 1263 and/or the Treaty of Perth in 1266 provide a convenient end-point; while in the Isle of Man 1266 is the end of the reign of the last Scandinavian king, Magnus.

It is ironic that the records for the Northern Isles of Orkney and Shetland are so meagre that no single date can be given for the beginning of the Viking period there, for it was here that Scandinavian influence lasted longest of all in the British Isles. Formally, they remained under Scandinavian rule until the impignoration of the Isles in 1468–9. However, it is likely that the succession of Scottish earls in the Orkney Earldom from 1231

began a process of 'Scottification' (F.T.Wainwright 1962c, 190), and, as
Barbara Crawford has argued (1977, 113–15), 'by the mid-thirteenth
century, Caithness had become to some extent an integral part of the
Scottish kingdom'. Although Shetland was linked more directly to Norway
from 1195 (B.E.Crawford 1971, 353), in Orkney the main period of
cultural influence from Scandinavia had ended by the mid-thirteenth century. Wainwright saw the death of Earl Ragnald in 1158 as a particularly
significant stage in the process: this was the end of the Golden Age.
Convenience of terminology, rather than strict chronological logic, therefore, maintains the term 'Viking' for the period up to the mid-eleventh
century and 'Late Norse' for the following two centuries, when these Isles
(and Caithness to the south) were still quite distinctively Scandinavian in
cultural (as well as political) orientation.

Such convenience has its drawbacks, in that it cannot easily be maintained for archaeological material. Though the Late Norse period is marked
by an increase in documentary source-material for the historian, it is not
marked by any fundamental change in the material culture of the inhabitants of Orkney. The problem is compounded by the lack of fine calibration
for the dating of artefacts on their own, and the inherent difficulties involved
in the dating of distinctive artefact-types or artistic motifs in contexts
distant from their source. The inevitable haziness of the chronological
distinctions certainly cannot be dispelled, and no attempt to do so will be
made here. Nor can the chronological problems be sidestepped by a retreat
into a pure, unsullied *pre*-history that ignores the, admittedly sparse,
documentary material, and the not-so-sparse institutional and linguistic
material. For better or worse, the Viking and Late Norse periods are
'text-aided', and hence *proto*-historic.

The *Orkneyinga Saga*, written *c.* 1192–1206, is a fundamental source
for the Late Norse period in Orkney as it gives much detail of the events of
the previous century. It also is valuable in that it paints pictures of some of
the most powerful men of Viking Britain, such as the Orkney Earls Sigurd
the Stout and Thorfinn (for modern translation, see A.B.Taylor 1938 and
Pálsson and Edwards 1978). It has provided the basis of some modern
historical accounts of the Norse Earldom (e.g. Clouston 1932), as well as
giving insights into life in this earldom. However, it has long been recognised that for the Viking period its information is very partial. Indeed,
Wainwright's account of the early part of the Viking period in the Northern
Isles (F.T.Wainwright 1962b, 126–40) deliberately asserts the primacy of
the chronology derived from archaeological and linguistic sources over that
of the Saga. More circumstantial evidence of historical references from
other parts of Britain is then used to bolster the argument. The present
writer would prefer to see archaeology as one of several interconnecting or
interpenetrating approaches to the past (see Biddle 1971, 391, 403), with an

obligation placed on the student of protohistoric periods to extract the maximum information from each discipline, within its academic limits. Thus, while this chapter will emphasise the material evidence, and not concern itself with the minutiae of evidence from allied disciplines, it should be remembered that this is a matter of convenience, rather than an approach that is, of itself, academically justifiable.

The origin of the Orkney Earldom traditionally lies in a gift from the Norwegian King. The *Orkneyinga Saga* tells of 'vikings (who) used to raid in Norway over summer and had Shetland and Orkney as their winter base', and of how one summer Harold Fine-hair sailed west over the North Sea in order to teach them a lesson. He conquered what amounts to the Northern and Southern Isles, and gave Shetland and Orkney to Earl Rognvald of Möre, who promptly (and probably shrewdly) gave them to his brother Sigurd. Subsequently, Harold gave Sigurd the title of 'earl' (Pálsson and Edwards 1978, 30). A similar account in the *Saga of King (Saint) Olaf* in *Heimskringla* by Snorri Sturluson (Laing and Simpson 1964, 218) tells us that:

> It is related that in the days of Harold Haarfager the King of Norway, the islands of Orkney, which before had been only a resort for vikings, were settled.

Elsewhere in *Heimskringla*, in the *Saga of Harold Fine-hair*, the western voyage of Harold is put after the battle of *Hafrsfjord* (now dated *c.* 890 AD). A further source, the twelfth-century *Historia Norvegiae*, makes the pirates a group related to Jarl Rognvald, who in Harold's day deprived the native Picts of their habitations and utterly destroyed them, subjecting the islands to themselves (quoted by Wainwright 1962a, 99, n.3).

It is of course possible that these saga accounts are untrustworthy. Haakon Shetelig in 1940 discussed the lack of contemporary foreign corroboration for Harold Fine-hair's expedition to the west, and concluded that 'we feel inclined to doubt that the story of Harold's expedition contains any nucleus of historical truth whatever' (Shetelig 1940, 24–5). The information in an Irish source and the *Historia Norvegiae* supports a hypothesis of independent annexation of the Orkneys by the family of the Earls of Möre a full generation before the time of Harold : it would be held, then, not as a fief of the King of Norway, but by means of inherited title from Möre, applied to wherever this dominion was extended. More recently, Professor Peter Sawyer has taken the argument a stage further, noting the absence of references to Harold's expedition in Irish annals, and preferring to see the tradition as 'best understood as a later elaboration, probably modelled on the expeditions of Magnus' (Magnus Barelegs), who led two expeditions in 1098 and 1102 (which are referred to in insular sources). To Sawyer, it would be a sudden and improbable assertion of power by Harold Fairhair late in the ninth or early in the tenth century (Sawyer 1976, 107 and 109).

As far as dating the earlier phases of Viking activities in the Earldom is concerned, scholars have preferred to take the indirect evidence from contemporary insular sources, such as annals referring to Viking raids elsewhere in Britain, to assert that Viking settlement in the Northern Isles must have occurred by the beginning of the ninth century (e.g. Wainwright 1962b, 129–30). Also, the equally indirect evidence of Dicuil, probably referring to the fleeing from the Faeroes of Celtic anchorites and priests *c*. 825 in the face of pirate raids, has been cited (e.g. Wainwright 1962b, 131–2; G. Jones 1968, 269–70). Indeed, the dating of phase 1 at Jarlshof, Shetland, to *c*. 800 AD is done merely by implication on these bases (Hamilton 1956, 93–4, 106). These are flimsy grounds upon which to date settlements in the north, and, using them, we get no more than the implication that raiding took place in the early ninth century: it does not seem enough to support theories of wide-ranging settlement, even though they support the likelihood of some gradual settlement in certain places. It could be that the saga and other sources may refer to a second, and more formalised, stage in the Viking contact with the north of Scotland.

Much ink has been spilled over the interpretation of these accounts, and play made of the dislocation in date between the saga accounts and the archaeological evidence. Most archaeologists have followed Shetelig and Wainwright in explicitly or implicitly rejecting the saga accounts. Other scholars, perhaps more cautious in their handling of the sagas, have made the point that this material does clearly seem to imply Viking activity before Harold's time, and that it is settlement that is specifically mentioned in them (e.g. Clouston 1932, 6, 20). 'Settlement' in the terms of the author of the *Jarlasaga* (as the *Orkneyinga Saga* was originally called) may very well have meant organisation of the land settled by the new Earl. Alternatively, as both H. Shetelig (1940, 25) and J. R. C. Hamilton (1956, 93) have pointed out (following Steenstrup), an Irish source relates that Raghnall or Rognvald, a Norwegian chieftain, after being driven from home by trouble, was established in Orkney from about 860 AD. The conclusion, therefore was that:

> It is . . . improbable that the Earldom of Orkney was founded by Harold. The Orkney earls certainly belonged to the same family as Earl Rognvald of Möre but appear to have been established in the islands at least a generation before the events related in the Sagas.

THE ARCHAEOLOGICAL RECORD

We need not necessarily be as strict in condemnation of sagas as Wainwright, Shetelig and Sawyer, and we might also be somewhat more cautious as archaeologists over the dating of the artefacts found in graves and settlements. D. M. Wilson's strictures (in reference to England) on the exact dating of artefacts in graves, are apposite:

The grave finds are difficult to date. I am sceptical in the matter of accurate typological dating in the Viking period, believing, with Almgren, that it is difficult to date any object to a period within a hundred years if there is no documentary source to assist the dating. It is easy to classify the swords found in Scandinavian graves, but it is impossible to say whether they represent people buried in the period of the raids or in the period of settlement. (1976a, 397)

We may add that the problem becomes even more acute when the comparison is made between material found in the homeland and in the colonies: is there a time-lag, and if so, how do we assess its length?

The traditional *typological* method of archaeology can offer us only an imprecise tool for the assessment of the origin and dating of Viking settlement in Orkney. It is subject to legitimate query just as the written sources are. Resolution of the problem can come only with some form of independent dating, and in the circumstances this must be archaeological – whether coin-dating or the use of radiocarbon determinations. Such methods have been used elsewhere in Scotland with some degree of success, in the Early Historic period (Alcock 1976), and the beginnings of a chronology exists at the Udal, North Uist (Crawford and Switsur 1977). But in both these cases – and the point is of fundamental importance – the independent dating provided by radiocarbon determinations has been related to the other evidence, whether documentary, artefactual or stratigraphical. If the radiocarbon dates are 'up for trial, or at least for calibration, before the historical dates' (Alcock 1981, 156; cf. Campbell, Baxter and Alcock 1979), they yet provide us with the potential for an advance with a particularly intractable problem, especially if interlocking groups of determinations can be undertaken.

Twenty years ago, Wainwright discussed the nature of the Scandinavian settlement in the Northern Isles as reflected in the archaeological record (Wainwright 1962b, 147–56), and naturally placed considerable emphasis upon the evidence from Jarlshof, Shetland: 'For a picture of a Viking settlement in the Northern Isles we are at present dependent almost entirely upon Jarlshof. Fortunately Jarlshof gives us a very full picture'. Some of the problems he faced are with us still: neither the excavations at Aikerness (Gurness), or the Brough of Birsay excavations, have yet been published, and the difficulties attending the study of pagan Viking graves, while considerably eased as far as Pierowall (Westray) is concerned (Thorsteinsson 1968), are far from resolved. Although Wainwright could enthusiastically assert that 'The material culture of the Scandinavian settlers comes before us most vividly in an archaeological context of graves, houses, hoards, isolated finds and runic inscriptions' (Wainwright 1962b, 147), we are looking at a small sample, the result of work of uneven quality. Considerable resources have been channelled into the archaeological study of

Orkney in the twenty years since Wainwright wrote, but they have not been part of a concerted or co-ordinated research strategy; indeed, much work has been of the nature of 'rescue' archaeology. Given the archaeological wealth of Orkney, it is perhaps inevitable that most excavation work must be of a 'rescue' nature, to record at least part of the disappearing data base: it is not a satisfactory situation and leads to an unbalanced picture. Much of what follows is either unpublished or only partially published in interim or summary accounts. Some could be rendered obsolete by new discoveries.

If in 1962 the picture of settlement in the Northern Isles was dominated by Jarlshof in Shetland, it has remained so since, even though other sites have later emerged. It has provided us with a detailed picture of the growth of the settlement over several centuries from one 'parent' dwelling to a complex which Alan Small has described as a 'township' (Small 1968, 9). The impression of complexity, however, is due as much to the successive building from the early prehistoric period until the post-medieval, as to the nature of the Viking settlement. Even in the Viking period, several phases are superimposed on top of one another. It is quite clear from J.R.C. Hamilton's analysis of the stratigraphy and phasing that at any one time there were probably no more than three families living at this site (see figure in Small 1968, 9). As a nucleated settlement, it could be seen as an early 'township' (cf. Clouston 1920; H. Marwick 1952, 216–23; Fenton 1978, 23–32, 40–8). As for function, the material found here has been interpreted in agricultural terms; and, perhaps surprisingly for a site so near to good fishing, exploitation of the sea's resources appears to have been secondary (Hamilton 1956, 137, 157). There is very little exotic imported material such as might have been expected from a trading-post or town.

A second Viking-age settlement site in Shetland was excavated by Small at Underhoull on Unst, which was a smaller single-building unit, possibly with a second unit nearby (Small 1966). On the basis of these two sites, Small has constructed a model of the ideal basic environmental factors for a settlement of the Viking Age (Small 1971, 75–9). It envisages an economy based on mixed agriculture with fishing also playing an important role. To provide utensils and tools, access to sources of bog-iron and steatite (soapstone) was desirable, and peat would be necessary for fuel. This model for the background to Viking settlement units is valuable in focusing our attention on the key features, but one needs to remember that essentially it applies to Shetland and Faeroe – very different landscapes from Orkney (cf. Brogger 1929, 35). Small himself has mapped the available land for such settlement in Shetland, and environmental factors make a very small percentage of the land mass suitable (Small 1969). Orkney, on the other hand, is very fertile (cf. maps (after O'Dell) in J. W. Hedges 1975, 65), and it need not surprise us if the resulting pattern may turn out to be somewhat different from Small's model for Shetland.

FROM PICT TO VIKING: BUCKQUOY AND BIRSAY

The Viking settlement in Orkney needs to be seen in its own terms, and not as a reflection of settlement elsewhere. In the present state of knowledge, it seems better to look at the particular evidence of Orkney, and await further excavated evidence before proceeding to any generalised statements about the nature of Viking settlement in the northern and western areas of Scotland. The debate over the relationship of incoming Viking to native Pict has been with us for many years, and if it has been given new twists, it is because there has now emerged some new evidence from the particular sites of Buckquoy, Orkney (cf. A. Ritchie 1974); and Udal, North Uist (I. A. Crawford 1981). It is a pity that a contentious tone has entered the debate: Crawford's disparaging remarks upon both the Buckquoy excavations and the wider interpretation of them by Ritchie are as unnecessary as they are misplaced. The value of the Udal excavations for discussion of the wider implications will be the greater when the full range of evidence is fully published, but methodologically it is unconvincing simply to cite this particular case in opposition to the particular case of Buckquoy. It may well be that 'the archaeological evidence cited for the Western Isles is as conclusively in favour of conquest as we are ever likely to get'; but, if it is based solely on the evidence from one site, one cannot accept this generalisation as it stands for the Western Isles, and the following sentence, that 'at present no evidence conflicts with the assumption of a similar pattern for the Northern Isles' (I. A. Crawford 1981, 268), therefore carries no weight at all.

Buckquoy in Birsay, described above (figure 9.1), is the only site in Orkney to have achieved final publication (A. Ritchie 1977). The picture here is one of the replacement of distinctive forms of Pictish period buildings by a rectangular building ascribed to the Viking period, itself replaced successively by two other buildings also ascribed to the Viking period. While the artefact assemblage for the later two buildings (phases IV and V) included some possible Viking artefacts, Ritchie has argued (A. Ritchie 1977, 192) that 'the artefact assemblage from the Norse levels is dominated by native products'. It is also the case that little of the artefact assemblage associated with the earlier, rectangular building was culturally distinctive or easily datable. There will always be a doubt about how earlier material in later contexts is to be interpreted. Few archaeologists will disagree with Crawford that 'disturbance or the retention of spoil could amount for their presence' (I. A. Crawford 1981, 265), but Ritchie's careful distinction for phase III between the finds from the interior of building 3 and those outside that were sealed by later structures (1977, 185) gives authority to her analysis. The ascription to the Viking context is based upon the change of building form from the characteristically cellular houses of the Pictish period. Unless an argument were to be advanced that the buildings of phases III, IV and V were native rather than Viking, it would be difficult to understand the repeated occurrence of native types in association with these rectangular forms other than in terms of continuity of usage of Pictish types. While, in theory, the presence of native artefacts could be the result of repeated disturbance, in the Viking period, of Pictish occupation debris, in practice, the very absence of distinctive Viking types of artefacts in association with the *occupation* of the buildings would seem to argue for the longevity of the native types.

It is unfortunate that the dating of phase III–V of the Buckquoy site is relative to that of a phase VI burial, ascribed to the tenth century, and not based on absolute dating criteria such as coins or radiocarbon determinations. There are other sites in the Birsay Bay area which, like Buckquoy, appear to have been occupied in the Pictish period, and followed by Viking period occupation and/or abandonment. A figure-of-eight shaped building from nearby (Birsay 'Small Sites' Area 3: Morris 1979b, 16–18) also had an absence of distinctively Viking artefacts, as did the fragmentary remains of a building in an adjacent area (Area 5: Morris 1980, 27–8). A second cliff-side site produced incoherent, yet definite, evidence of structural features, together with long-cist burials below cairns, apparently Pictish in character (Ashmore 1980), overlain by midden deposits into which cist-graves, probably Viking in date, were cut (Areas 1 and 2: Morris 1979b, 13–16). The site of Saevar Howe, at the south end of the Bay, has a sequence of Pictish settlement to Viking settlement to long cist cemetery (J. W. Hedges 1983b). Examination of the artefacts from Saevar Howe has demonstrated the existence of a substantial number of pre-Norse or native types of artefact. Although a large proportion of the collection is, in effect, unstratified, some of the native types exist alongside Viking types in the later phases of occupation of the site.

On the Brough of Birsay there is clear evidence from recent excavations in several different areas (figure 10.1) of occupation and structural phases, probably Pictish in date, being replaced by buildings from the Viking period (Morris 1981a, 35–7, 40; Hunter and Morris 1981, 254–7). Earlier excavations had already indicated that the nature of the site had changed from a religious to a secular settlement in the earlier part of the Viking period (Cruden 1958; 1965; Radford 1959). It was also evident in all previous excavations that, in the areas to the east of the chapel on the Brough, Viking period buildings had replaced earlier constructions and midden deposits (Radford 1959, 14–15; Hunter and Morris 1982). Through the building of these structures on a large scale, it has been argued that the site achieved a higher status, being associated with the Earls of Orkney (Cruden 1958; 1965; Radford 1959). Subsequently, by the erection of a church and buildings to the north of it, the site again became essentially a religious one,

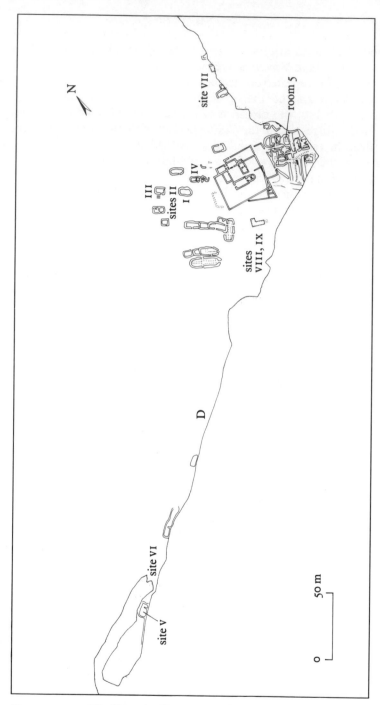

FIGURE 10.1. The Brough of Birsay: overall site survey.
(Crown copyright.)

218

although its interpretation as Christ Church minster is a matter for debate (see below; colour plate 23).

PLATE 10.1. Beachview, Birsay: 'studio' site. Final photograph 1980. (C. D. Morris: Crown copyright.)

It is evident that there is much new evidence to be analysed from the Birsay Bay area which has a direct bearing upon the problems of the nature of the initial Viking settlement there (figure 10.2). It is clear that on each of these sites, as at Jarlshof in Shetland, buildings were regularly abandoned and replaced. With plentiful supplies of flagstone on the beach, and the potential for re-use of the stones from earlier buildings, the settlers here could easily adapt the buildings to current needs, or sweep them away and start afresh. This makes for extremely complex archaeological sequences, which are sometimes composed of many fragments of different structural elements (cf. Area IV North: Morris 1982a). However, major changes have been distinguished: Radford and Cruden (Radford 1959, 16–18; Cruden 1965, 26–8) and Hunter (1983) have noted, on the Brough of Birsay, changes in layout and orientation of buildings, and at the recently discovered Beachview 'studio' site (plate 10.1), it appears that the major building discovered so far (Morris 1980, 28–30; 1981a, 38–9) was abandoned and infilled with stones and midden debris which has received an initial radiocarbon determination of 940 ± 55 bp (GU-1191). It was apparently replaced by another building represented so far mainly by the found-

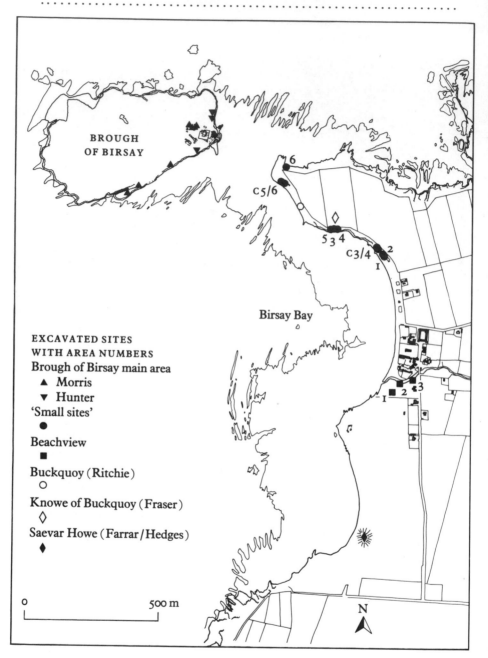

FIGURE 10.2. The Bay of Birsay: excavated sites. (Crown copyright.)

ations of a small circular chamber with central hearth. There were also building remains stratigraphically earlier than the main building. Similarly, on the 'Peerie Brough', at least three major alterations and / or replacements of buildings have been noted (Area V: Morris 1980, 24–5; 1981a, 37–8).

Despite this flurry of excavation on various sites around the Birsay Bay area (for summary see Morris forthcoming) it is not yet possible to generalise about the settlement evolution of the area in the Viking period. Both absolute and relative dating 'markers' will eventually serve to provide chronological limits for each of the various sites, which should then enable statements to be made about contemporaneity, or otherwise, of particular structures and sites. It is a tragedy that so much evidence has already been destroyed, and a sobering thought that the many visible archaeological features on the coast (see Donaldson, Morris and Rackham 1981, fig.5) will appear to give Birsay a picture of dense settlement in contrast to the known evidence from elsewhere in Orkney.

OTHER CURRENT EXCAVATION

Although it is conceivable that, as Birsay was the seat of the Earls of Orkney, a large entourage was attracted there, such evidence as is available from other sites seems to suggest that our present picture of Viking settlement in Orkney is unrepresentative. Dr Ritchie has elsewhere referred to the 'amazingly small body of evidence for such a major phase of Scotland's history' (A. Ritchie 1977, 189), and it can only be put down to a lack of archaeological initiative. Where serious, sustained, work has been undertaken, results have been forthcoming. Peter Gelling's summary of his work at Skaill (Deerness) will shortly be available (Gelling forthcoming and this volume). It is sufficient to note here that, apart from prehistoric occupation, clear excavated evidence has emerged for pre-Norse structures as well as Viking and Later Norse buildings. In the immediate vicinity (figure 10.3) there was also an old church and a hogback monument (Low 1879, 53–5; Lang 1974, 232) and, within a couple of miles in either direction, further secular and ecclesiastical sites ('The Howie'; Brough of Deerness, Morris 1977). There can be little doubt that the position here is likely to be of similar complexity to that in Birsay.

Similarly in Rousay, a major grouping of sites of the Viking period is evident from the area around the Bay of Westness (figure 10.4). A series of excavations is taking place under the direction of Sigrid Kaland. The impetus for the series came from the discovery of a richly-furnished female grave (R. B. K. Stevenson 1968), which has been followed up by examination of the cemetery (Kaland 1973; Youngs and Clark 1981, 183). The indications are that it is a ninth-century cemetery. Nearby are the foundations of two boat-nausts, one replacing the other, and fine stone-built buildings which are later in date than the graves (Wilson and Hurst 1964,

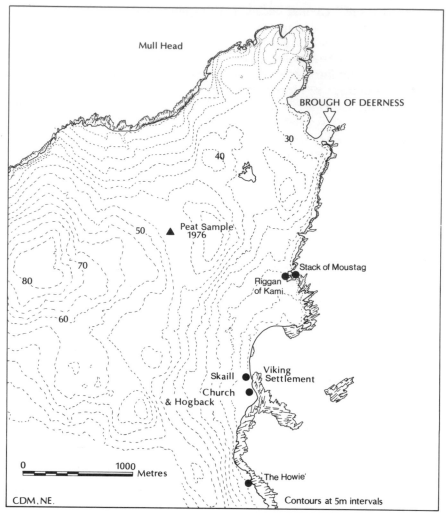

FIGURE 10.3. Deerness: Skaill, the Brough and nearby sites.
(Crown copyright.)

240; Kaland 1973). In the nineteenth century, a Viking sword and shield boss were allegedly found at the Knowe of Swandro, although it is possible that they represent secondary usage (Grieg 1940, 88–90) or may even be from the cemetery (Kaland pers. comm.). The complexity of settlement evolution in this area is further indicated by the place-name Skaill, to the west of the site and now associated with a deserted settlement (H. Marwick 1947, 87) and the probable castle-site known as 'The Wirk' (Clouston 1931, 27–31).

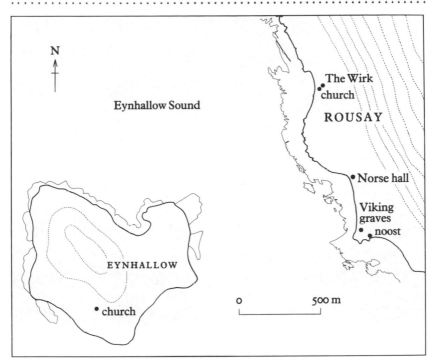

N
↑

Eynhallow Sound

The Wirk
church

ROUSAY

Norse hall

Viking
graves
noost

EYNHALLOW

church

0   500 m

FIGURE 10.4. Norse settlement at Westness, Rousay.

Recent investigation on a more modest scale has indicated that the area of Orphir is likely to be no different. As with other sites, *Orkneyinga Saga* proved a spur to earlier investigators: references (ch.LXVI) to a church and drinking-hall here were well known (Pálsson and Edwards 1979, 112–13). Excavations took place in 1899–1901 and at other times, uncovering walls of buildings, which were generally identified with those of the Bu (Johnston 1903, 22–3). The site of the church was near these (plate 10.2). Work to the north and east of the Bu has investigated other structural remains, notably a tunnel (possibly a souterrain), below midden deposits probably of Viking date. Additionally, it is possible that an industrial site, located at Lavacroon nearby, may date from this period (Batey 1980, 35; 1981, 34), and a Viking grave was found at Greenigoe (Henshall 1952, 17). A runic inscription in Tankerness House, apparently from St Nicolas' Church, and a number of stray finds of steatite and other material, both from Bu Farm and Swanbister nearby, help to fill out the picture (Batey, pers. comm.).

The picture of Viking settlement in Orkney from excavated sites is unrepresentative, not least on distributional grounds, for many areas are unexamined; and intensive examination is the result of particular factors, rather than part of an overall policy to investigate settlement-patterns of the

PLATE 10.2. Orphir, Orkney: Earl's Bu and Round Church.
(C. D. Morris: copyright Durham University.)

period. It is also unrepresentative because four of the sites are high status sites. Skaill (Deerness) and Westness (Rousay) can probably be associated with particular Saga figures, and Birsay and Orphir were directly linked with the Earls of Orkney. Only Buckquoy, and the buildings found on top of earlier Pictish buildings set around Gurness broch (A. Ritchie 1974, 25–6), are as yet exceptions – and the latter has a tenuous archaeological existence as far as published data are concerned (Richardson 1948, 7–8).

VIKING 'CASTLES'

Another group of sites, probably also associated with high-status personages, at least extends the range of site type. There are a number of small fortified or 'castle' sites worthy of note (see Clouston 1926; 1929; 1931; RCAHMS 1946, 49–50; Cruden 1960, 20–1; Talbot 1974). The best-known is undoubtedly that on Wyre, where a small square tower, set within defensive ditches and banks, is reasonably associated with the castle of Kolbein Hruga, mentioned in *Orkneyinga Saga* (Pálsson and Edwards 1978, 139). The site is locally known as 'Cubbie Roo's Castle' (plate 10.3) and both its position on Wyre adjacent to a church and a farm called the Bu of Wyre, and the absence of any other castle site on the island, if circumstantial evidence, is enough to accept the identification (H. Marwick 1928,

21. Westness, Rousay. Ninth-century male burial in a 'boat grave'. The man was buried with some of his possessions, including a shield boss, arrows, and dice.

22. Westness, Rousay. This splendid brooch, perhaps dating from the 8th century, was found in 1968 in a richly furnished female grave, probably of 9th-century date. The brooch is not of Orcadian origin.

PLATE 10.3. 'Cubbie Roo's Castle', Wyre. (C. D. Morris:
copyright Durham University.)

9–11). A second castle site mentioned in the *Saga*, *c.* 1152 (Pálsson and
Edwards 1978, 67) has been associated by J. Storer Clouston and A. B. Taylor with buildings at Cairston in Stromness (A. B. Taylor 1938, 398, n.8),
but later writers have not yet accepted the visible remains as necessarily
indicative of a date consistent with that in the *Saga*, or indeed this place with
Kjarreks-staðir. A third *kastali* is on Damsey, where Swein Asleifsson stayed
overnight in 1136 (Pálsson and Edwards 1978, 113), but such evidence as
there is on the ground has yet to be examined closely. On the basis of the
archaeological evidence from Wyre, the site of the 'Wirk' on Rousay has
sometimes been interpreted as a similar Norse castle (Marwick 1924, 17;
A. B. Taylor 1938, 384, n.5). Comparable to this site is that of Castle Howe,
Holm, which Clouston associated with the Bu of Paplay (see A. B. Taylor
1938, 372–3, no.2). On the other hand, Clouston's interpretation of the site
of *Gernanes*, near Nether Bigging, in Stenness loch, as a Norse castle has not
been universally accepted. The tower at Stenness Kirk, the Castle of Stackel
Brae, Eday, 'Castle' Ellibister (Evie and Rendall), a mound between Lang-
skaill and Netherskaill, Birsay and Harray, and Work, Kirkwall have
all also been put forward as possible candidates for Norse castle status.
Recently, Raymond Lamb has suggested that major structural features
visible in the eroding cliffs near Crosskirk, Tuqoy (Westray) may be
comparable to 'Cubbie Roo's Castle' (Lamb pers. comm., see *The Orcadian*

23.7.1981). Excavations in 1982 by Olwyn Owen will undoubtedly clarify the archaeological issues, if hardly bearing on Lamb's further suggestion that these buildings represent the Hall of Haflidi. It is evident in general that a renewed research programme of archaeological excavation would be desirable to assess this group of sites, and the suggestions first put forward with great enthusiasm and persuasion by J.S.Clouston.

Renewed fieldwork has brought to the fore in recent years the potential importance of multi-period mound-sites. The Beachview, 'studio' site, Birsay, mentioned above, has every appearance of being on top of a large mound created by the successive building of structures, and the repeated dumping of midden material in this area. Certainly observation of, and trial excavations in an area of the site to the north, exposed by flooding of the Burn of Broadhouse, have demonstrated this to be the case, and very limited work in a third area of the Beachview site to the north-east produced the same picture (see Donaldson, Morris and Rackham 1981, 74; Morris forthcoming). It seems likely that the mound of Saevar Howe, to the south, was created by continued building and occupation. As emphasised by the excavator, the recent excavations have explored only a fraction of the deposits belonging to the Pictish and Viking periods of occupation, and these may indeed be 'the upper end of a much longer period of occupation than we have evidence for' (J.W.Hedges 1983b). A number of other sites in the islands appear to be the remains of mounds created by this process. Lamb, in his survey of Sanday and North Ronaldsay, has drawn attention to some. The relationship of such very large mounds, possibly covering up to a hectare of ground, to place-names of particular Norse types have been examined, and indicate that the primary Norse occupation was often late in the archaeological history of the mound (RCAMS 1980, 7–8; nos 69–114). Since none has as yet been excavated, it is difficult to attribute specific dating to them, but some sites are probably entirely prehistoric (e.g. Northskaill, Sanday; RCAMS 1980, no.81, 17), while others have produced Norse artefacts (e.g. Pool, Sanday RCAMS 1980, no.84, 18). A number of these sites are subject to violent coastal erosion, and resulting exposed sections, for instance at Pool (Sanday) have proved very valuable for the elucidation of the basic archaeological sequence (J.R.Hunter pers. comm.). Their relationship to adjacent sites is also intriguing, as for instance in the case of Stromness (North Ronaldsay) (RCAMS 1980, no.114, 20), adjacent to the broch of Burrian (MacGregor 1974).

ENVIRONMENTAL ARCHAEOLOGY

It is with sites of this group that a new avenue of research opens, with the application of modern methods of analysis of the palaeoeconomy and palaeoenvironment. In urban contexts these methods are producing valuable results for our understanding of the Viking period (see Kenward *et al.* 1978 and Morris 1982b), and it is already clear that we can expect to place the study of the economy and environment of sites of this period on a more secure basis in this way. Again, the results from Buckquoy, Birsay are the only ones to have reached final publication (A. Ritchie 1977), and a preliminary attempt has been made to integrate results from more recent excavations in the Bay of Birsay to these (Donaldson, Morris and Rackham 1981). As Dr Ritchie has emphasised above (chapter 9), cereal crops, especially bere and oats, were more commonly grown in this area in the past. It is clear from the sampling of the later deposits in Areas 1 and 2 besides the Brough Road, and also from the Beachview 'studio' site, that this was the case in the Viking/Late Norse periods. Their existence was also demonstrated in the Viking contexts at Saevar Howe (Dickson, in Hedges 1983b). There is a hint that, as far as oats were concerned, it was during this period that common oat (*Avena sativa*) was introduced, for only wild oat (*Avena fatua*) is found in earlier contexts – but this will need support from the results of other samples in this area and elsewhere. Some weeds may also have been used in their own right for making bread (Donaldson, Morris and Rackham 1981, 80). Of considerable interest was the occurrence at Saevar Howe, in phase II, of a significant number of examples of seeds of cultivated flax. Flax has been found elsewhere in the early Viking midden at Barvas machair, Lewis, and could as well have been utilised for consumption as for spinning and weaving (Dickson, in Hedges 1983b). As with the Pictish period, it is evident that animal husbandry was fundamental to the economy. At Saevar Howe, cattle, sheep and pig were all found in significant numbers, and there was no major change in the proportion of these between the Pictish and Viking periods. In both periods, sheep outnumbered cattle (Rowley-Conwy, in Hedges 1983b). At Buckquoy, despite the general problems relating to the excavation of middens (A. Ritchie 1977, 191), and to the natural history of waste middens (Noddle 1977, 201), it was clear that cattle, sheep and pig were all exploited. There are some interesting variations between the three Norse phases: for instance, the percentage of minimum number of individuals of cattle varied from 29 per cent in Norse III to 55 per cent in Norse IV, and 47 per cent in Norse V, whereas sheep were 50 per cent in III and V (Noddle 1977, 202, table 1). Miss Noddle is inclined to see 'the availability of livestock [as] dictated by the environment rather than by direct choice' (1977, 202), but it must not be forgotten that Man, to an extent, structures the environment to his choice: it is, for instance, a conscious decision to grow crops, even if the yield is affected by non-human factors, and the same must be true of animal husbandry. Even if we accept that there are several different possible explanations of the presence from Norse III onwards of more bones per individual among smaller genera, that fact alone is significant (Noddle 1977, 202–3). That there are changes in the way in which Man exploits the environment is also evident: there is a much greater range of fish species represented in the Norse phases than in the Pictish (Wheeler 1977, table 12, 212 and 214). It has been pointed out that the importance of fishing in the later Viking periods is observable elsewhere (Donaldson, Morris and Rackham 1981, 77), but on the contrary, no great difference between the fish evidence from the Pictish and Viking periods was seen at Saevar Howe (Colley, in Hedges 1983b).

Judgements such as this must be based on reliable data. The interrelationship of artefacts and eco-facts demand more rigorous analysis in future. The relative importance of fish and cattle at Buckquoy, for instance, cannot be stated in quantitative terms on the basis of the data presented, and the preliminary judgements about this for the 'Room 5' excavation on the Brough of Birsay must, despite the use of wet-sieving, be regarded as indicative of a trend rather than as absolute figures. Here sieving was only conducted down to 5 mm: had sieving been carried out to 1 mm presumably a greater proportion of small bones would have been recovered, and therefore the relative percentages of fish and other bone affected. Both Colley and Rowley-Conwy (Hedges 1983b) have similarly emphasised the implications of partial recovery of fish material at Saevar Howe in relation to the total sample. It is hoped that more reliable quantitative data will emerge from the sampling programme of the deposits on the Beachview sites (Donaldson, Morris and Rackham 1981, 74 and 82). If it is true, as Ritchie has said above (chapter 9), that the 'factor of partial survival limits many of the conclusions about economic life that can be drawn', the factor of selective recovery in the past has limited them even more. If we can at least attempt to recover a reliable cross-section of the environmental and economic evidence, we shall have cut down the number of variables affecting the interpretation of the results and be able to concentrate on the problems of partial survival and partial excavation (see, for example, Carver 1979; Meadow 1980). In analysing the Saevar Howe material, both Colley and Rowley-Conwy (Hedges 1983b) have underlined the need for more refined techniques of analysis of date. In particular, they have emphasised the need to make a distinction not only on the basis of period, but also of type of deposit within a period – for example whether within or outside a structure.

Sites such as Pool (Sanday), Stromness (North Ronaldsay), and Beachview (Birsay), offer the possibility of large-scale recovery and detailed examination of environmental and economic data. This kind of evidence is as fundamental to our understanding of the Viking period in Orkney as is the evidence of particular artefacts; and the design of excavations, whether as responses to threats of destruction of particular sites, or as investigations of unthreatened monuments, must include provision for the examination of this material. It is fundamental because our understanding of exchange networks and the relationships of settlements to an economic system is still at a generalised level (e.g. Small 1968, 7–9). In north Norway, where a similar group of sites has been located, some of these problems are now being faced. Pioneering work was done on these mounds in the 1960s, and a basic chronology worked out for them (Munch 1966). More recently attention has been paid to wider issues, and the observation made that 'Although there is great potential, little work has been done with environmental data' (Bertelsen 1979, 53). It is here, perhaps, that there lies the possibility for fruitful comparison with the mounds in Orkney. Parallel work on these relatively unusual forms of site from two parts of the Viking world ought to provide direct and meaningful insights – perhaps more immediately relevant than the research programme on the Mesoamerican village cited by Bertelsen (1979, 55).

PLACE-NAMES

Of course, this 'new' evidence from environmental archaeology must be related to other material, and cannot exist in a vacuum. Economic factors do not respect the boundaries between academic disciplines, and as relevant here are the insights from the studies of place-names and the organisation of land as reflected in Later Medieval rentals. By their very existence, the large numbers of names in the Isles and certain coastal mainland areas of Scotland carry implications for the understanding of settlement patterns, and the nature of the archaeological record of these patterns.

Wainwright discussed at length work on Orkney place-names prior to 1962, such as the fundamental work by Hugh Marwick (F. T. Wainwright 1962b, 119–26 and 133–40). Marwick's work was largely concerned with the *sequence* of settlement, and he arranged the farm-names into a chronological order (1952, Part III). He based his attempt on the geographical characteristics of the sites in relation to their size, as recorded in fifteenth- and sixteenth-century rentals. He also related it to the *skatting* of land (or imposition of a land tax) which he took to be an event of the end of the ninth century, on the basis of the Harold Fine-hair tradition. However, Professor Sawyer's strictures on this tradition have led him to propose that 'the origin of the skatland should probably be sought in the thirteenth or perhaps the twelfth century' (Sawyer 1976, 109). Though Marwick's use of the absence of *skatting* to suggest that *-quoy* names were later than 900 AD, and the presence of skat or *land, garðr* and *bolstaðr* names to suggest they were pre-900, may well have to be abandoned, his observations on relative chronology may stand, for the argument was not wholly based upon this. He noted that the geographical position of *-quoys* tended to be on the fringes of a *tunship*, as *setr* names, whereas the group of names in *land, garðr* and *bolstaðr* were notable for their position on fertile and attractive areas in central positions. However, they appeared still to be secondary to the original settlements, which he saw as represented by some *skaill* names but

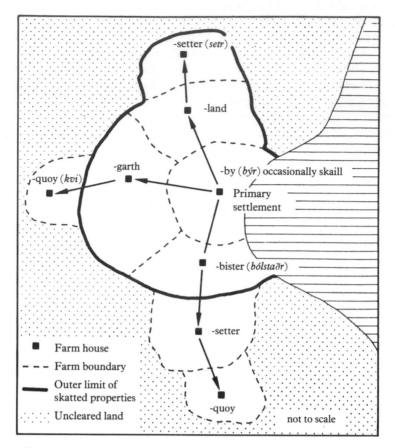

FIGURE 10.5. Orkney place-names sequence: an idealised model.

particularly *byr* names.

This sequence of place-names has been represented graphically by Patrick Bailey (1971, 76): his idealised model (figure 10.5) in fact emphasises the point that Marwick was proposing a *relative* chronology of names on the local level, not an absolute chronology (e.g. H. Marwick 1952, 248). There is no reason why *setr* names in one locality should not in strict chronology come before, say, *land* or *bolstaðr* names in another. Marwick was at pains to emphasise his use of the term 'secondary' as being in relation to geography, and, apart from the argument about skatting, not in absolute chronological terms. His work provides us with a sequence for the spread of settlement at the local level, not a widespread sequence of name-forms tied to an absolute chronology. It would be useful to have other local sequences from other areas, with which to compare this sequence.

On a more general level, Professor Nicolaisen has studied three settlement names, *staðr*, *setr*/*saetr* and *bolstaðr*, in north and west Scotland (Nicolaisen 1976, 85–96). He argued that the distribution of these indicated a relative chronology in the names, and also an expansion of the Viking settlement. He felt that the expanding distribution of *staðr* and *setr* represents the settlement in the earlier and later parts of the ninth century, whereas that of *bolstaðr* supplies 'an overall visual impression of Scandinavian settlement in the north and west when at its most extensive', in contrast to *dalr* which represented the area of influence (1976, 96). As an overall visual impression of the Viking settlement in Scotland, Nicolaisen's maps are very impressive, and, if detailed arguments in favour of the early dates are accepted, then even more important in terms of gauging the scale of this settlement. But, do we have to assume expansion to be constant? In fact, do we not have to reckon with the possibility of fluctuation with periods of contraction as well as expansion? Also, is it possible that the elements may refer to different types of settlement and therefore not be successive, but contemporary? Or, even if a word such as *saetr* refers to a specific sort of settlement, could it as well precede as succeed *bolstðr* in the local sequence? Further work by Nicolaisen is eagerly awaited.

Both the names, and their distribution as small farms, reflect in Orkney the *odal* system of land-tenure (cf. Drever 1933). It is likely that successive generations took into cultivation outlying portions of a landholding, with new farms being established on the margins around the original farm – as is represented graphically in Bailey's model. Marwick has suggested that often these outlying settlements were as productive as the original ones, because of the outfield system of summer-grazing which meant that the constant manuring of the animal fold or *kvi* outside the farm boundary wall (or *garðr*) rendered this area fit for establishment of a new farm which was then given the -*quoy* suffix (H. Marwick 1952, 227–8). The aggregate of the farms growing out in such a way from the original settlement, which would often hold arable and grazing land in common, and have common sources of peat on the moors, became known as *tunships*, and represent nucleated settlements of a form entirely different from the familiar villages to the south (Clouston 1920).

It is clear that such analyses as these of the system of land-holding and settlement-patterns, if subject still to detailed scrutiny, are essential for the understanding of the archaeological material, as the archaeological evidence is essential for the understanding of them. To make an obvious point: the place-name of Buckquoy is an example of a *kvi* (H. Marwick 1970, 60–1) which presumably on Marwick's model would be *relatively* late in the local sequence. But, we may ask, relative to what? Can our archaeological evidence answer this question yet? Dr Ritchie's archaeological sequence at the farmstead on the Buckquoy peninsula is not unbroken and continuous from Pictish to Viking (1977, 181) and so it is conceivable that her site may not come from the primary phase of settlement in Birsay. But, *if* this is the case, where is the primary settlement? Questions such as these are basic, but until there is more direct archaeological evidence it will be difficult to begin to answer them, and to test the models and sequences derived from other disciplines. A similar set of questions arise over the nature of place-names deriving from *skáli*. Clouston (1932, 14–18) and Hugh Marwick (1952, 237–40) both asserted that, despite the apparently humble origin of this name (meaning a hut or shed), places with such names represented early, primary settlements of the Viking period. Clearly the archaeological evidence from Peter Gelling's work at Skaill, Deerness (Gelling forth-coming) will be of very great interest in this connection.

ADMINISTRATION AND EXCHANGE

Other questions arise from study of institutional aspects of the Earl-dom of Orkney. Fundamental work has been done on such matters by J. Storer Clouston, both in a long series of papers and in his *History of Orkney* (1932). It is abundantly clear from this work that, especially in the social sphere, many features to be found in Orkney, such as the *godings*, the great *bus* and their owners, the *þings* or assemblies, directly reflect arrangements in the rest of the Viking world. The granting of land, the arrangements for collection of *skat* or tax, and some of the administrative features connected with these, such as the provision for defence of the area, have also been examined in some detail, especially by Hugh Marwick, with connections made between the Orkney Earldom and other Viking settlements in the British Isles, notably the Hebrides and Isle of Man (H. Marwick 1935; 1949a). A further detail, that of the *huseby* system – royal administrative farms of a military nature – has been demonstrated by Asgaut Steinnes to have existed in Orkney as in Scandinavia. Four such names still exist, in Birsay, Rousay, Shapinsay and Stronsay; a fifth may be near Braeswick on Sanday, and Steinnes infers that the earl's seat at Orphir was a sixth (Steinnes 1959). It is interesting that, when Thorfinn established himself at Birsay, he appears to have chosen a sea-board site. This may have super-seded the *huseby* site, a few miles inland (Steinnes 1959, 46n; H. Marwick 1970, 83–5), but this cannot on present evidence be proved. However, it does seem significant that a site in the west of the mainland should have been chosen by Thorfinn, one can but speculate that it offered him not only strategic advantages in terms of access to the sea, but also possibly eco-nomic, in that it was ideally situated to monitor commercial (and other) traffic going northwards and avoiding the unpredictable (and often treach-erous) Pentland Firth. To progress in our understanding of this period, it is essential that an attempt be made to relate the archaeological evidence from sites such as Birsay and Orphir to the evidence for institutional arrangements. At present, as with the linguistic evidence, scholars in the different fields have come to conclusions without apparent reference to evidence in the fields adjacent to their own.

At Jarlshof there was little evidence to suggest the status of a trading-post or town. It is the same for Orkney. Small has already observed (1971, 86) that, while Brogger (1929, 121) and A. B. Taylor (1938, 386) identified the *Hǫfn* of the *Orkneyinga Saga* (Pálsson and Edwards 1978, 120–1) with Pierowall on Westray, A. R. Lewis had (1958, 277, note 102) elevated this into the principal Viking port in the Orkneys – for which there is no evidence. Kirkwall seems to have been considered a market town in the early twelfth century (Pálsson and Edwards 1978, 96). Even so, it is said to have had few houses, and it is likely that development of Kirkwall followed the establishment of the Cathedral there (Gourlay and Turner 1977, 2 and 13). There is no clear evidence from elsewhere for a trading-centre, and we must assume that Dublin was the major centre for all northern and western Britain, with routes running north as well as south (Small 1971, 86). There are merchant-graves in the Western Isles (Grieg 1940, 29–30 and 48–61) and Smyth has argued, on the basis of a study of various written sources, for a 'slave-trade' centering on Dublin (Smyth 1977, chs x and xi). In addition, a Hiberno-Manx coinage existed in the Kingdom of the Isles (Dolley 1976b; 1976a, pl.61), and the Hiberno-Norse coinage is well known (Dolley 1966). While such coinages could scarcely have had much value outside their origin centre (Dolley 1966, 121), there is no doubt that commercial transactions took place – perhaps on the basis of units of measure of silver in the form either of ring-money, ingots or hack-silver (Graham-Campbell 1976a, 125; Warner 1976). These units are found in hoards from Orkney, and indeed the arm-rings from Skaill are the earliest dated examples from Scotland (Graham-Campbell 1976a, 125) (plate 10.4).

It would be foolish to explain all exotica and material from other parts of the British Isles, found in Orkney, as the result of commercial contact. There was a considerable period of raiding, of which records in annals and insular material in western Norwegian graves provide incontrovertible evidence (Morris 1979a). It is, however, harder to assess the Orcadian evidence in this context. Even the discovery of the fine insular brooch from Westness, Rousay (R. B. K. Stevenson 1968; colour plate 22) is not con-clusive, for there are various means by which it could have arrived in Orkney: raiding is one, exchange another. Nevertheless, the evidence of hoard material is witness to the political importance of Orkney, and to the considerable wealth owned by certain individuals.

Hoards from Burray and Skaill inevitably dominate the picture (Graham-Campbell 1976a, 119–28). The Skaill hoard probably weighed over 8 kg and Burray 1.9 kg. In both cases, less than 0.5 per cent was in silver coin; the rest was in silver objects and hack-silver. In both, particularly note-

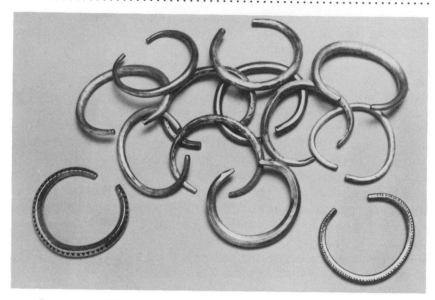

PLATE 10.4. 'Ring-money' from Viking silver hoard, Skaill.
(Copyright NMAS)

worthy were 'thistle' brooches and arm-rings, and the hoards have the appearance of containing both ready units of measure, and material yet to be cut to specific units. This is important, for it lessens Wilson's argument that hoards reflect instability or internecine quarrel (Wilson 1976b, 101). The latest work on these hoards by Olwyn A. Owen (pers. comm.), suggests that their deliberate deposition in particular places might be less related to raiding than to economic activity. Previous work has emphasised the particular position of these two Orcadian hoards in the overall Scottish distribution and the conclusion drawn that 'overseas trade, other than in basic commodities, did not play a central part in the economic life of the Norse settlers in Scotland' (Graham-Campbell 1976a, 115 and 127). It may, perhaps, be worth reiterating the point that the concepts of 'Scotland' and 'Ireland' are largely anachronistic at this time, and that Dublin could well have acted as an economic focus for a hinterland, both within its own island, and along the western seaboard of the Isles. It seems reasonable to interpret the Irish material in terms of the trading connections of the Norse towns in Ireland (Graham-Campbell 1976b), but too great a contrast with material from Scotland should not be drawn (see Morris forthcoming).

CHURCH BUILDING

The wealth of the Orkney Earls is reflected in building projects such as Thorfinn's minster at Birsay, the Round Church at Orphir, and the Cathedral of St Magnus in Kirkwall (all recorded in *Orkneyinga Saga*, Pálsson and Edwards 1978, 71, 113, 118). Each of these buildings is fascinating in its own right as an architectural project. The unusual shape of the Orphir church was undoubtedly inspired, though probably at second-hand, by the Church of the Holy Sepulchre (Radford 1962, 181–2). The minster at Birsay was built following Earl Thorfinn's procession/pilgrimage, and Earl Rognvald went on a two-year round-trip to the Holy Land that was dignified with the description 'crusade' (*Orkneyinga Saga*, chs LXXXVI–XC). If Rognvald, like Thorfinn before, was putting Orkney onto the European political map, he also had brought Europe to Orkney, for he was responsible for the building of the Romanesque Cathedral at Kirkwall (Cruden 1977). At Birsay, too, considerable resources must have been expended on the building of Christ Church minster by Thorfinn. It is at present a matter for debate as to whether this is to be looked for on the Brough of Birsay or on the mainland side of the Bay (Lamb 1974).

Such diversion of resources into church-building projects was widespread in Orkney. Despite problems of chronology, the distribution of mediaeval stone chapels in Orkney is remarkable (figure 10.6). It is generally accepted that many were the private chapels of prominent personages, and that there is a relationship between their foundation and rental districts or *eyrislands*. This organisation of private chapels had been, it may be argued, imposed upon the remnants of an order derived from the pre-Norse, Celtic period, and was itself superseded by a parochial system. Some of the chapels became, with the re-organisation of ecclesiastical arrangements, head-churches of a parish, while others were no longer used (Clouston 1932, ch.XIII; Cant 1973, 1–2, 10–11; 1975, 8–9, 11–13). In addition, Lamb has argued strongly for the existence of a Norse monastic system, as well as the eremitical tradition of the Celtic Church (Lamb 1976).

The archaeology of the church in the pre-Norse and Norse periods, if fascinating, is one that is fraught with difficulties of attribution and chronology. Dr Radford in 1962 brought forward material that he considered related to the Celtic and Norse churches (Radford 1962). Apart from Lamb's important work, the subject in general has hardly advanced since then, and repetition here is not in order. Two particular sites have been excavated since 1962. At Newark Bay, below a sixteenth- or seventeenth-century fortified house, there was uncovered a chapel with an associated cemetery, being eroded at the seashore. The chapel was thought by the excavator, D. Brothwell, to be of tenth century date (on the basis of coins below the flooring), and the skeletons are a very important group from the Viking period. Below the chapel and cemetery were two earth-houses (Brothwell 1977, 182). At the Brough of Deerness, excavations and survey by C. D. Morris on the site traditionally interpreted as a Celtic monastery (Radford 1962, 166–7; C. Thomas 1971, 34–5), raised questions about the

FIGURE 10.6. Distribution of chapels in part of Orkney.

identification. The new survey (figure 10.7) showed a regularity of plan not noted before, which can either be interpreted in terms of a Norse monastery (Lamb 1973, 93–6) or perhaps a secular settlement analogous to the Brough of Birsay (Morris 1977). Excavations showed that there were two major phases of chapel construction, and a very-worn tenth-century Anglo-Saxon coin was found between them. There were very few burials in the churchyard (Morris 1976; 1978). Interesting as these two particular chapel-sites may be, their position within the overall ecclesiastical system of the Viking/Late Norse periods in the parish of Deerness is not immediately clear. The recent survey work by Lamb on North Ronaldsay and Sanday has brought to the fore the urgent need for systematic work on the identification of such sites as a prerequisite for a deeper understanding of the

236

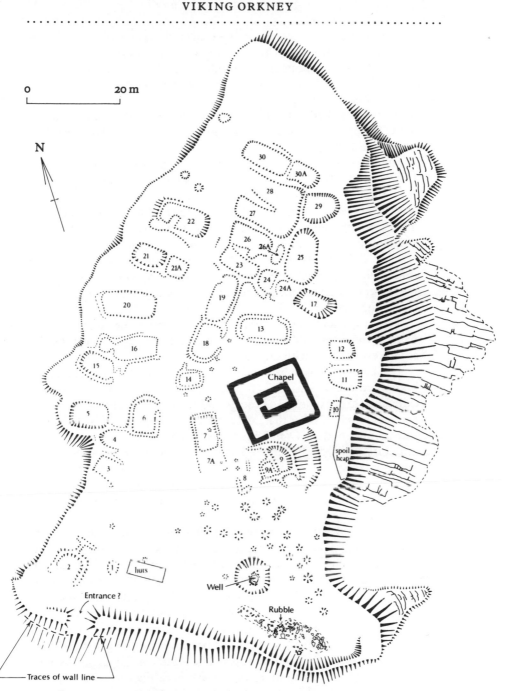

0   20 m

N

30
30A
28
29
27
22
26
26A
25
21
23
21A
24
24A
20
19
17
13
18
12
16
Chapel
15
14
11
5
6
10
4
7
spoil
heap
3
7A
9
8
9A

huts
2
1
Well
Entrance ?
Rubble

Traces of wall line

FIGURE 10.7. The Brough of Deerness: site survey 1977.
(Crown copyright.)

church life of mediaeval Orkney (RCAMS 1980, 8). There is an immediate parallel with the situation in the Isle of Man, and current research by Christopher Lowe on aspects of the church archaeology of these two areas of the Norse world should supplement the work of R. G. Cant and the overall survey by Lamb. (Colour plate 24.)

The traditional date for the introduction of Norse Christianity to Orkney is *c.* 995, and is based on a colourful tale in the *Orkneyinga Saga* (Pálsson and Edwards 1978, 39):

> After his return from Wendland, Olaf Tryggvason spent four years looting in the British Isles. Then he was baptised in the Scillies and from there sailed to England where he married Gyda, the sister of King Kvaran of Ireland. Next he spent a while in Dublin till Earl Hakon sent Thorir Klakka out west to lure him away from there.
>
> Olaf sailed east with five ships and didn't break his journey until he reached Orkney. At Osmundwall he ran into Earl Sigurd, who had three ships and was setting out on a viking expedition. Olaf sent a messenger to him, asking Sigurd to come over to his ship as he wanted a word with him.
>
> 'I want you and all your subjects to be baptised,' he said when they met. 'If you refuse, I'll have you killed on the spot, and I swear that I'll ravage every island with fire and steel'.
>
> The Earl could see what kind of situation he was in and surrendered himself into Olaf's hands. He was baptised and Olaf took his son, called Hvelp or Hundi, as a hostage and had him baptised too under the name of Hlodvir. After that, all Orkney embraced the faith.

The tale is also told in *Olaf Tryggvason's Saga* where accounts of the contemporary 'conversions' in Norway and Iceland are also given (Laing and Simpson 1964, chs 32–104 *passim*; G. Jones 1968, 32–5). Jones has suggested that Olaf's motives for his apparent missionary zeal were political and that 'He stands before posterity as one who in his day and place was Christ's best hatchet-man' (1968, 134–5). It is clear that the sagas do not tell the whole story, whether in Norway or Orkney, but it is not as clear, perhaps, as Wainwright would have it, that Christianity had been accepted by 900 (1962b, 158–62). While it may seem inherently likely, the evidence cited in its favour is not unchallengeable. For instance, the argument about the dating of the place-name elements such as *bolstaðr* and *kirkjubolstaðr* by Hugh Marwick (1952, 232–4) is now re-opened with Sawyer's rejection of the skatting theory (see above). Equally, the Bressay stone and Whiteness axe are used in the argument, and it must be axiomatic that generalisations should not be based on single examples. The argument for assimilation or overlap, if suggestive, is no more conclusive here than in other parts of Britain (see Morris 1981b, 233–5), and the dating of both the stone and the axe can hardly be regarded as fixed and secure, being based on typological and stylistic considerations. One might hope, in the future, for clearer dating of chapels, which would throw light on this problem: the evidence from Newark Bay and the Brough of Deerness, when published, will need careful scrutiny.

BURIAL PRACTICES

It is clear that there was a range of burial practice among the pagan Scandinavians of Orkney: burial within existing mounds, burial under new mounds, boat burial, burial under stone cairns, in stone-lined oval graves, in stone-lined rectangular cists, and in simple dug graves. Shetelig, in a pioneering paper (1945) attempted to place the Orkney material in a wider British context. It is now necessary to place them in a longer time sequence in Orkney, for both cist burials and cairn burials are recorded from the Pictish period (see A. Ritchie, chapter 9 above). From the period after the adoption of Christianity, burial necessarily involved the deposition of no grave-goods, and poses problems of association and dating for the archaeologist. However, one cist-grave, unaccompanied with grave-goods, from Sandside, Graemsay, has been C-14 dated to 865–55 bp (J. W. Hedges 1978, 377), and it seems reasonably clear now that the cemetery found by Farrer at Saevar Howe in the nineteenth century (Farrer 1864; 1868) was later than the Viking buildings uncovered recently by J. W. Hedges and is therefore dated to the tenth century at the earliest (Hedges 1983b). With the Pictish period burials from the Brough of Birsay, Buckquoy, Brough Road Areas 1 and 2, and Oxtro broch as well as the Viking and Christian Norse burials from the first three sites and Saevar Howe (see A. Ritchie, this volume), it is clear that, when these sites are fully published, evidence from Birsay will offer a chance for a more detailed understanding of burial practices.

The pagan Viking graves have been discussed by Wainwright, and, quite apart from the general dating problem, have the specific difficulty of poor initial recording (1962b, 148–50; 160–1). His conclusions regarding paganism therefore seem unduly exact, and the argument almost circular when he states that:

> Many more pagan graves will be found, of course, but perhaps not so many as might have been expected a few years ago, for the period of paganism is now being reduced from two hundred years to one hundred or less.

Dr Arne Thorsteinsson has undertaken an invaluable task in disentangling the information from Pierowall, Westray, but his criticism of *Viking Antiquities* is salutary. If he has re-established this cemetery as a major site, it is nevertheless the case that there is an inbuilt limitation to the evidence (1968). It is therefore all the more valuable that a major series of excavations has taken place on the cemetery at Westness, Rousay (R. B. K. Stevenson

1968; Kaland 1973, 93–7, 100; Youngs and Clark 1981, 183). After excavation, there will at last be one complete Viking graveyard recorded to modern standards. It is evident already that in its range of graves it offers examples of types hitherto imperfectly understood, such as the oval grave. If the richest grave remains the one found first, yet the boat-burial recently uncovered goes some way to illumine the defective Pierowall evidence. All graves were unmarked on the present surface, although it appears possible that they originally had some sort of grave-marker (Kaland, pers. comm.). There is in this group the best opportunity for examining Wainwright's statements about the length of usage of the pagan traditions of burial.

Other evidence that has come from pagan graves since Wainwright's day has been of single finds. Dr Ritchie, for instance, excavated a coin-dated late tenth-century male inhumation placed within the ruins of the Phase V buildings at Buckquoy (Ritchie 1977, 190–1). Recent examination of the material from a grave uncovered in 1939 at the Broch of Gurness, has also dated that female grave to the tenth century on the basis of the type of oval brooch represented (Robertson 1969). Similarly, a recently excavated male burial in a cist from Area I, Brough Road, Birsay (Morris 1979b, 14) would be attributed to the tenth century on the basis of the comb type.

A related group of monuments are the house-shaped recumbent monuments known as hogbacks. Their origin lies in Northern England, probably in the tenth century, and this short-lived type was also adopted in particular areas of Scotland (Lang 1974). Five are recorded from Orkney, of which four survive, and all appear to be of a plain, non-illustrative type with tegulation. It is likely that this isolated group is of considerably later date, and the result of late copying of an unusual form of monument normally found far to the south. However, the presence of a low headstone at St Boniface (Papa Westray) (Lang 1974, 211, 230, pl. 17a) and late folk-lore traditions (Kirkness 1921, 132; E. W. Marwick 1975, 61) confirm that they were nevertheless still perceived as grave-monuments.

CONCLUSIONS

With the hogbacks, we have moved well into the Late Norse period, rather than the Viking period proper. For that reason, it will suffice to mention the evidence of runic inscriptions such as those from Maes Howe (Liestøl 1968), the Ring of Brodgar, the Brough of Birsay (Marwick 1922) and Orphir (C. E. Batey pers. comm.). They are currently under study by Dr Aslak Liestøl (Liestøl forthcoming). As we move forward in time, so there arises the fascinating subject of the transmission of Scandinavian culture to later periods. At one time, it was thought that Norse building-customs could be detected *in extenso* in later crofts of the Northern and Western Isles (Roussell 1934). More recent work, notably by Fenton, has modified this view (e.g. Fenton 1978, chs 14–15; 1979) and care is needed

23. Brough of Birsay. The aerial view shows the Norse church and churchyard, with what may be earlier buildings to the west.

24. Brough of Deerness. General view of what is now thought to be a Norse monastery, or else a secular settlement similar to that at Brough of Birsay (see plan, page 237).

25. St Magnus, Egilsay. An aerial view, from the east, of this lovely Norse church on the small island of Egilsay.

over cultural assumptions in chronology. However, there are any aspects of the transmission of material culture in which a Scandinavian contribution can be detected, and needs to be weighed against other contributions (see Fenton forthcoming).

It is clear from work in Shetland and Fair Isle that Viking traditions in sea transport continued right up to the modern age (A. Morrison 1973, ch.3; 1978; T. Henderson 1978). A study of the small boats of Orkney in relation to the Scandinavian tradition is an area of study that needs specialist attention before vital evidence disappears under the impact of modern technology. It is hoped that study currently being undertaken by the National Maritime Museum, Greenwich, on a cast of the small boat from the Viking period graveyard at Westness, Rousay, at one end of the chronological spectrum, will illumine this topic (Youngs and Clark 1981, 183). It is curious that there appears to be less evidence for a Norse ancestry of Orcadian boats than those from Shetland (Lethbridge 1952, 144; Mather 1964).

In comparison to other areas of Scotland, the archaeology of Orkney has fared well in terms of resources allocated and research pursued, and yet much needs to be done, even for the Viking and Late Norse periods. Our picture is at present very partial, and in each particular field of study it is incredible how inadequate our knowledge is. In part, this is due to the fact that some major pieces of work have not yet been fully published, but also to the particularistic nature of the work carried out. The balance of our knowledge is based entirely on the chance of individual initiative or personal interest. Dr Lamb has drawn attention to the vast untapped archaeological potential of the Northern Isles of Orkney, and his Orkney Survey will, in supplementing the work of the Royal Commission, bring to light particularly important sites or areas for these periods. This is already clear from his work on the scattered finds from Sties and on the mound-sites such as Stromness and Pool (RCAMS 1980, nos 132, 84, 114, 248–9). Detailed survey in other areas has done the same: for instance, recently, Kenneth Steedman's survey of Deerness parish brought to light the finds from Quoys, which appear to be Norse in origin (Steedman 1980; pers. comm.). Recent work in Orkney has already added much to our knowledge of these periods, but even if it will not be possible to examine archaeologically even a fraction of all the potential sites, it is essential that the impetus and momentum are not lost. The richness of Orkney's archaeology is comparable to that of Wessex in the Prehistoric period. Viking Orkney was not peripheral: it was a key area of the Viking World.

Acknowledgements. Although brought together in its final form for this publication, the content of this chapter has been in preparation for some time. Parts of it have been presented on various occasions to particular societies and institutions too numerous to list. The invitation from Professor Robert T. Farrell of Cornell University to talk upon this topic within the Cornell Viking Series 1980 provided the stimulus to carry out a more systematic and rigorous study of the topic. Some of the wider implications have been discussed in my paper in the volume edited by Professor Farrell, and will receive further discussion in my projected book on the Vikings in Britain and Ireland. In preparing this chapter, I have benefited enormously from discussion of both detail and general matters with many colleagues and students. In particular, I am most grateful to Dr Anna Ritchie and Dr Sigrid Kaland whose willingness to discuss in detail the results of their excavations in Orkney, as well as more general matters, has been most heartening. To other excavators and researchers who have provided information, and whose names appear in the text, I am indeed indebted. Without open co-operation between scholars working in as compact an academic field as this, progress on the general front would be impossible. In relation to my own work in Orkney, I must acknowledge the considerable support of both the Inspectorate of Ancient Monuments, Scottish Development Department, and of the University of Durham. The results of the Birsay Bay Project would not have been possible without the hard work and support of my Assistant Supervisors, and in particular the enthusiasm of my colleagues, Alison Donaldson and James Rackham, who have widened both the scope of the Project and my own academic frame of reference. The latest stages of bringing this work together – albeit in an interim form – has depended to a great extent on the active support of my wife and colleague, Colleen Batey. Not only has she assisted with the collection and ordering of data, but has also spurred me on to complete the work at a time when it was in danger of being submerged by the obligations of running the Birsay Bay Project.

11 Colin Renfrew **Epilogue**

Yea, hid wis thir lullaby,
The dunder o' the loom, the fleean shuttle i' the skilly haan'
That keepid them a catloup fae starvation.
Here they lived, an' loved an' dee'd.
Bit thoo needsno peety them,
They hid pace i' thir time, an' a trust that teuk them t'row.
They hid fish an' maet fae the ebb,
An' they could mak' a banquet wae a heid o' kail,
An' held Aald Yeul wae snorran keks an' draps o' eel.

From C. M. Costie (1974) 'The Auld Hoose Spaeks'

With the passing of Viking Orkney, the prehistory of the islands comes to an end, although the language was, for many centuries to come, to remain the Norn, the Norse dialect still spoken in the northern islands in the eighteenth century. It lingers today in the lilting intonation and the rich dialect vocabulary of Orcadian speech, admirably captured in the poems of Miss Costie.

In a sense, of course, prehistoric Orkney did not come to an end, for one of the strongest experiences which a visitor to Orkney encounters is an almost overwhelming sense of the continuity of things.

It is still very much less than a century since many of the old ways disappeared with the onset of mechanisation of transport and of farming, the stationing of great fleets in Scapa Flow during two world wars, and now the commercial pressures from the oil installations on Flotta. In his *Reminiscences of an Orkney Parish*, John Firth (1920) described the farming ways and the life in the long houses which, now ruined, still form a prominent feature in the Orkney landscape. In the words of Miss Costie once again:

The waa's aa' blackened,
An' the reuf's faa'n in,
Noo only seelence hings
Whar eence gay laughter bade.

To the student of the past, a visit to one of these houses – or still better to the rural museum at Corrigal – is an illuminating experience. For one sees the very building conventions which were in use five thousand years ago at Skara Brae. The neuk beds (the stone-built beds set in the wall) closely resemble the beds of the neolithic village. And the partitions of sandstone flag in the byres are almost identical to the divisions in the compartmented long cairns, such as one sees clearly today at the cairn of Midhowe on Rousay. This need not be unbroken continuity, of course: it is simply the local sandstone, which fractures into these magnificent flags, being used in a manner for which it is admirably suited. The wonderfully gaunt Standing Stones of Stenness exploit this same property of the stone, which is responsible also for some features of the building style of the chambered cairns of Quanterness type, with their drystone walling, and their long and narrow corbelled roofing (plate 11.1).

The continuities are there, nonetheless, persisting through period after period. The organisation of this book has inevitably focused upon separate time periods, and so has perhaps not sufficiently stressed these elements of continuity, nor considered enough the reasons for the changes which did occur.

The economy of Orkney was essentially based on smallholdings. From the first introduction of farming on to very recent times the basic realities have been corn, livestock and the produce of the sea. That applies as much to Viking as to neolithic times, and other staples today such as kail (cabbage) and potatoes, for instance, are comparatively recent introductions.

ENVIRONMENT AND TECHNOLOGY

There are however some basic changes in environment and life in Orkney which should not be overlooked. In chapter 7 we have seen that during the Bronze Age Orkney underwent a climatic deterioration which may conceivably be associated with the comparative paucity of archaeological finds from that time. Arguably, too, this may have been the time when peat was first widely used as a fuel: certainly the coverage of blanket peat was greatly increased. It is certainly the period of formation of many of the mounds of burnt stone on the islands. Why they came into widespread use then is not yet clear. That one of their chief functions was the boiling of meat in their impressive stone troughs seems to be well documented now. The heat was conveyed to the troughs by hot stones, which were brought to a high temperature in a peat fire. Is it perhaps possible that until that time

PLATE 11.1. Quanterness chambered cairn: a vertical view
showing the oversailing courses narrowing to the roof.

there had been sufficient fuel in the form of small trees or shrubs, twigs or driftwood to allow meat to be roasted? It may be that declining wood resources and the simultaneous spread of peat made the technology of trough boiling with peat as the fuel the more effective. Arguably it would not have been superseded until the ready availability of bronze cauldrons in the Iron Age. These would allow water to be boiled (and meat with it) over a peat fire without all the inconvenience and the dirt of heating stones and plunging them into water. In the brochs we no longer see the great middens formed of burnt stone and peat ash, although peat may well have remained the principal fuel. The alleged discovery of its combustible properties by Torf Einar, as related in the *Orkneyinga Saga,* is either apochryphal, or it reflects the rediscovery of a technique which the Pictish predecessors of the Norseman could surely have taught them.

Technologies too certainly changed: most notably, metals were now used. Orkney does not seem to have been rich in bronze: few bronze artefacts have been found and there are no clear signs of metalworking from the prehistoric period. Iron may have been produced locally, but certainly the few items of gold (notably the Early Bronze Age discs from the Knowes of Trotty) and the great quantities of silver from the Pictish period were imports.

The most evident and interesting changes which took place in early Orkney were, however, those in social structure and organisation, and it is to these that we must turn.

SOCIAL CHANGE IN EARLY ORKNEY: EXTERNAL FACTORS

Despite the relative abundance of finds from early Orkney, the social organisation of the periods in question is far from clear. Still less so are the underlying factors responsible for the transition from one social form to another. In a sense it is still too early to tackle convincingly the problems that are raised by the finds, and I have much sympathy with the cautionary view expressed in chapter 6 by Dr Graham Ritchie: 'not to imply that we know more than we do'. I myself, however, adhere to the first school of archaeological interpretation to which he refers, seeing the deliberate articulation of hypothetical social frameworks as the way forward, while admitting that the evidence is often very thin. Such frameworks are therefore to be seen as devices to aid thought and to further research rather than as claims to reconstruct the past in any definitive way.

This book has been organised in a series of chapters focusing upon separate time periods and partly for that reason there has been in it relatively little discussion of change or of causal factors.

In the archaeology of earlier days it was common to see each change in the material record as the result of the arrival of a new group of people. Immigrants with new technologies and new ideas were seen as the principal agency of innovation. Thus not only were the first farmers of Orkney seen as immigrants – which can hardly be doubted – but so were the builders of the passage graves; the users of grooved ware; the people who built the henge monuments; the Beaker People; those who introduced bronze to the islands; the people first using cremation burial; the broch builders; the Picts and of course the Norsemen. Today this migrationist view is largely discounted, so that while many of these innovations are still accepted as the product of the diffusion of ideas, the arrival of substantial new populations is less willingly admitted.

Only in the case of the Norsemen is large-scale immigration generally accepted. The critic of the current reluctance to accept migrationist views might well comment that in the case of the Norsemen, the anti-migrationist has very little choice, since the advent of the Norse Earls of Orkney is historically well documented. And he might go on to say that what was true of Viking times could well have been true earlier also. But this would be to overlook the special nature of the Viking phenomenon, where the social developments in Scandinavia which created the pressure to sail westwards were accompanied by the necessary developments in ship design and ship building without which such voyages would not have been possible.

The nature and intensity of early Norse settlement in the Orkney Islands is still a matter for discussion. In her chapter on the Picts (chapter 9), Dr Anna Ritchie notes the evidence from her excavations at Buckquoy which suggests that the process of settlement may have been a gradual and fairly peaceful one.

The linguistic evidence, however, remains puzzling. The Orkney Norn, the Norse dialect which became the language of the islands until replaced by Scottish dialect under the Stewart earls, seems to have contained no words clearly derived from the language of the Picts. More surprisingly, the place-names of Orkney are almost entirely Norse, with hardly any toponyms clearly surviving from Pictish times. Why is this? Does it imply a total extermination of the Pictish population, in contradiction to the suggestions of Anna Ritchie? Or can we propose some mechanism by which the incomers would assign to different places in the islands names which had meaning in their own language? There has been, so far as I am aware, very little serious discussion of the precise circumstances in which place-names are either accepted from local inhabitants with a pre-existing system of nomenclature, or created afresh *de novo*. It is possibly true, in general, however, that a new, hierarchically structured society with the incomers as the dominant group, may readily impose the terminology of that group upon the landscape. On the other hand, when the pattern of immigration is one of incomers in small groups, infilling a pre-existing settlement pattern without disrupting it, many place-names in the language of the original population are more likely to survive. In the modern world many nation states seeking to assert their ethnic identity have suppressed place-names of a different ethno-linguistic origin, and perhaps a similar outlook may have operated in Norse Orkney.

On this view, then, it is possible that there are few if any large-scale incursions of new groups of people into Orkney between the initial population by the first farmers and the arrival of the Vikings from the east. The lack of Pictish place-names need not, on the view argued here, indicate a discontinuity in population. Anna Ritchie's view of a more gradual and perhaps peaceful process is equally plausible. Many of the apparent continuities in material culture throughout the first millennium AD could be explained in this way. Raymond Lamb has suggested that the distribution of mediaeval chapels in Orkney, which is itself related to the Norse system of rental districts, may show a continuity with the preceding Pictish tenurial system, and may indeed extend back to the first millennium BC.

VISIBILITY IN THE ARCHAEOLOGICAL RECORD

If we take a hasty and perhaps superficial view of the archaeological record in Orkney, there are three major episodes or phases of very evident building activity which we might be tempted to regard as 'climaxes' in the trajectory of development.

The first of these is a long one spanning the entire period of construction of the chambered tombs, starting with the first, probably well before 3500 BC, and encompassing the building of Maes Howe in around 2800 BC and the two major henge monuments at very approximately the same time. We can consider further below the extent to which this 'cycle' was a single, unitary phenomenon.

Whatever its nature it seems to have come to an end around 2300 BC when the tombs ceased to be used. It is conventional to regard the succeeding period in Orkney, from the end of the construction and use of chambered tombs (which are usually considered as 'neolithic') as assignable to the 'Bronze Age'. This designation, however, while so useful in Scandinavia and in England and southern Scotland, is really rather inappropriate to the Northern Isles, where metal finds are so few. But in any case, the second millennium BC, and much of the first, were until recently very much a gap in the Orcadian record, filled in part by a few earth mounds and some cist burials. The recent increase in our information is reviewed in chapter 7: cemeteries like that of Quoyscottie are now known, and the mounds of burnt stone can be assigned to this period. But, for all this new evidence, we have no public monuments, no major constructions, and very few sites, other than the mounds of burnt stone, which can be considered domestic.

This picture changes dramatically with the construction of the brochs. Their remarkable frequency in Orkney and in Shetland has long been recognised, and they make the earlier part of the 'Iron Age' a period of high

. . . .

visibility in the record, in contrast to the preceding Bronze Age.

For quite how long brochs continued to be built is not yet very clear. Evidently they did continue in use, often as the nucleus of large village structures, for a long time after broch-building had ended – well into the Pictish period. The latter has, like the Bronze Age, until recently been a period of low visibility, although Anna Ritchie's excavation at Buckquoy, and the recent work on the Pictish village at the broch at the Howe of Howe Farm have enhanced our knowledge.

It is not until the Norse period with its conspicuous remains, including the Earl's Palace at Birsay, the round church at Orphir and above all the great cathedral of St Magnus that we again see prominent architectural monuments.

Viewed, then, in rather soft focus, the prehistory of Orkney looks like three periods of high achievement, when the extant monuments allow us to say a good deal, interrupted by two periods (the Bronze Age and the Pictish Iron Age) where activities appear to have been on a more modest scale. Such a division into periods, episodes or phases is, of course, an arbitrary one. We would much prefer to study the various features of society – the demography, the subsistence economy, the social organisation, the belief system – along their trajectory through time without the imposition of such arbitrary divisions. But the changing nature of the record prevents it. In the period of the chambered cairns and that of the brochs, we have sufficient datable sites to prepare distribution maps and to consider the spatial patterns of activity as Fraser (1983) has done for the earlier period. J.W. Hedges (1975) has attempted this for the period of the mounds of burnt stone, but their identification is in many cases less certain. And for the Pictish period, after the brochs, we have observed very few sites: archaeologically they have a very low profile, which is not to say that they are not there.

INTERACTION IN ORKNEY AND IN BRITAIN

While we have accepted that trend of contemporary thought which is cautious in explaining changes in the archaeological record as the result of invasion or immigration, that is not to say that significant contact between different areas was not occurring. And while 'diffusionist' explanations are themselves not currently fashionable, it would not be realistic to discuss the appearance of artefacts of metal in Orkney as anything other than the result of contact with the Scottish mainland. This is one case, given the absence of metal sources in the islands and the paucity of actual finds, where Orkney can be regarded unhesitatingly as the receiver, and the lands to the south as the donor: a relationship where Orkney is in the secondary position. To use the terminology currently favoured by Marxist anthropologists (and others), Orkney was from the standpoint of metallurgical trade and industry at the periphery of a 'world system' whose 'core' lay well to the south. But the simplicities of what some choose to call 'dominance theory', where the world is divided into advanced cores and retarded peripheries, are seldom applicable to societies which are not at a state level of social complexity. Indeed they recall in many ways the old-fashioned diffusionist view which operated on the principle of *ex Oriente lux,* with the Near East as the source of all progress.

Recently a different perspective has emerged where an analysis of change is sought in terms of interactions between neighbouring areas which do not need to be expressed in terms of dominance, or of core and periphery. Often we see changes taking place over a broad area, which clearly embraces many independent social units, or polities as one might term them (without any suggestion that they are urban communities). It is the interactions between these equal-status polities which are often worth studying. This peer-polity interaction approach (Renfrew and Cherry, in press) has recently been applied to a number of cases in prehistoric Europe, and I feel it may be helpful here also.

Let us take the case of the brochs. Many writers, most recently MacKie (1965), have taken the core/periphery view of culture diffusion, with Orkney as the receiver at the fringe, and some other area, in this case south-west England, as the source. The alternative, which some have been tempted to offer, is to see Orkney, or Shetland, or the Western Isles as the source, the focus of innovation. The peer-polity interaction approach would lead one instead to look for parallel developments within many of the localities of the interaction area, including all three insular groups, and Caithness and Sutherland too.

As Hedges rightly stresses, there is now no reason to look for points of origin outside these areas. The early round house at Quanterness (Renfrew 1979, 181) and the structure at the Bu near Stromness (Hedges forthcoming a) allow us to see a possible typological development for early circular structures seen also at Jarlshof in Shetland. And the forts of the Western Isles indicate a background of defensive architecture. The approach invites us to consider the communications and interactions within the area which may have shaped the common developments observed right across it.

Above all we need a clear picture of the social organisation of the time. And to the extent that the brochs were of approximately the same size, and often well spaced in the landscape (rather than placed close together like towers in some larger system of defence), they may be regarded as representing small communities of roughly equal scale and rank (Renfrew 1976). Unless some are much larger and more elaborate than the usual norm, there would seem no case for a hierarchical order, with prominent chiefs or kings controlling large areas from their fortified fastnesses. On the contrary, these seem to be simply the well-defended farmsteads of relatively small rural communities which were the approximate equivalent in territorial scale of the tomb-building groups of the neolithic age.

We begin to see Early Iron Age society in Orkney then as a segmentary society without pronounced personal ranking, in many ways similar to that of the builders of the chambered cairns. The contents of the brochs themselves indicate some disparities in rank perhaps, with objects of fine craftsmanship, but there is none of the wealth during this period which we are to see in the great silver hoards of the next.

What we are apparently seeing in the years up to *c.* 600 BC and to the building of the early brochs is the emergence or consolidation of a society divided primarily into small groups of between perhaps ten and fifty people, usually perhaps extended families. These groups may have had internal ranking in the existence of a prominent household leader. But we have no evidence yet for larger alliances, where a whole number of these households or 'towns' (in the traditional Orcadian sense of the word) would be grouped under a single more powerful leader or chief. To say that we do not see it is not to establish that it did not exist. We can infer alliances, perhaps clan affiliations, such as are present in many segmentary societies, but not yet the concentration of real power into the hands of individuals.

Now one interesting feature of this pattern is that it was a local one, local that is to the area in question in northern Scotland. The rest of the British Isles seems to have functioned in a different way. In most areas around this time there are clear signs of a more centralised society, with a whole hierarchy of 'hillforts' often functioning as tribal centres. This is true for much of Scotland as well as for the south, but not for the more northerly regions where the brochs are found.

The brochs are thus significant in ways going beyond their architectural uniqueness. This is not simply an autonomous architectural tradition, developed perhaps by a process of peer-polity interaction. It represents also a social reality which appears to have differed markedly from that operating further south. Instead, the segmentary societies perhaps represented by the brochs, look, to the modern observer, much more like those represented for us also by the chambered tombs of three thousand years earlier.

We should note also that the society which followed, that of the Picts (who were, of course, quite simply the descendants of the broch builders), although at first sight rather impoverished, does in distinction show signs of more prominent internal ranking. In the first place, we know now that some at least of the Pictish settlements, still centred upon an earlier broch, were very much larger than the original brochs themselves. There were large villages, like that at Howe or Gurness, and more houses, like Buckquoy. Secondly, we have the occasional hoard of silver ornaments, which indicates a fondness for display and conspicuous consumption not hitherto in evidence. And then there are the symbol stones which, although not easy to interpret, may well be making statements claiming or asserting the ascendency of individuals or families over specific territories, just as did the slightly later inscribed stones of the Viking period in Denmark (Randsborg 1980, 131). All of this may possibly belong within a new social order in which local independence was lost, as the Orkneys came within the jurisdiction of the reported Pictish king, whose seat was further south in Scotland. The story of the Orcadian *regulus* (perhaps sub-king) who met St Columba at the Pictish court, as Adomnan relates, may hint at this. But the archaeological record does not yet document the top tier of our proposed hierarchy, and one would need the discovery of the seat of this king, or perhaps of some royal burials in what is now Scotland to illustrate it for us.

NEOLITHIC PROBLEMS

With the autonomous development of the brochs within the northern highlands and islands as a model, we can now turn to some of the more difficult problems of the neolithic period. Here we are no longer faced merely with the old choice between diffusion and local independent invention. We can now consider the role of Orkney within larger areas of intercommunicating polities, within which innovation could occur and be reinforced by competition and by emulation between them.

The beginning of the story – the arrival of the first farmer settlers – seems clear enough, although it would still not be surprising to find that Orkney had been visited or even inhabited on a year-round basis by hunter-gatherer communities without the domesticated plants and animals favoured by the first farmers who subsequently arrived. These earlier groups, concentrating on marine resources, would have enjoyed a way of life generally termed mesolithic. Such a pattern of life is well documented on the Hebridean island of Oronsay around 4500 BC (Mellars 1978). There are just a few indications from surface finds of chipped stone tools, that such communities may have lived in Orkney, but as yet no excavated remains.

In any case, one must regard the first farmers as immigrants, as Anna Ritchie describes, and their way of life is best represented for us so far by her excavations at the Knap of Howar. No doubt other sites as early will be discovered, and one may predict that amongst them will be some chamber tombs of the Orkney–Cromarty type. Of course, it would be possible to argue an extreme 'independent origin' position, and suggest that collective burial in chamber tombs developed independently among the farming communities of Orkney, as it seems to have done in such different parts of Europe as Brittany, Iberia and Scandinavia. But the form of some of the simpler Orcadian cairns compares so closely with those of north Scotland, as Audrey Henshall indicates in chapter 5, that this suggestion seems unnecessary. One may rather suppose that the first agricultural population came to Orkney with a set of beliefs and social or religious conventions which included clear views about the sort of community they belonged to and the manner in which it was fitting to dispose of the dead.

It is after this that the questions arise. Did the Orcadian passage graves like Quanterness and Quoyness simply develop locally from the simple chambered cairns of the first farmers? This is perfectly conceivable, since the flags of Orkney sandstone which are so readily available favour the development of a local architectural style with corbelled roofs over long and narrow chambers, and with numerous side chambers. If there was such a local development in architecture, culminating in the construction of Maes Howe, it may have run alongside a rather different series of developments resulting in the grander stalled cairns such as Midhowe.

Some writers have long argued, however, that the Orcadian passage graves must be related to those of Ireland, notably in the Boyne valley, which show the same feature of a central chamber set in a round mound and reached by a long entrance passage. The Irish passage graves, such as Newgrange, are certainly earlier than the Orcadian examples so far dated. The artefacts in Orkney and the Boyne show little resemblance in general. The carved stone from Pierowall in Westray, recently discovered, may however prove an important clue (plate 5.4), for the style of the carving is very like that of the Boyne tombs – a similarity already hinted in Orkney by the more modest carvings from Eday Manse and the Holm of Papa Westray. This may provide the more convincing indication of the influence upon Orkney of ideas and symbols from the Boyne which is necessary to substantiate the proposed origin for the passage graves. Bradley and Chapman (in press) have recently applied the idea of peer-polity interaction to the later neolithic of the British Isles, and the concept is helpful here. For what one may be seeing here is a convergence of traditions. We may have been wrong to have in mind a 'family tree' model, with a common source for features in different areas followed by an increasing divergence, as developments go their own way and depart increasingly from the common prototype. Instead there may be an early period with much local variation, followed by the general establishment of beliefs and norms of behaviour over an increasingly wide area, accompanied by the widespread adoption of specific symbols and styles of expression.

On this view it would be perfectly possible for the Orkney passage graves to have begun their development locally, from a starting point in the simpler Orkney-Cromarty cairns, and to have profited during their later development from contacts with the Western Isles and with Ireland.

Such an approach to the question may be necessary if we are to understand the origins of henge monuments and the development of the pottery known as grooved ware – both problems clearly posed in chapter 6 by Graham Ritchie.

Once again, there is so far no evidence of the arrival of new groups of people at this time. Moreover, it should be remembered that in Orkney there is no chronological separation between the building of chambered cairns on the one hand and the construction of henge monuments and the use of grooved ware on the other. In south Britain the long barrows and the Severn-Cotswold tombs belong to an early phase, along with the cause-wayed camps, while the henge monuments and the accompanying grooved ware are a good deal later. The Orcadian chambered cairns naturally have an origin much later than their southern counterparts, since farming reached Orkney comparatively late. But the two Orcadian henges are as early as most of those of Wessex, and are certainly contemporary with the continuing use of some of the chambered cairns, including Quanterness, Isbister and Maes Howe.

It is again difficult to conceive of so specific a form of ritual monument as the henge originating independently in north and south – especially when the form is effectively restricted to Britain and is not seen in continental Europe. Moreover, as Graham Ritchie points out, the custom of digging circular ditches is not likely to have originated in Orkney where ditches usually have to be rock-cut. There is a convenient prototype in the cause-wayed camps of the chalklands in the south.

But this does not mean that we must assume a southern origin for the whole ritual complex. The peer-polity interaction approach leads us not to expect a single specifically localised point of origin for the entire ritual complex. Clearly there must have been rather wide contacts at this time, and we may sometimes exaggerate the difficulties of travel. The early radiocarbon dates for the henge at Balfarg in Fife, cited by Graham Ritchie, remind us that Scotland may have played a role in the developmental process. It is possible to argue, too, that the astronomical concepts which may be reflected in the layout of some of the Scottish ritual sites, such as Callanish, may be more at home in the north than in southern lowland England. It might be as valid to see Avebury, for instance, as a southern transformation of the Ring of Brodgar as it would be to assert the converse; yet both may be the product of a process of ritual and architectural development in which the whole of Britain participated. Comparable arguments may be necessary to explain the similarities in the pottery of the time, the grooved ware, which, whatever the local variants, seems evidently related, from Orkney in the north to Clacton in the south.

These may seem somewhat abstract arguments, but they are necessary if we are to set the ritual monuments of Orkney within their broader British context. We do not have to consider them either as derivative, situated at the periphery of some 'world system', nor as a unique point of origin at some notional core. They are better seen as an integral part of a more complex system of interacting parts, making a contribution, although not necessarily a preponderant one, to the evolving belief system.

In human terms this means that we are not necessarily better thinking of distinct stages – an earlier egalitarian phase with chambered cairns and a later, chieftain phase with henge monuments. We can conceive instead of a developing society, in which public ritual was increasingly taking on an important role, and where the religious ideas of one area might have a considerable impact not only on immediately neighbouring communities but more widely.

PREHISTORIC PILGRIMAGES?

Indeed one is tempted to wonder whether there may not have been some *agency of greater mobility* at work in the spread of ritual ideas. Were there perhaps seasonal festivities at many of the great ritual centres and holy places of Britain, which attracted worshippers and adherents not simply from the outlying parts of their own territories, but from much further afield? Is this the underlying human reality behind some of the peer-polity interactions which we have inferred? 'To goon on pilgrimages', as Chaucer puts it in the *Canterbury Tales*, may be a practice of vastly greater antiquity in Britain than the Late Middle Ages.

The notion of the 'periodic central place' is a familiar one for the geographer of the market economy (Skinner 1964), and Isobel Smith long ago suggested something comparable for the causewayed camps of the earlier neolithic of southern Britain (Smith 1965, 19). I have suggested that the great ritual monuments of the south, like Avebury or Durrington Walls, as well as Brodgar and Stenness, may have been the ritual foci of chiefdom societies (Renfrew 1983). Their distribution in space, as the possible foci of quite large territories, supports this idea. But perhaps I have insufficiently stressed that the ritual focus of one territory can exercise a powerful influence upon the inhabitants of *other* regions. The great church of St James of Compostela, for instance, may have been the chief ritual focus for northern Spain in the Middle Ages, but it was also more than that. More relevantly perhaps, the shrine of St Thomas à Becket was undoubtedly the pride of the archdiocese of Canterbury, yet it attracted pilgrims from many lands. Of course, in these cases we are talking about a more developed belief system, a religion of the Book, with an international organisation centred upon Rome. We must not project the religious customs of the High Middle Ages unthinkingly upon the British Neolithic. We are talking here of what we may instead regard as peasant cults amongst totally illiterate populations. And Isobel Smith may also have been right in thinking of medieval fairs and cattle markets – the religious dimension may not, in earlier times, have excluded the practical and economic one. It seems a frequent feature of the behaviour of human societies, or polities (to use the terminology favoured here), that outside and beyond the social and territorial units of political control there are periodic meetings and gatherings. This is true of many hunter-gatherer bands, which occasionally meet together at large gatherings or corroborees, to use the Australian term. It is true also of the ancient Greeks, whose fiercely competitive civic pride was canalised and to some extent overcome at pan-Hellenic festivals, of which that at Olympia is today the most famous. We have mentioned the medieval Christian pilgrimage; and its Muslim equivalent, the visit of the faithful to Mecca, should not be forgotten.

Evidence of very long-distance travel is already available for the British Neolithic. When the polished stone axes, found in the southern counties, were first being examined, and as their sources were identified in Cornwall, at Langdale Pike in Cumbria, etc., it was noticed that some of the causewayed camps had axes from a remarkably wide range of sources (see Smith 1971, 102). No specific human mechanism was offered to account for this, although Grahame Clark (1965) put forward the useful suggestion of ceremonial gift exchange to explain their general widespread distribution. But perhaps we should now add the further religious dimension to the discussion, and suggest that the driving force behind the movement of many of the travellers was the desire to attend the great seasonal religious ceremonies at one site or another. Seasonality is one of the most obvious features in such monuments as Stonehenge, and Thom has suggested that various stone circles of Britain show alignments upon a variety of seasonal solar phenomena. Many of these examples, of course, come from a date after the British Neolithic, but the point may apply to the period of the henges also.

Against such a background of movement – which is securely documented for Scotland (although not yet Orkney) by finds of jade axes ultimately derived from continental Europe (Campbell Smith 1965) – the parallel development of rituals, of monuments, and of symbolic systems in different parts of Britain becomes much easier to comprehend.

From this perspective the development of the Orcadian henges has to be seen as part of a larger British phenomenon. No doubt one aspect of the process was the emergence of more centralised social structures – chiefdoms in modern anthropological parlance. But here I am stressing rather the emergence of what must have been a remarkably powerful body of religious beliefs, with accompanying ritual observances. These are reflected in the notable uniformity of the henges over the whole of Britain, and in the very widespread distribution of grooved ware. Here Orkney, with its still continuing tradition of communal burial, was well equipped to play a part, and this was one of the very few areas where the use and perhaps even the construction of the monuments in the older tradition (the chambered cairns) persisted alongside the new ritual practices in the henges.

SOCIAL TRANSFORMATIONS

In this Epilogue it has been possible to make suggestions about some of the factors underlying the three great cycles of Orcadian prehistory. The development of neolithic ritual, culminating in the two great Orcadian henges, can be seen as part of a religious or ritual movement common to Britain as a whole. I have suggested that it may have been sustained by quite widespread travels of individuals, on what we might imagine as prehistoric pilgrimages.

But why did this tradition come to so dismal an end around 2300 BC? This is a question we cannot yet answer. One might appeal to internal factors: perhaps some agricultural difficulties resulting in population decline (although the evidence for climatic deterioration comes rather later). Alternatively, however, we might note that the whole British ritual complex associated with the henges declined at about the same time. It is now commonly associated with the development of a different set of values, laying more emphasis perhaps on personal prestige (Renfrew 1973; Shennan 1983), seen reflected perhaps in the Beaker burials. Such developments are less marked in the north: indeed it is interesting that it is in the north that the stone circles of the Bronze Age continue some of the old traditions. Orkney, however, was not on any of the trade routes which may have allowed the élites in the south the opportunity of amassing wealth and prestige. Perhaps in this circumstance lies the underlying cause for her decline in the Bronze Age.

The rise in the Early Iron Age of the brochs, whose distribution has been compared above with that of the much earlier chambered cairns, represents a remarkable re-assertion of northern individuality. Once again, Orkney (with Shetland, the Hebrides and the northern counties of the Scottish mainland) produced distinctive architectural forms. It is tempting to suggest that this was again a time of relative autonomy, of isolation even. Certainly in the succeeding Pictish period, when Orkney may have come under the sway of a ruler based in Scotland, the architectural finds are less impressive. Prestige was expressed in other ways again – in silver ornaments, and perhaps by the symbol stones.

The Norse arrival, unlike these other cases, seems to have been an essentially external event, brought about by a mixture of social and technological developments in Scandinavia. The social background to the early Viking raids has been much discussed, and of course they depended heavily on the new technology of the Norse sailing ships. But if the initial shift from Pictish to Norse was essentially an exogenous change, the stability of the new system was a feature of the suitability of the Orkneys for the new exploitation, and of the effectiveness of that system in relation to Orkney.

PROSPECT

One general point indeed emerges as the *Leitmotiv* of the present review: that more work is needed on a number of fronts if we are to reach a really satisfactory understanding of the Orcadian past. This is not a negative conclusion. Quite to the contrary, it is remarkable how far the great upsurge of excavation work in Orkney over the past decade, with which all the contributors of this volume have been associated, has succeeded in giving positive answers to a whole series of questions, as well as bringing to the fore some of the new ones which have been discussed here. The need, of course, is for further work, and here I think we can take comfort from three aspects of the current scene.

The first positive feature in very recent years has been the appointment, by the Orkney Heritage Society, of a resident Orkney Archaeologist. His prime task is rightly seen as one of survey rather than of excavation, and the early results of his work have been nothing less than spectacular. In his survey of two of the north isles of Orkney, Sanday and North Ronaldsay (RCAMS 1980b), Raymond Lamb has brought to light a striking number of new sites, and of new classes of site. In doing so he has documented the extent to which the monuments of rural Orkney are under threat, both from coastal erosion and from the mechanisation and intensification of farming, which today is increasingly departing from the traditional methods which for so long left many sites undisturbed. The survey, moreover, goes beyond the identification of individual sites and moves towards a larger vision of the landscape, the prehistoric landscape, as an object of study. This shift is in keeping with current developments in other areas, and already it has brought to attention some important issues.

When the landscape rather than the individual site is considered the whole question of land use becomes relevant – our attention moves to the fields, rather than focusing solely upon the focal settlements: to whole areas, as it were, rather than to discrete points. And whenever early fields and field systems are studied, whether in Gotland or Wessex or in Dartmoor, field divisions and boundaries take on a new importance. In studying areas, the linear features which divide them are often more interesting than the individual settlement points which they contain. So it has proved in Orkney. Dr Lamb has recognised a class of monument, hitherto largely overlooked in Orkney: the treb dykes. Treb dykes are massive linear earthworks (RCAMS 1980b, 9), and it is Dr Lamb's suspicion, as yet unconfirmed by excavation, that some of them may go back perhaps as far as the Bronze Age. That would certainly harmonise with findings in other areas, such as the impressive Bokerley Dyke system in Wessex. Their study is just beginning, but we can certainly recognise that the investigation of early land use in Orkney is likely to be one of the growth points of archaeological research. This is particularly germane since our earliest systematic records for Orkney relate to taxation in the period of Scottish rule. There is no doubt that many of the land divisions there recorded go back to Norse times, so that there is a potential source of historical information about Norse land tenure to be set alongside the findings of field survey. The great potential of such survey information makes the task all the more urgent, since mechanisation is a constant threat to early field systems, and much has already been lost.

A second encouraging aspect of current research is the contribution now being made by environmental specialists. The work of the pollen analyst formed the basis for many of the observations by Davidson and Jones in their contribution, although much more has yet to be undertaken before we have a full and detailed picture of the vegetational history of the area. The potential contributions of the geomorphologist and soil scientist remain to be fully exploited, not least in the context of the study of land use just discussed. Another interesting topic is the nature of the farm mounds of the north isles. These were again first noticed by Lamb (RCAMS 1980, 7) and are now the subject of study by Davidson (Davidson, Lamb and Simpson 1983). Initial study suggests a resemblance with the 'gardshauger' of Arctic Norway (Bertelsen 1979), and it may be that here we shall have a useful new source of data about early subsistence and settlement.

Finally it is appropriate to refer to the great contributions currently being made by rescue archaeology in Orkney. In Britain in general it has been widely realised, in recent years, that developments within our town centres have been destroying a very high proportion of the evidence relating to early urban development. Such important excavation projects as those of Winchester, York and the City of London have sprung from this realisation – in contrast with Dublin where a terrible desecration has been effected at the Wood Quay site, with the wanton destruction, without adequate prior investigation, of one of the most important Viking sites of Europe. (It should be remarked here that the archaeological potential of Kirkwall itself has not yet been fully appreciated, and a coherent plan for its investigation is much to be desired, for what must surely be the most important Viking settlement in Scotland.) But while British urban archaeology has in general responded to the most pressing threats, this has not been the case with the rural landscape. Whole areas containing a great variety of field monuments have been destroyed in England and in Scotland by deep mechanised ploughing. Happily the problem is rather different in Orkney, since most of the prehistoric settlements and monuments in question are stone-built, and are not so easily eradicated by simple ploughing. Although it is distressing to learn that one of the few single standing stones in Orkney, overlooking the Loch of Stenness, was destroyed by a farmer with a tractor a couple of years ago, and that a broch site, a scheduled Ancient Monument, has been deliberately destroyed by its owner – both these acts being contraventions of the law – such infractions are happily rather rare. The monuments of the past are respected in Orkney. Moreover the Scottish Development Department has responded magnificently to the general situation by sponsoring an organisation, North of Scotland Archaeological Services, whose role it is to undertake rescue excavations in cases where the threat to sites cannot easily be averted.

Several of the important recent excavations in Orkney have been conducted under their aegis, including those at the broch of Bu near Stromness and at the broch at Howe. The latter has been one of the most interesting and rewarding excavations in recent years in the whole of Britain. For in addition to the Pictish remains discussed by Anna Ritchie and the broch mentioned by Hedges, there are earlier or pre-broch remains, and these are now seen to have been constructed upon the site of a neolithic chambered cairn. Of course the full publication of these excavations is now eagerly awaited, but there are encouraging signs that this important enterprise will not go the way of the ill-fated pre-war excavations at the Broch of Gurness and the Brough of Birsay and evade publication altogether. For I have on my shelf an impressive series of well-documented preliminary reports, produced by North of Scotland Archaeological Services for this and other sites, which show that at least the preliminary work has been done, and that this important site is well on the way to publication.

It should be mentioned here also that many of the excavations discussed in this volume were funded either in whole or in part by the Scottish Development Department (Ancient Monuments). The threat to the heritage is as great in Orkney as anywhere else, but the action of the Orkney Islands Council in employing an Orkney Archaeologist and of the Scottish Development Department in supporting North of Scotland Archaeological Services have together succeeded so far in averting disaster.

This is as it should be. For in Orkney, somehow more markedly than in many other areas, the past has the quality of a present reality. The monuments are there, obvious in the landscape, and the evident continuities have a meaning, not just for the archaeological specialist, but for everybody. It is no coincidence, then, that the poets of Orkney have felt and expressed these feelings with great conviction. For Edwin Muir this was one of the deep sources of his poetic writing, and today the work of George Mackay Brown expresses anew the timeless quality of the world of Orkney. The Orcadian today is the inheritor, in this way, of the Orkney of yesterday. And so too, in a sense, are we all who seek to know the heritage of the islands, to the extent that we can gain an understanding of our common early past from a study of prehistory.

The possession of so great a heritage brings with it great obligations, which are not always easy to meet. And that is the thought which Miss

Costie so well expressed in the concluding lines of her poem 'The Auld Hoose Spaeks', with whose beginning I introduced this chapter and with whose ending I shall now conclude:

> Peety! Na min, raither thoo should lift thee kep,
> An' say thanks for thee gret heritage,
> . . . .
> An thoo're the culmination o' id aa'
> An' thine's the trust tae see 'id disno dee,
> Bit gets skailled oot amang the folk o' this wir land,
> Tae mak them read, an' see, an' understand.

Colin Renfrew and Simon Buteux **Radiocarbon Dates from Orkney**

In the list which follows, we have set out all the radiocarbon dates currently available from archaeological contexts in Orkney. The dates are given first in radiocarbon years, bc or ad, together with the associated standard error and the laboratory measurement number.

There is as yet no universally agreed procedure for the calibration of radiocarbon dates, which is necessary to express the date in 'true' or calendar years BC or AD. We have used here the procedure proposed by Dr Malcolm Clark (Clark 1975). It should be noted that the accompanying standard error is also modified. The calibrations currently in use are based upon the Californian bristlecone pine, *Pinus aristata*. It is likely that an independent calibration, based on wood samples preserved in Irish bogs, will also soon be available. Current indications are that these figures may not differ very much from those obtained from the bristlecone pine (Ottaway 1983). It is likely, therefore, that further refinements in measurement and calibration will ultimately permit more precise datings (i.e. dates with smaller standard errors). But in most cases such calibrated dates will probably not differ substantially from the calibrated figures set out here. It should be noted however, that to achieve a 95 per cent probability level it is necessary to quote dates with a ±2 sigma range. The range thus lies between the mean date plus 2 sigma and the mean date minus 2 sigma, where the mean date is the calibrated date quoted here, and sigma is the standard error, after calibration, as listed.

Acknowledgement. We wish to thank all the contributors to this volume for supplying the radiocarbon dates listed here, and Dr V.R. Switsur for his advice.

263

KNAP OF HOWAR

Lab no.	Context	Material	Radiocarbon date bc/ad	Calendar date BC/AD
Birm 816	Lower midden	Mixed animal bone	2820 bc ± 180	3600 BC ± 190
SRR 349	Lower midden	Mixed animal bone	2472 bc ± 70	3205 BC ± 110
Birm 813	Midden filling wall of House 2 (= lower midden)	Mixed animal bone	2320 bc ± 100	2995 BC ± 115
Birm 815	Lower midden	Mixed animal bone	2300 bc ± 130	2970 BC ± 145
SRR 347	Midden filling wall of House 1 (= lower midden)	Mixed animal bone	(3756 bc ± 85)	(4560 BC ± 110)
SRR 452	Re-run of sample SRR 347	Mixed animal bone	2131 bc ± 65	2725 BC ± 110
SRR 348	Upper midden contemporary with House 1	Mixed animal bone	2815 bc ± 70	3595 BC ± 110
Birm 814	House 2, floor deposit	Mixed animal bone	2740 bc ± 130	3520 BC ± 145
SRR 346	House 1, floor deposit	Mixed animal bone	2582 bc ± 70	3350 BC ± 110
SRR 344	Upper midden contemporary with House 1	Mixed animal bone	2501 bc ± 70	3245 BC ± 110
SRR 345	House 1, floor deposit	Mixed animal bone	2398 bc ± 75	3090 BC ± 110

SKARA BRAE

Lab no.	Context	Material	Radiocarbon date bc/ad	Calendar date BC/AD
Birm 795	Occupation deposits on old land surface	Mixed animal bone	2520 bc ± 120	3270 BC ± 135
Birm 480	Occupation deposits on old land surface	Mixed animal bone	2370 bc ± 100	3055 BC ± 115
Birm 794	Occupation deposits on old land surface	Mixed animal bone	2330 bc ± 100	3005 BC ± 115
Birm 637	Beginning of phase I village	Mixed animal bone	2480 bc ± 100	3215 BC ± 115
Birm 638	Beginning of phase I village	Mixed animal bone	2480 bc ± 120	3215 BC ± 135
Birm 639	Beginning of phase I village	Mixed animal bone	2450 bc ± 100	3175 BC ± 115
Birm 636	Beginning of phase I village	Mixed animal bone	2400 bc ± 130	3095 BC ± 145
Birm 790	End of phase I village	Mixed animal bone	2420 bc ± 150	3125 BC ± 160
Birm 789	End of phase I village	Mixed animal bone	2360 bc ± 120	3045 BC ± 135
Birm 791	End of phase I village	Mixed animal bone	2340 bc ± 100	3020 BC ± 115
Birm 788	Beginning of phase II village	Mixed animal bone	2340 bc ± 120	3020 BC ± 135
Birm 786	Beginning of phase II village	Mixed animal bone	2330 bc ± 120	3005 BC ± 135
Birm 787	Beginning of phase II village	Mixed animal bone	2200 bc ± 100	2850 BC ± 115

Lab no.	Context	Material	Date (bc)	Date (BC)
Birm 436	End of phase II village	Mixed animal bone	2090 bc ± 110	2655 BC ± 125
Birm 434	End of phase II village	Mixed animal bone	2070 bc ± 110	2625 BC ± 125
Birm 435	End of phase II village	Mixed animal bone	1920 bc ± 100	2415 BC ± 115
Birm 433	End of phase II village	Mixed animal bone	1880 bc ± 100	2355 BC ± 125
Birm 793	Base of waterlogged layer in midden deposits at periphery of domestic area	Mixed animal bone	2110 bc ± 130	2685 BC ± 145
Birm 477	Base of waterlogged layer in midden deposits at periphery of domestic area	Mixed animal bone	2000 bc ± 100	2520 BC ± 115
Birm 478	Base of waterlogged layer in midden deposits at periphery of domestic area	Mixed animal bone	1900 bc ± 140	2385 BC ± 150
Birm 438	Top of waterlogged layer in midden deposits at periphery of domestic area	Mixed animal bone	2190 bc ± 120	2830 BC ± 135
Birm 792	Top of waterlogged layer in midden deposits at periphery of domestic area	Mixed animal bone	1980 bc ± 110	2495 BC ± 125
Birm 437	Top of waterlogged layer in midden deposits at periphery of domestic area	Mixed animal bone	1830 bc ± 110	2275 BC ± 125

LINKS OF NOLTLAND

Lab no.	Context	Material	Date (bc)	Date (BC)
GU 1429	Secondary ploughsoil immediately preceding main midden deposition in West Midden area	Bone of Bos	2265 bc ± 65	2930 BC ± 110
GU 1428	Secondary ploughsoil immediately preceding main midden deposition in West Midden area	Bone of Bos	2190 bc ± 65	2830 BC ± 110
GU 1431	Midden around articulated deer skeletons in West Midden	Bone of Bos	2000 bc ± 65	2520 BC ± 110
GU 1430	Upper layer of midden deposition in West Midden area	Bone of Bos	1910 bc ± 60	2400 BC ± 110
GU 1433	Midden material used to fill in the structure at Grobust	Mixed animal bone	1890 bc ± 60	2370 BC ± 110
GU 1432	Deer butchering site in accumulating sand deposit behind a field boundary in Central Dunes immediately underlying Beaker occupation	Bone of Cervus elephas	1772 bc ± 60	2190 BC ± 110

RINYO

Lab no.	Context	Material	Date (bc)	Date (BC)
Q 1226	No context	Animal bone probably Bos	1900 bc ± 70	2385 BC ± 110

QUANTERNESS (ORK 43)

Lab no.	Context	Material	Radiocarbon date bc/ad	Calendar date BC/AD
Q 1294	Main chamber, stratum 1	Organically rich soil	2640 bc ± 75	3420 BC ± 110
SRR 754	Main chamber, Pit A, stratum 2 (same burial as Q 1479 and Pta 1626)	Human bone	2410 bc ± 50	3110 BC ± 110
Pta 1626	Main chamber, Pit A, stratum 2 (same burial as SRR 754 and Q 1479)	Human bone	2350 bc ± 60	3030 BC ± 110
Q 1479	Main chamber, Pit A, stratum 2 (same burial as SRR 754 and Pta 1626)	Human bone	2220 bc ± 75	2875 BC ± 110
Q 1363	Main chamber, stratum 3	Human bone	2590 bc ± 110	3360 BC ± 125
Q 1451	Main chamber, stratum 3	Human bone	2160 bc ± 100	2775 BC ± 115
Pta 1606	Main chamber, Pit C, stratum 5 (same burial as SRR 755 and Q 1480)	Human bone	2180 bc ± 60	2810 BC ± 110
Q 1480	Main chamber, Pit C, stratum 5 (same burial as SRR 755 and Pta 1606)	Human bone	1955 bc ± 70	2460 BC ± 110
SRR 755	Main chamber, Pit C, stratum 5 (same burial as Q 1480 and Pta 1606)	Human bone	1920 bc ± 55	2415 BC ± 110

ISBISTER (ORK 25)

Lab no.	Context	Material	Radiocarbon date bc/ad	Calendar date BC/AD
GU 1179	Foundation deposit immediately prior to building of tomb	Human bone	2480 bc ± 55	3215 BC ± 110
GU 1178	Foundation deposit immediately prior to building of tomb	Human bone	2295 bc ± 100	2965 BC ± 115
GU 1182	Deposit under intact shelf, Stall 5 (same sample as Q 3013)	Human bone	2530 bc ± 80	3285 BC ± 110
Q 3013	Deposit under intact shelf, Stall 5 (same sample as GU 1182)	Human bone	2425 bc ± 50	3135 BC ± 110
GU 1185	Deposit in undisturbed Side cell 3 (same sample as Q 3016)	Human bone	2470 bc ± 95	3205 BC ± 110
Q 3016	Deposit in undisturbed Side cell 3 (same sample as	Human bone	2410 bc ± 55	3110 BC ± 110

Lab no.	Context	Material	bc date	BC date
GU 1180	Deposit on floor of undisturbed Stall 4	Human bone	24?0 bc ± 90	3?3? BC ± 110
GU 1181	Deposit on floor of undisturbed Stall 4	Human bone	2460 bc ± 130	3190 BC ± 145
GU 1184	Deposit in undisturbed Side cell 3 (same sample as Q 3015)	Human bone	2415 bc ± 90	3120 BC ± 110
Q 3015	Deposit in undisturbed Side cell 3 (same sample as GU 1184)	Human bone	2310 bc ± 55	2980 BC ± 110
Q 3018	Backfill behind hornwork abutting tomb (same sample as GU 1190)	Deer bone	2335 bc ± 45	3010 BC ± 110
GU 1190	Backfill behind hornwork abutting tomb (same sample as Q 3018)	Deer bone	2310 bc ± 55	2980 BC ± 110
GU 1183	Deposit under intact shelf, Stall 5 (same sample as Q 3014)	Human bone	1960 bc ± 80	2470 BC ± 110
Q 3014	Deposit under intact shelf, Stall 5 (same sample as GU 1183)	Human bone	1880 bc ± 50	2355 BC ± 110
GU 1186	Stone infilling sealing tomb (same sample as Q 3017)	Human bone	2090 bc ± 100	2655 BC ± 115
Q 3017	Stone infilling sealing tomb (same sample as U 1136)	Human bone	2080 bc ± 50	2640 BC ± 110
GU 1187	Cist burial inserted in backfill behind North hornwork	Human bone	1300 bc ± 55	1595 BC ± 110
KNOWE OF RAMSAY (ORK 30)				
Q 1223	No context	Animal bone	2390 bc ± 65	3080 BC ± 110
Q 1224	No context	Deer bone	2350 bc ± 60	3030 BC ± 110
Q 1222	No context	Animal bone	2060 bc ± 60	2610 BC ± 110
KNOWE OF ROWIEGAR (ORK 31)				
Q 1221	No context	Cattle bone	2355 bc ± 60	3035 BC ± 110
Q 1227	No context	Deer bone	2055 bc ± 60	2600 BC ± 110
QUOYNESS (ORK 44)				
SRR 753	No context	Human bone	2315 bc ± 50	2990 BC ± 110
SRR 752	No context	Human bone	2240 bc ± 50	2900 BC ± 110

KNOWE OF YARSO (ORK 32)

Lab no.	Context	Material	bc date	BC/AD date
Q 1225	No context	Animal bone	2275 bc ±60	2940 BC ±110

PIEROWALL QUARRY

Lab no.	Context	Material	bc date	BC/AD date
GU 1582	Material used in construction of structure beside ruined chambered tomb	Bone of *Bos*	2190 bc ±60	2830 BC ±110
GU 1583	Secondary occupation of structure beside ruined chambered tomb	Bone of *Bos*	2190 bc ±60	2830 BC ±110
GU 1584	Secondary occupation of structure beside ruined chambered tomb	Bone of *Bos*	2080 bc ±65	2640 BC ±110

MAES HOWE (ORK 36)

Lab no.	Context	Material	bc date	BC/AD date
SRR 791	Naturally formed peat layer below bank in North ditch section	Peat	3145 bc ±60	3930 BC ±110
SRR 505	Basal organic material above bedrock, 0.70 m below ground level, in North ditch section (same sample as Q 1482)	Silty peat	2185 bc ±65	2820 BC ±110
Q 1482	Basal organic material in North ditch section (same sample as SRR 505)	Silty peat	2020 bc ±70	2550 BC ±110
Q 1481	Basal organic material in South ditch section (same sample as SRR 524)	Silty peat	1815 bc ±70	2250 BC ±110
SRR 524	Basal organic material in South ditch section (same sample as Q 1481)	Silty peat	1495 bc ±50	1830 BC ±110
SRR 504	Lower organic layer of two on inner slope of ditch in North section, 0.85 m below ground level	Silty peat	1710 bc ±45	2110 BC ±110
SRR 523	Organic mud layers in South ditch section	Silty peat	930 bc ±45	1145 BC ±110
SRR 522	Organic layer in South ditch section	Silty peat	ad 265 ±45	AD 300 ±70
SRR 521	Uppermost organic layer in South ditch section, 0.46 m below ground surface	Silty peat	ad 715 ±40	AD 730 ±70
SRR 792	Burnt material from within secondary bank overlying primary low stone bank in South ditch section	Soil with organic material	ad 905 ±65	AD 955 ±80

STONES OF STENNESS

Lab no.	Context	Material	Radiocarbon date bc/ad	Calendar date BC/AD
SRR 350	Basal ditch deposit in main ditch section – organic layer	Animal bone	2356 bc ±65	3040 BC ±110
SRR 351	Central setting associated with calcined bone and grooved ware sherds	Wood charcoal	2238 bc ±70	2895 BC ±110
SRR 592	Bedding trench of possible rectangular timber setting	Fragments of decomposed wood	1730 bc ±270	2135 BC ±275
SRR 352	Pit C	Wood charcoal	ad 519 ±150	AD 560 ±160

RING OF BRODGAR

Lab no.	Context	Material	Radiocarbon date bc/ad	Calendar date BC/AD
SRR 502	Basal organic deposit overlying deep silt infill in north ditch section – depth 0.7 m	Organic mud	255 bc ±60	375 BC ±80
SRR 503	Lower peat in north ditch section – depth 0.6 m	Organic mud	375 bc ±45	440 BC ±70

Lab no.	Context	Material	Radiocarbon date bc/ad	Calendar date BC/AD
BEAQUOY (Burnt Mound)				
SRR 1001	In rubble infill of cooking trough of secondary structure	Animal bones and teeth	1677 bc ± 65	2065 BC ± 110
SRR 999	Twigs from silt at base of well-like structure relating to secondary structure	Twigs	511 bc ± 80	615 BC ± 95
POINT OF BUCKQUOY, BIRSAY CUTTINGS 5 & 6 (Midden)				
GU 1222	Carbonised grain from midden deposits associated with structural feature	Carbonised naked barley	1310 bc ± 180	1605 BC ± 190
LIDDLE (Burnt Mound)				
SRR 1000	From base of localised peat deposit over which the structure was built. The date has no connection with the occupation	Peat	2111 bc ± 40	2690 BC ± 110
SRR 525	First peat formed in a flag-lined gully which formed part of the occupational structure	Peat	958 bc ± 45	1185 BC ± 110
SRR 701	Organic detritus from bottom of cooking trough	Organic detritus, mainly heather roots	876 bc ± 75	1065 BC ± 110

KNOWES OF QUOYSCOTTIE

Lab no.	Context	Material	Radiocarbon date bc/ad	Calendar date BC/AD
UB 2161	F 103, cremation deposit cut into natural clay, overlain by clay	Wood charcoal	1195 bc ± 120	1490 BC ± 135
UB 2162	F 64, cremation deposit in Knowe 1	Wood charcoal	990 bc ± 85	1235 BC ± 110
UB 2158	F 15, cremation deposit cut into natural clay and concealed by thin layer of clay	Wood charcoal	900 bc ± 40	1100 BC ± 110
UB 2163	F 91, cremation deposit cut into old land surface	Wood charcoal	710 bc ± 85	890 BC ± 100

HOLLAND

| GU 1373 | Secondary burial in short cist inserted into primary mound (same burial as GU 1374) | Human bone | 995 bc ± 60 | 1240 BC ± 110 |
| GU 1374 | Secondary burial in short cist inserted into primary mound (same burial as GU 1373) | Human bone | 930 bc ± 60 | 1145 BC ± 110 |

QUANTERNESS ROUND HOUSE

Lab no.	Context	Material	Radiocarbon date bc/ad	Calendar date BC/AD
Q 1465	Primary occupation of round house, prior to wall F	Organically rich soil	620 bc ±85	815 BC ±100
Q 1464	Primary occupation of round house, prior to wall F	Organically rich soil	490 bc ±85	580 BC ±100
Q 1463	Secondary occupation subsequent to construction of wall J and feature W within round house	Organically rich soil	180 bc ±60	185 BC ±80

PIEROWALL QUARRY ROUND HOUSE

Lab no.	Context	Material	Radiocarbon date bc/ad	Calendar date BC/AD
GU 1580	Occupation immediately preceding construction of round house	Bone of Bos	560 bc ±80	765 BC ±95
GU 1581	Occupation contemporary with use of round house	Bone of Bos	475 bc ±60	545 BC ±80

BU BROCH

Lab no.	Context	Material	Radiocarbon date bc/ad	Calendar date BC/AD
GU 1228	In floor deposits in broch	Charcoal	520 bc ±95	670 BC ±110
GU 1154	In floor deposits in broch	Animal bone	510 bc ±80	615 BC ±95
GU 1152	At base of rubble filling broch interior	Cow's skull	490 bc ±65	580 BC ±80
GU 1153	In floor deposits of earth-house built into disused broch	Animal bone	595 bc ±65	795 BC ±80

SKAILL, DEERNESS

Lab no.	Context	Material		
Birm 413	Occupation of 'Iron Age' site	—	260 bc ± 120	375 BC ± 130
Birm 397	Occupation of 'Iron Age' site	—	150 bc ± 110	160 BC ± 110
Birm 764	Primary context in 'Iron Age/Dark Age' site	—	70 bc ± 100	40 BC ± 110
Birm 763	Primary context in 'Pictish'	—	ad 530 ± 100	AD 570 ± 110
Birm 762	Primary context in 'Pictish level'	—	ad 600 ± 100	AD 640 ± 110

BROUGH OF BIRSAY, AREA IV, SITE E

Lab no.	Context	Material		
GU 1251	Burnt layer below north wall of Structure E	Charcoal (Salix/Populus)	ad 570 ± 55	AD 615 ± 75
GU 1252	Burnt layer below north wall of Structure E	Charcoal (Salix/Populus)	ad 670 ± 50	AD 700 ± 70
GU 1253	Burnt layer below north wall of structure E	Charcoal (Salix/Populus)	ad 690 ± 50	AD 715 ± 70

BROUGH OF BIRSAY, AREA IV, NORTH OF SITE E

Lab no.	Context	Material		
GU 1254	Charcoal spreads in levelling material sealing features cut into natural clay	Charcoal (Salix/Populus)	ad 675 ± 50	AD 705 ± 70
GU 1318	Charcoal spreads in levelling material sealing features cut into natural clay	Charcoal (Salix/Populus)	ad 690 ± 50	AD 715 ± 70

BROUGH OF BIRSAY, AREA IV, SITE S

Lab no.	Context	Material		
GU 1319	Burnt layer within blocked entrance, possibly re-used as hearth, of wall in north of area	Carbonised seaweed and charcoal (Pinus, Quercus)	ad 795 ± 55	AD 810 ± 75

BROUGH OF BIRSAY, AREA I, SITE N

Lab no.	Context	Material		
GU 1192 & 1195	Features below northern wall of Structure N	Charcoal (Salix/Populus)	ad 815 ± 55	AD 835 ± 75
GU 1194	Features below northern wall of Structure N	Charcoal (Salix/Populus)	ad 750 ± 85	AD 760 ± 100

BROUGH OF BIRSAY, ROOM 5

Lab no.	Context	Material	Radiocarbon date bc/ad	Calendar date BC/AD
GU 1229	Phase 2b	Charcoal (*Salix*/*Populus*)	ad 645 ± 55	AD 680 ± 75
GU 1193	Phase 3a	Charcoal (*Salix*/*Populus*)	ad 955 ± 60	AD 995 ± 80

SAEVAR HOWE

Lab no.	Context	Material	Radiocarbon date bc/ad	Calendar date BC/AD
GU 1402	Midden-enriched ground surface contemporary with lowest of three superimposed Norse houses (phase II (a))	Charcoal of spruce	ad 690 ± 60	AD 715 ± 80
GU 1400	Central path of middle one of three superimposed Norse houses (phase II (b))	Charcoal of willow	ad 750 ± 90	AD 760 ± 105
GU 1401	Infill of drain belonging to uppermost of three superimposed Norse houses (phase II (c))	Mixed fish, mammal and shell remains	ad 555 ± 60	AD 600 ± 80

BIRSAY 'SMALL SITES', AREA 3

Lab no.	Context	Material	Radiocarbon date bc/ad	Calendar date BC/AD
GU 1230	Rubble and debris fill representing end of use of figure-of-eight building of pre-Norse type	Carbonised grain (*Hordeum vulgare*, *Avena fatua*)	ad 915 ± 60	AD 960 ± 80

BEACHVIEW 'STUDIO SITE', BIRSAY

Lab no.	Context	Material	Radiocarbon date bc/ad	Calendar date BC/AD
GU 1191	Midden post-dating wall and rubble collapse of large building	Carbonised grain (*Avena fatua*, *Hordeum* etc.) and charcoal (*Pinus*)	ad 1010 ± 55	AD 1040 ± 75

Note: All dates from Birsay are provisional.

SANDSIDE, GRAEMSAY

Lab no.	Context	Material	Radiocarbon date bc/ad	Calendar date BC/AD
GU 1067	Skeleton inside long cist	Human bone	ad 1085 ± 55	AD 1110 ± 75

Bibliography

Alcock, L. (1976) A multi-disciplinary chronology for Alt Clut, Castle
  Rock, Dumbarton, *Proc. Soc. Antiq. Scot.* 107 (1975-6), 103-13.
— (1980) Populi bestiales Pictorum feroci animo: a survey of Pictish
  settlement archaeology, *in* Hanson, W. S. and Keppie, L. J. F.,
  Roman Frontier Studies 1979 (= British Archaeol. Reports,
  International Series, no.71), Oxford, 61-95.
— (1981) Early historic fortifications in Scotland, *in* Guilbert, G.,
  Hill-fort studies: essays for A. H. A. Hogg, Leicester, 150-80.
Anderson, A. O. (1922) *Early Sources of Scottish History*, vol.1,
  Edinburgh.
Anderson, A. O. and Anderson, M. O. (1961) *Adomnan's Life of
  Columba*, London.
Anderson, J. (1868) On the horned cairns of Caithness, *Proc. Soc.
  Antiq. Scot.* 7 (1866-8), 480-512.
— (1873) *The Orkneyinga Saga*, Edinburgh.
— (1874) Notes on the relics of the Viking period of the Northmen in
  Scotland, illustrated by specimens in the Museum, *Proc. Soc.
  Antiq. Scot.* 10 (1872-4), 536-94.
— (1883) *Scotland in Pagan Times, The Iron Age*, Edinburgh.
— (1890) Notice of the excavation of the brochs of Yarhouse . . . in
  Caithness, *Archaeol. Scotica* 5 (1874-90), 131-98.
Anderson, M. O. (1973) *Kings and Kingship in Early Scotland*,
  Edinburgh and London.
Ashmore, P. J. (1974) Excavations at Summersdale, Orkney, by F. G.
  Wainwright in July 1960, *Proc. Soc. Antiq. Scot.* 105 (1972-4),
  41-2.
— (1980) Low cairns, long cists and symbol stones, *Proc. Soc. Antiq.
  Scot.* 110 (1978-80), 346-55.
Bailey, P. (1971) *Orkney*, Newton Abbot.

de Bakker, H. (1979) *Major Soils and Soil Regions in the Netherlands*, Centre for Agricultural Publishing and Documentation, Wageningen, Netherlands.

Baldwin, J. (1978) *Scandinavian Shetland. An Ongoing Tradition?*, Scot. Soc. for Northern Studies, Edinburgh.

Barron, D. G. (1895) Notice of a small cemetery of cremated burials, with cinerary urns of clay, recently discovered at Culla Voe, Papa Stour, Shetland, *Proc. Soc. Antiq. Scot.* 29 (1894-5), 46-8.

Barry, G. (1805) *The History of the Orkney Islands*, Edinburgh.

Batey, C. E. (1980) Excavations at Orphir 1979, *Univs Durham & Newcastle upon Tyne, Archaeol. Reps for 1979*, Durham, 33-5 (also *Northern Stud.* 15, (1980), 17-22).

— (1981) Excavations at the Earl's Bu at Orphir, Orkney, *Univs Durham & Newcastle upon Tyne, Archaeol. Reps for 1980*, Durham, 33-5.

Batey, C. E. and Morris, C. D. (1983) The finds, *in* Hedges, J. W. (1983b), 85-108.

Bekker-Nielsen, H., Foote, P. and Olsen, O. (1981) *Proceedings of the Eighth Viking Congress, Arhus 1981*, Odense.

Bell, B. and Haigh, D. (1981) Howe of Howe, *Discovery and Excavation in Scotland in 1981*, 25.

Bertelsen, R. (1979) Farm mounds in North Norway. A review of recent research, *Norwegian Archaeol. Rev.* 12 (1979), 48-56.

Biddle, M. (1971) Archaeology and the beginnings of English society, *in* Clemoes, P. and Hughes, K., *England before the Conquest. Studies in primary sources presented to Dorothy Whitelock*, Cambridge, 391-408.

Bigelow, G. F. (1978) *Preliminary report of the 1978 excavations at Sandwick, Unst, Shetland Islands*.

— (forthcoming) Sandwick, Unst and late Norse Shetland economy, *in* Smith, B., *Archaeology in Shetland*, Lerwick.

Birks, H. H. (1975) Studies in the vegetational history of Scotland. IV. Pine stumps in Scottish blanket peats, *Phil. Trans. Royal Soc. Lond.* B 270 (1975), 181-226.

— (1977) The Flandrian forest history of Scotland: a preliminary synthesis, *in* Shotton, F. W., *British Quaternary Studies: Recent Advances*, Oxford, 119-35.

Bourke, C. (1980) Early Irish hand-bells, *J. Royal Soc. Antiq. Ireland* 110 (1980), 52-66.

Bradley, R. (1978) *The Prehistoric Settlement of Britain*, London.

— (1982) Position and possession: assemblage variation in the British Neolithic, *Oxford J. Archaeol.* 1(1) (1982), 27-38.

Bradley, R. and Chapman, J. (forthcoming) The nature and development of long-distance relations in later Neolithic Britain and Ireland, *in* Renfrew, C. and Cherry, J. F. (forthcoming).

Bramwell, D. (1977) Bird and vole bones from Buckquoy, Orkney, *in* Ritchie, A. (1977), 211-14.

— (1979) The bird bones, *in* Renfrew (1979), 138-43.

Brøgger, A. W. (1929) *Ancient Emigrants: A History of the Norse Settlements of Scotland*, Oxford.

Brothwell, D. (1977) On a mycoform stone structure in Orkney, and its relevance to possible further interpretations of so-called souterrains, *Bull. Inst. Archaeol. London* 14 (1977), 179-90.

Brown, G. M. (1975) *Letters from Hamnavoe*, Edinburgh.

Bullard, E. R. (1975) Orkney habitats: an outline ecological framework, *in* Goodier (1975), 19-28.

Bullard, E. R. and Goode, D. A. (1975) The vegetation of Orkney, *in* Goodier (1975), 31-46.

Burgess, C. (1969) Chronology and terminology in the British Bronze Age, *Antiq. J.* 49 (1969), 22-9.

— (1974) The Bronze Age, *in* Renfrew, A. C., *British Prehistory*, London, 165-232.

— (1980) *The Age of Stonehenge*, London.

Burgess, C. and Miket, R. (1976) *Settlement and Economy in the Third and Second Millennia BC*, (= British Archaeol. Reports, no.33), Oxford.

Calder, C. S. T. (1937) A neolithic double chambered cairn on the Calf of Eday, Orkney, *Proc. Soc. Antiq. Scot.* 71 (1936-7), 115-54.

— (1939) Excavations of iron age dwellings on the Calf of Eday in Orkney, *Proc. Soc. Antiq. Scot.* 73 (1938-9), 167-85.

— (1950) Report on the excavation of a Neolithic temple at Stanydale in the parish of Sandsting, Shetland, *Proc. Soc. Antiq. Scot.* 84 (1949-50), 185-205.

— (1956) Report on the discovery of numerous stone age house sites in Shetland, *Proc. Soc. Antiq. Scot.* 89 (1955-6), 340-97.

Callander, J. G. (1934) The bronze age pottery of Orkney and Shetland, *Proc. Orkney Antiq. Soc.* 12 (1933-4), 9-13.

— (1936) Bronze age urns of clay from Orkney and Shetland, with a note on vitreous material called 'cramp', *Proc. Soc. Antiq. Scot.* 70 (1935-6), 441-53.

Callander, J. G. and Grant, W. G. (1934) The Broch of Midhowe, Rousay, Orkney, *Proc. Soc. Antiq. Scot.* 68 (1933-4), 444-516.

— (1935) A long stalled cairn, the Knowe of Yarso, in Rousay, Orkney, *Proc. Soc. Antiq. Scot.* 69 (1934-5), 325-51.

Campbell, J. (1979) *Bede's Reges and Principes*, Jarrow Lecture, Newcastle upon Tyne.

Campbell, J. A., Baxter, M. S. and Alcock, L. (1979) Radiocarbon dates for the Cadbury massacre, *Antiquity* 53 (1979), 31-8.

Campbell Smith, W. (1965) The distribution of jade axes in Europe with a supplement to the catalogue of those from the British Isles, *Proc. Prehist. Soc.* 31 (1965), 25-33.

Cant, R. G. (1973) The church in Orkney and Shetland and its relations with Norway and Scotland in the middle ages, *Northern Scotland* 1 (1972-3), 1-18.

— (1975) *The Medieval Churches and Chapels of Shetland*, Shetland Archaeol. & Hist. Soc. Lerwick.

Carver, M. O. H. (1979) Notes on some general principles for the analysis of excavated data, *Science & Archaeology*, 21 (1979), 3-24.

Caseldine, C. J. and Whittington, G. (1976) Pollen analysis of material from the Stones of Stenness, Orkney, *in* Ritchie, J. N. G. (1976), 37-40.

Chesterman, J. T. (1979) Investigation of the human bones from
Quanterness, *in* Renfrew (1979), 97-111.
— (1983) The human skeletal remains, *in* Hedges, J. W. (1983a),
73-132.
Childe, V. G. (1931) *Skara Brae. A Pictish Village in Orkney*, London.
— (1935) *The Prehistory of Scotland*, London.
— (1946) *Scotland before the Scots*, London.
— (1950) *Ancient dwellings at Skara Brae*, Edinburgh.
— (1952) Re-excavation of the chambered cairn of Quoyness,
Sanday, on behalf of the Ministry of Works in 1951-2, *Proc. Soc.
Antiq. Scot.* 86 (1951-2), 121-39.
— (1956) Maes Howe, *Proc. Soc. Antiq. Scot.* 88 (1954-6), 155-72.
— (1962) The earliest inhabitants, *in* Wainwright, F. T. (1962), 9-25.
Childe, V. G. and Grant, W. G. (1939) A Stone Age Settlement at the
Braes of Rinyo, Rousay, Orkney, *Proc. Soc. Antiq. Scot.* 73
(1938-9), 6-31.
— (1947) A Stone Age Settlement at the Braes of Rinyo, Rousay,
Orkney (Second Report), *Proc. Soc. Antiq. Scot.* 81 (1946-7),
16-42.
Clark, J. G. D. (1952) *Prehistoric Europe. The Economic Basis*, London.
— (1965) Traffic in stone axe and adze blades, *Econ. Hist. Rev.* 18
(1965), 1-28.
— (1980) *Mesolithic Prelude*, Edinburgh.
Clark, R. M. (1975) A calibration curve for radiocarbon dates, *Antiquity*
49 (1975), 251-66.
Clarke, D. L. (1970) *Beaker Pottery of Great Britain and Ireland*,
Cambridge.
— (1978) *Mesolithic Europe: the economic basis*, London (originally *in*
Sieveking *et al.* (1976), 449-81).
Clarke, D. V. (1976a) *The Neolithic Village at Skara Brae, Orkney.
Excavations 1972-3: An Interim Report*, Edinburgh.
— (1976b) Excavations at Skara Brae: a summary account, *in* Burgess
and Miket (1976), 233-50.
— (1983) Rinyo and the Orcadian Neolithic, *in* O'Connor, A. and
Clarke, D. V., *From the Stone Age to the 'Forty Five. Studies
presented to R. B. K. Stevenson*, Edinburgh, 45-56.
Clarke, D. V., Hope, R. and Wickham-Jones, C. (1978) The Links of
Noltland, *Curr. Archaeol.* 6(2) (1978), 44-6.
Close-Brooks, J. (1975) A Pictish pin from Golspie, Sutherland, *Proc.
Soc. Antiq. Scot.* 106 (1974-5), 208-10.
— (1980) Excavations in the Dairy Park, Dunrobin, Sutherland,
1977, *Proc. Soc. Antiq. Scot.* 110 (1978-80), 328-45.
Clouston, J. S. (1920) The Orkney townships, *Scot. Hist. Rev.* 17
(1919—20), 16-45.
— (1926) An early Orkney castle, *Proc. Soc. Antiq. Scot.* 60 (1925-6),
281-300.
— (1929) Three Norse strongholds in Orkney, *Proc. Orkney. Antiq.
Soc.* 7 (1928-9), 57-74.
— (1931) *Early Norse Castles*, Kirkwall.
— (1932) *A History of Orkney*, Kirkwall.

Clutton-Brock, J. (1979) Report of the mammalian remains other than
    rodents from Quanterness, in Renfrew (1979), 112-34.
Coles, J. M. (1960) Scottish late bronze age metalwork, Proc. Soc.
    Antiq. Scot. 93 (1959-60), 16-111.
— (1964) Scottish middle bronze age metalwork, Proc. Soc. Antiq.
    Scot. 97 (1963-4), 82-156.
— (1969) Scottish early bronze age metalwork, Proc. Soc. Antiq. Scot.
    101 (1968-9), 1-110.
Colley, S. (1983) Marine resource exploitation, in Hedges, J. W.
    (1983b), 111-13.
Coope, G. R. and Pennington, W. (1977) The Windermere interstadial
    of the Late Devensian, Phil. Trans. Royal Soc. Lond. B 280 (1977),
    337-9.
Corcoran, J. X. W. P. (1966) Excavation of three chambered cairns at
    Loch Calder, Caithness, Proc. Soc. Antiq. Scot. 98 (1964-6), 1-75.
Costie, C. M. (1974) The Collected Orkney Dialect Poems, Kirkwall.
Craw, J. H. (1934) A mound containing short cists at Trumland,
    Rousay, Orkney, Proc. Soc. Antiq. Scot. 68 (1933-4), 68-70.
Crawford, B. E. (1971) The Earls of Orkney-Caithness and their relations
    with Norway and Scotland: 1158-1470, unpublished D.Phil. thesis,
    University of St Andrews.
— (1977) The earldom of Caithness and the kingdom of Scotland,
    1150-1266, Northern Scotland 2 (1974-7), 97-117.
Crawford, I. A. (1972) Excavations at Coileagean an Udail (The Udal)
    N. Uist, 9th interim report, Christ's College, Cambridge.
— (1973) Excavations at Coileagean an Udail (The Udal), N. Uist,
    10th interim report, Christ's College, Cambridge.
— (1974) Scot (?), Norseman and Gael, Scot. Archaeol. Forum 6
    (1974), 1-16.
— (1981) War or Peace-Viking colonisation in the Northern and
    Western Isles of Scotland reviewed, in Bekker-Nielson et al.
    (1981), 259-69.
Crawford, I. A. and Switsur, R. (1977) Sandscaping and C 14: the
    Udal, N. Uist, Antiquity 51 (1977), 124-36.
Cruden, S. H. (1958) Earl Thorfinn the Mighty and the Brough of
    Birsay, in Eldjárn, K., Third Viking Congress, Reykjavík (1956),
    Reykjavík, 156-62.
— (1960) The Scottish Castle, Edinburgh and London.
— (1965) Excavations at Birsay, Orkney, in Small (1965), 22-31.
— (1977) The Cathedral and Relics of St Magnus, Kirkwall, in
    Apted, M. R. et al., Ancient Monuments and their Interpretation,
    London and Chichester, 85-97.
Curle, C. L. (1974) An engraved lead disc from the Brough of Birsay,
    Orkney, Proc. Soc. Antiq. Scot. 105 (1972-4), 301-7.
— (1982) Pictish and Norse Finds from the Brough of Birsay, Orkney
    1934-74, (= Soc. Antiq. Scot. Monograph, no.1), Edinburgh.
Cursiter, J. W. (1887) Notice of the bronze weapons of Orkney and
    Shetland and of an iron age deposit found in a cist at Moan,
    Harray, Proc. Soc. Antiq. Scot. 21 (1886-7), 339-46.
— (1898) The Scottish Brochs: their Age and their Destruction. A Theory,
    Kirkwall.

Cursiter, J. W. (1908) Notices (1) of a bronze dagger, with its handle of horn, recently found in the island of Rousay, and (2) of an inscription in tree-runes, recently discovered on a stone in the stone circle of Stennis, Orkney, *Proc. Soc. Antiq. Scot.* 42 (1907-8), 74-8.

— (1923) The Orkney brochs, *Proc. Orkney Antiq. Soc.* 1 (1922-3), 49-52.

Davidson, D. A., Jones, R. L. and Renfrew, C. (1976) Palaeoenvironmental reconstruction and evaluation : a case study from Orkney, *Trans. Inst. British Geogr.* 1 (1976), 346-61.

Davidson, D. A., Lamb, R. G. and Simpson, I. (1983) Farm mounds in North Orkney : a preliminary report, *Norwegian Archaeol. Rev.* 16 (1983), 39-44.

Davidson, J. L. and Henshall, A. S. (1982) Staney Hill, *Discovery and Excavation in Scotland in 1982*, 17-18.

Davidson, J. M. (1943) A Pictish symbol stone from Golspie, Sutherland, *Proc. Soc. Antiq. Scot.* 67 (1942-3), 26-30.

Dickson, C. (1983) The macroscopic plant remains, *in* Hedges, J. W. (1983b), 114.

Dimbleby, G. W. (1978) *Plants and Archaeology*, 2nd ed., London.

Dolley, R. H. M. (1966) *The Hiberno-Norse Coins in the British Museum*, London.

— (1976a) Two near contemporary findings of Hiberno-Norse coins from Maughold, *J. Manx Mus.* 7 (1976), 236-40.

— (1976b) *Some Irish Dimensions to Manx History*, Belfast.

Donaldson, A. M., Morris, C. D. and Rackham, D. J. (1981) The Birsay Bay Project. Preliminary investigations into the past exploitation of coastal environment at Birsay, Mainland, Orkney, *in* Brothwell, D. and Dimbleby, G., *Environmental Aspects of Coasts and Islands*, Symposia of the Association for Environmental Archaeology, no.1, (= British Archaeol. Reports, International Series, no.94), Oxford, 65-85.

Drever, W. P. (1933) Udal Law, *in* Viscount Dunedin, Lord Wark and Black, A. C., *Encyclopaedia of the Laws of Scotland*, vol.15, Edinburgh, 321-36.

Dryden, H. (n.d.) Orkney and Shetland, circles, broughs and etc. Plans, Soc. Antiq. Scot. MS 170, National Monuments Record of Scotland.

Dryden, H. and Petrie, G. (n.d.) The Broughs of Skara and Lingrow, Orkney, Soc. Antiq. Scot. MS 30, National Monuments Record of Scotland.

Dumville, D. N. (1976) A note on the Picts in Orkney, *Scot. Gaelic Stud.* 12 (1976), 266.

Edwards, A. J. H. (1926) Excavation of a number of graves in a mound at Ackergill, Caithness, *Proc. Soc. Antiq. Scot.* 50 (1925-6), 160-82.

— (1927) Excavation of graves at Ackergill . . ., *Proc. Soc. Antiq. Scot.* 51 (1926-7), 196-209.

Edwards, K. J. and Ralston, I. (1978) New dating and environmental evidence from Burghead fort, Moray, *Proc. Soc. Antiq. Scot.* 109 (1977-8), 202-10.

Ellesmere, Earl of (1848) *Guide to Northern Archaeology*, London.

Erdtman, G. (1924) Studies in the micropalaeontology of post-glacial deposits in northern Scotland and the Scotch isles with especial reference to the history of woodlands, *J. Linnean Soc. Bot.* 96 (1924), 449-504.

Evans, J. G. (1969) The exploitation of molluscs, *in* Ucko, P. J. and Dimbleby, G. W., *The Domestication and Exploitation of Plants and Animals*, London, 479-84.

— (1975) *The Environment of Early Man in the British Isles*, London.

— (1977) The palaeoenvironment of coastal blown sand deposits in western and northern Britain, *Scot. Archaeol. Forum* 9 (1977), 16-26.

Evans, J. G. and Spencer, P. J. (1977) The mollusca and environment, Buckquoy, Orkney, *in* Ritchie, A. (1977), 215-19.

Evans, J. G., Limbrey, S. and Cleere, H. (1975) *The effect of man on the landscape: the Highland Zone*, (= Council for British Archaeology, Research Report, no.11), London.

Fairhurst, H. (1971) The wheelhouse site at A' Cheardach Bheag on Drimore machair, South Uist, *Glasgow Archaeol. J.* 2 (1971), 72-106.

Farrer, J. (1857) Notice of a 'Burgh', recently opened in the island of Burray, Orkney, *Proc. Soc. Antiq. Scot.* 2 (1854-7), 5-6.

— (1864) An account of the discoveries at the Knowe of Saverough, *Proc. Soc. Antiq. Scot.* 5 (1862-4), 9-12.

— (1868) Note respecting various articles in bronze and stone; found in Orkney, and now presented to the Museum, *Proc. Soc. Antiq. Scot.* 7 (1866-8), 103-5.

Fenton, A. (1972) A fuel of necessity: animal manure, *in* Ennen, E. and Wiegelmann, G., *Festschrift Matthias Zender, Studien zu Volkskultur, Sprache und Landesgeschichte*, Bonn, 69-75.

— (1974) Seaweed manure in Scotland, *in In memoriam António Jorge Dias*, vol.3, Lisbon, 147-86.

— (1978) *The Northern Isles: Orkney and Shetland*, Edinburgh.

— (1979) *Continuity and Change in the Building Tradition of Northern Scotland*, (= Asa G. Wright Memorial lecture no.4), Reykjavik.

— (forthcoming) Aspects of continuity, *in* Fenton and Pálsson (forthcoming).

Fenton, A. and Pálsson, H. (forthcoming) *Continuity and Tradition in the Northern and Western Isles.*

Fergusson, J. (1877) *Short Essay on the Age and Uses of the Brochs and the Rude Stone Monuments of the Orkney Islands and the North of Scotland*, London.

Firth, J. (1920) *Reminiscences of an Orkney Parish*, Stromness.

Fleming, A. (1971) Bronze age agriculture on the marginal lands of north-east Yorkshire, *Agric. Hist. Rev.* 19 (1971), 1-24.

Fraser, D. (1980a) Investigations in neolithic Orkney, *Glasgow Archaeol. J.* 7 (1980), 1-14.

— (1980b) Redland area, chambered cairn, *Discovery and Excavation in Scotland in 1980*, 25.

— (1983) *Land and Society in Neolithic Orkney*, (= British Archaeological Reports, no.117), Oxford.

Fraser, J. (1923) Some antiquities in Harray parish, *Proc. Orkney Antiq. Soc.* 1 (1922-3), 31-7.

— (1924) Antiquities of Sandwick parish, *Proc. Orkney Antiq. Soc.* 2 (1923-4), 22-9.

— (1925) Antiquities of Birsay parish, *Proc. Orkney Antiq. Soc.* 3 (1924-5), 21-30.

— (1927) The antiquities of Firth parish, *Proc. Orkney Antiq. Soc.* 5 (1926-7), 51-6.

Frenzel, B. (1966) Climatic change in the Atlantic/Sub-Boreal transition on the northern hemisphere: botanical evidence, *in* Sawyer, J. S., *World Climate from 8000 to 0 BC*, Royal Meteorological Society, London, 89-123.

Gelling, P. S. (forthcoming) Excavations at Skaill, Deerness, Orkney, *in* Fenton and Pálsson (forthcoming).

Godwin, H. (1956) Report on the peat samples, *in* Childe (1956), 169-72.

— (1975) *The History of the British Flora*, 2nd ed., Cambridge.

Goodier, R. (1975) *The Natural Environment of Orkney*, The Nature Conservancy Council, Edinburgh.

Goodwin, A. J. H. and van Riet Lowe, C. (1929) *The Stone Age cultures of South Africa*, (= Annals South Africa Mus. 27, 1929).

Graeme, A. S. (1914) An account of the excavation of the Broch of Ayre, St Mary's Holm, Orkney, *Proc. Soc. Antiq. Scot.* 48 (1913-14), 31-51.

Graham, A. (1947) Some observations on the brochs, *Proc. Soc. Antiq. Scot.* 81 (1946-7), 48-99.

Graham-Campbell, J. A. (1976a) The Viking-age silver and gold hoards of Scandinavian character from Scotland, *Proc. Soc. Antiq. Scot.* 107 (1975-6), 114-35.

— (1976b) The Viking-age silver hoards of Ireland, *in* Greene, D. and Almquist, B., *Seventh Viking Congress, Dublin (1973)*, Dublin, 39-74.

— (1980) *The Viking World*, London.

Grant, W. G. (1933) Excavation of a denuded cairn, containing fragments of steatite urns and cremated human remains, in Rousay, Orkney, *Proc. Soc. Antiq. Scot.* 67 (1932-3), 24-6.

— (1937) Excavation of bronze age burial mounds at Quandale, Rousay, Orkney, *Proc. Soc. Antiq. Scot.* 71 (1936-7), 72-84.

Grieg, S. (1940) *Viking Antiquities in Scotland, Viking Antiquities in Britain and Ireland*, vol.2, Shetelig, H., Oslo.

Hamilton, J. R. C. (1956) *Excavations at Jarlshof, Shetland*, Edinburgh.

Hedges, J. W. (1975) Excavation of two Orcadian burnt mounds at Liddle and Beaquoy, *Proc. Soc. Antiq. Scot.* 106 (1974-5), 39-98.

— (1978) A long cist at Sandside, Graemsay, Orkney, *Proc. Soc. Antiq. Scot.* 109 (1977-8), 374-8.

— (1983a) *Isbister: a chambered tomb in Orkney*, (= British Archaeol. Reports, British Series, no.115), Oxford.

— (1983b) Trial excavations on Pictish and Viking settlements at Saevar Howe, Birsay, Orkney, *Glasgow Archaeol. J.* 10 (1983), 73-124.

BIBLIOGRAPHY

— (forthcoming a) *Bu, Gurness and the Brochs of Orkney*.
— (forthcoming b) *The Broch of Gurness, Aikerness, Orkney:*
   A Catalogue of the Finds from the 1930-39 Excavations.
Hedges, J. W. and Bell, B. (1980) The Howe, *Current Archaeology* 7
   (1980), 48-51.
Hedges, M. E. (1977) The excavation of the Knowes of Quoyscottie,
   Orkney: a cemetery of the first millennium BC, *Proc. Soc. Antiq.
   Scot.* 108 (1976-7), 130-55.
Hedges, S. E. (1980) Spurdagrove, Orkney: a prehistoric farmstead,
   Scottish Development Department (Ancient Monuments),
   Edinburgh.
Hedges, S. E. and J. W. (forthcoming) Excavations at Tougs,
   Shetland; an agricultural settlement in Shetland.
Heggie, D. C. (1981) *Megalithic Science*, London.
Heizer, R. F. (1963) Domestic fuel in primitive society, *J. Roy.
   Anthrop. Inst.* 93 (1963), 186-94.
Henderson, I. (1958) The origin centre of the Pictish symbol stones,
   Proc. Soc. Antiq. Scot. 91 (1957-8), 44-60.
— (1967) *The Picts*, London.
— (1971) The meaning of the Pictish symbol stones, *in* Meldrum, E.,
   The Dark Ages in the Highlands, Inverness, 53-67.
Henderson, T. (1978) Shetland boats and their origins, *in* Baldwin
   (1978), 49-56.
Henshall, A. S. (1952) Early textiles found in Scotland, *Proc. Soc.
   Antiq. Scot.* 86 (1951-2), 1-29.
— (1963 and 1972) *The Chambered Tombs of Scotland*, 2 vols,
   Edinburgh.
— (1974) Scottish chambered tombs and long mounds, *in* Renfrew,
   A. C., *British Prehistory*, London, 137-64.
— (1979) Artefacts from the Quanterness cairn, *in* Renfrew (1979),
   75-93.
— (1983) The finds, *in* Hedges, J. W. (1983a), 33-59.
Higgs, E. S. and Jarman, M. R. (1972) The origins of animal and plant
   husbandry, *in* Higgs, E. S., *Papers in Economic Prehistory*,
   Cambridge, 3-13.
Hodder, I. (1982) *Symbols in Action. Ethnoarchaeological Studies of
   Material Culture*, Cambridge.
Hunter, J. R. (1983) Recent excavations on the Brough of Birsay,
   Orkney Heritage 2 (1983), 152-70, (= Proceedings of the Birsay
   Conference, 1982).
Hunter, J. R. and Morris, C. D. (1981) Recent Excavations at the
   Brough of Birsay, Orkney, *in* Bekker-Nielsen *et al.* (1981), 245-58.
— (1982) Excavation of Room 5, Brough of Birsay Cliff-top
   Settlement 1973-4, *in* Curle (1982), 124-38.
Huxtable, J. (1975) Dating – thermoluminescence, *in* Hedges, J. W.
   (1975), 82-4.
Huxtable, J., Aitken, M. J., Hedges, J. W. and Renfrew, A. C. (1976)
   Dating a settlement pattern by thermoluminescence: the burnt
   mounds of Orkney, *Archaeometry* 18 (1976), 5-17.
Jackson, A. (1971) Pictish social structure and symbol-stones, *Scot.
   Stud.* 15 (1971), 121-40.

Jackson, A. (1977) Faroese fare, *in* Kuper, J., *The Anthropologists' Cookbook*, London, 48-51.

Jackson, K. H. (1955) The Pictish language, *in* Wainwright, F. T. (1955), 129-60.

— (1977) The ogam inscription on the spindle whorl from Buckquoy, Orkney, *in* Ritchie, A. (1977), 221-2.

Jobey, G. and Tait, J. (1966) Excavations on palisaded settlements and cairnfields at Alnham, Northumberland, *Archaeol. Aeliana* 44 (1966), 5-48.

Joensen, J. P. (1976) Pilot whaling in the Faroe Islands, *Ethnol. Scandinavica* (1976), 5-42.

Johnston, A. W. (1903) Notes on the Earl's Bu at Orphir, Orkney, called Orfjara in the sagas, and on the remains of the round church there, *Proc. Soc. Antiq. Scot.* 37 (1902-3), 16-31.

Johnstone, P. (1980) *The sea-craft of Prehistory*, London.

Jones, G. (1968) *A History of the Vikings*, Oxford.

Jones, M. (1980) Carbonised cereals from Grooved Ware contexts, *Proc. Prehist. Soc.* 46 (1980), 61-3.

Jones, R. L. (1975) Environment – pollen, *in* Hedges, J. W. (1975), 84-8.

— (1977) Pollen identification, *in* Hedges, M. E. (1977), 149-50.

— (1979) Vegetational studies, *in* Renfrew (1979), 21-8.

Kaland, S. H. H. (1973) Westnessutgravningene på Rousay, Orknyøyene, *Viking* (1973), 77-102.

Keatinge, T. H. and Dickson, J. H. (1979) Mid-Flandrian changes in vegetation on Mainland Orkney, *New Phytol.* 82 (1979), 585-612.

Kenward, H. K. *et al.* (1978) The environment of Anglo-Scandinavian York, *in* Hall, R. A., *Viking Age York and the North*, (= Council for British Archaeol. Research Report, no.27), London, 58-70.

Kilbride-Jones, H. E. (1973) On some aspects of neolithic building techniques in Orkney, *Acta Praehistorica et Archaeologica* 4 (1973), 75-96.

Kirkness, W. (1921) Notes on the discovery of a coped monument and an incised cross-slab at the graveyard, St Boniface Church, Papa Westray, Orkney, *Proc. Soc. Antiq. Scot.* 55 (1920-1), 132-3.

Lacaille, A. D. (1954) *The Stone Age in Scotland*, London.

Laing, L. (1974) *Orkney and Shetland*, Newton Abbot.

Laing, S. and Simpson, J. (1964) Translation of Snorri Sturluson, *Heimskringla. Part One. The Olaf Sagas*, London, revised edition.

Lamb, R. G. (1973) Coastal settlements of the North, *Scot. Archaeol. Forum* 5 (1973), 76-98.

— (1974) The Cathedral of Christchurch and the monastery of Birsay, *Proc. Soc. Antiq. Scot.* 105 (1972-4), 200-5.

— (1976) The Burri Stacks of Culswick, Shetland, and other paired stack-settlements, *Proc. Soc. Antiq. Scot.* 107 (1975-6), 144-54.

— (1980) *Iron Age promontory forts in the Northern Isles*, (= British Archaeological Reports, no.79), Oxford.

Lang, J. T. (1974) Hogback monuments in Scotland, *Proc. Soc. Antiq. Scot.* 105 (1972-4), 206-35.

Legge, A. J. (1981) Aspects of cattle husbandry, *in* Mercer, R. J., *Farming practice in British prehistory*, Edinburgh, 169-81.

Lethbridge, T. (1952) *Boats and Boatmen*, London.

Lewis, A. R. (1958) *The Northern Seas: Shipping and Commerce in Northern Europe AD 300-1100*, Princeton, New Jersey.

Liestøl, A. (1968) The Maeshowe runes. Some new interpretations, *in* Niclasen (1968), 55-61.

— (forthcoming) The runic inscriptions of Scotland, *in* Fenton and Pálsson (forthcoming).

Limbrey, S. (1975) *Soil Science and Archaeology*, London.

Longworth, I. H. (1967) Further discoveries at Brackmont Hill, Brackmont Farm and Tentsmuir, Fife, *Proc. Soc. Antiq. Scot.* 99 (1966-7), 60-92.

Low, G. (1879) *A Tour through the Islands of Orkney and Schetland in 1774*, Anderson, J., Kirkwall.

Lynch, F. (1973) The use of the passage in certain passage graves as a means of communication rather than access, *in* Daniel, G. and Kjaerum, P., *Megalithic Graves and Ritual*, (=*Jutland Archaeological Society Publications*, no.11), 147-61.

Lysaght, A. (1974) Joseph Banks at Skara Brae and Stennis, Orkney, 1772, *Notes Records Royal Soc. London* 28 (1974), 221-34.

Macaulay Institute for Soil Research (1978) *Annual Report*, 1977-8.

McCrie, G. (1881) Notice of the discovery of an urn of steatite in one of the five tumuli excavated at Corquoy, in the island of Rousay, Orkney, *Proc. Soc. Antiq. Scot.* 15 (1880-1), 71-3.

MacGregor, A. (1974) The broch of Burrian, North Ronaldsay, Orkney, *Proc. Soc. Antiq. Scot.* 105 (1972-4), 63-118.

Mackay, R. R. (1950) Grooved Ware from Knappers Farm, near Glasgow, and from Townhead, Rothesay, *Proc. Soc. Antiq. Scot.* 84 (1949-50), 180-4.

MacKie, E. W. (1965) The origin and development of the broch and wheelhouse building cultures of the Scottish Iron Age, *Proc. Prehist. Soc.* 31 (1965), 93-146.

— (1974) *Dun Mor Vaul*, Glasgow.

MacLean, C. (1976) Cereals from Pits A-C, Stones of Stenness, Orkney, *in* Ritchie, J. N. G. (1976), 43-4.

Marwick, E. W. (1975) *The Folklore of Orkney and Shetland*, London.

Marwick, H. (1922) A rune-inscribed stone from Birsay, Orkney, *Proc. Soc. Antiq. Scot.* 56 (1921-2), 67-71.

— (1924) Antiquarian notes on Rousay, *Proc. Orkney Antiq. Scot.* 2 (1923-4), 15-21.

— (1928) Kolbein Hruga's Castle, Wyre, *Proc. Orkney Antiq. Soc.* 6 (1927-8), 9-11.

— (1935) Leidang in the West, *Proc. Orkney Antiq. Soc.* 13 (1934-5), 15-29.

— (1947) *The Place Names of Rousay*, Kirkwall.

— (1949a) Naval defence in Norse Scotland, *Scot. Hist. Rev.* 28 (1949), 1-11.

— (1949b) Notes on archaeological remains found in Orkney, *Proc. Soc. Antiq. Scot.* 83 (1948-9), 236-40.

— (1952) *Orkney Farm-Names*, Kirkwall.

— (1970) *The Place-Names of Birsay*, Nicolaisen, W. F. H., Aberdeen.

Mather, A. S., Ritchie, W. and Smith, J. (1975) An introduction to the morphology of the coastline, *in* Goodier (1976), 10-18.

Mather, J. Y. (1964) Boats and boatmen of Orkney and Shetland, *Scot. Stud.* 8 (1964), 19-32.

Maxwell, G. S. (1975) Casus Belli; native pressure and Roman policy, *Scot. Archaeol. Forum* 7 (1975), 31-49.

Meadow, R. H. (1980) Animal bones: problems for the archaeologist together with some possible solutions, *Paléorient* 6 (1980), 65-77.

Mellars, P. (1976) Settlement patterns and industrial variability in the British Mesolithic, *in* Sieveking *et al.* (1976), 375-99.

— (1978) Excavation and economic analysis of Mesolithic shell middens on the island of Oronsay (Inner Hebrides), *in* Mellars, P., *The Early Postglacial Settlement of Northern Europe*, London, 371-96.

Mercer, R. J. (1981) The excavation of a late neolithic henge-type enclosure at Balfarg, Markinch, Fife, Scotland, *Proc. Soc. Antiq. Scot.* 111 (1981), 63-171.

Miller, M. (1978) Eanfrith's Pictish son, *Northern History* 14 (1978), 47-66.

Miller, R. (1976) *Orkney*, London.

Moar, N. T. (1969) Two pollen diagrams from the Mainland, Orkney Islands, *New Phytol.* 68 (1969), 201-8.

Moore, P. D. (1975) Origin of blanket mires, *Nature* 256 (1975), 267-9.

Morris, C. D. (1976) Brough of Deerness, Orkney, Excavations 1975: Interim Report, *Northern Stud.* 7-8 (1976), 33-7.

— (1977) The Brough of Deerness, Orkney: a new Survey, *Archaeologia Atlantica* 2 (1977), 65-79.

— (1978) Brough of Deerness, Orkney. Interim report on excavations and Survey 1976-7, *Northern Stud.* 11 (1978), 16-19 (also *Univ. of Durham, Archaeol. Reps for 1977*, Durham, 26-8).

— (1979a) The Vikings and Irish monasteries, *Durham Univ. J.* 71 (1979), 175-85.

— (1979b) Birsay, Orkney: 'Small Sites' excavations and survey, *Univs of Durham & Newcastle upon Tyne, Archaeol. Reps for 1978*, Durham, 11-19 (also *Northern Stud.* 13 (1979), 3-19).

— (1980) Birsay: Excavation and Survey 1979, *Univs of Durham & Newcastle upon Tyne, Archaeol. Reps for 1979*, Durham, 22-32 (also *Northern Stud.* 16 (1980), 17-28).

— (1981a) Excavations at Birsay, Orkney, *Univs of Durham & Newcastle upon Tyne, Archaeol. Reps for 1980*, Durham, 35-40.

— (1981b) Viking and Native in Northern England: a case-study, Bekker-Nielsen *et al.* (1981), 223-44.

— (1982a) Excavations at Birsay, Orkney, *Univs of Durham & Newcastle upon Tyne, Archaeol. Reps for 1981*, Durham, 46-53.

— (1982b) The Vikings in the British Isles: some aspects of their settlement and economy, *in* Farrell, R. T., *Viking Civilisation*, Chichester, 70-94.

— (1983) Excavations around the Bay of Birsay, Orkney, *Orkney Heritage* 2 (1983), 119-51, (= Proceedings of the Birsay Conference, 1982).

Morrison, A. (1980) *Early Man in Britain and Ireland*, London.

Morrison, I. A. (1973) *The North Sea Earls*, London.

— (1978) Aspects of Viking small craft in the light of Shetland practice, *in* Baldwin (1978), 57-76.

Muir, E. (1965) *Selected Poems*, London.

Munch, G. S. (1966) Gårdshauger i Nord-Norge, *Viking* 30 (1966), 25-59.

Mykura, W. (1975) The geological basis of the Orkney environment, *in* Goodier (1975), 1-9.

— (1976) *British Regional Geology. Orkney and Shetland*, Edinburgh.

N.A.A. (1979) *Nordic Archaeol. Abstracts 1979*, Viborg.

Neil, N. R. J. (1981) A newly discovered decorated stone from Orkney, *Antiquity* 55 (1981), 129-31.

Niclasen, B. (1968) *Fifth Viking Congress, Tórshavn, 1965*, Tórshavn.

Nicolaisen, W. F. H. (1976) *Scottish Place-Names. Their Study and Significance*, London.

Noddle, B. (1977) The animal bones from Buckquoy, Orkney, *in* Ritchie, A. (1977), 201-9.

— (1978) A brief account of the history of domestic animals in Caithness and Orkney, *The Ark* 9 (1978), 309-12.

O'Kelly, M. J. (1954) Excavations and experiments in ancient Irish cooking-places, *J. Royal Soc. Antiq. Ireland* 84 (1954), 105-55.

— (1973) Current excavations at Newgrange, Ireland, *in* Daniel, G. and Kjaerum, P., *Megalithic Graves and Ritual*, (= Papers presented at the III Atlantic Colloquium, Mosegård, 1969), Copenhagen, 137-46.

O'Riordain, S. P. (1953) *Antiquities of the Irish Countryside*, London.

Osborne, P. J. (1977) Evidence from the insects of climatic variation during the Flandrian period : a preliminary note, *World Archaeol*. 8 (1977), 150-8.

OS Ordnance Survey Record Card (now incorporated with the National Monuments Record of Scotland).

Ottaway, B. S. (1983) *Archaeology, Dendrochronology and the Radiocarbon Calibration Curve*, Edinburgh.

Padel, O. J. (1972) *Inscriptions of Pictland*, Unpublished M.Litt. thesis, University of Edinburgh.

Pálsson, H. and Edwards, P. (1978) *Orkneyinga Saga. The History of the Earls of Orkney*, London.

Parry, G. (1977) Field survey of some Quoyscottie-type barrow cemeteries in Orkney, *in* Hedges, M. E. (1977), 151-4.

Peglar, S. (1979) A radiocarbon-dated pollen diagram from Loch of Winless, Caithness, north-east Scotland, *New Phytol*. 82 (1979), 245-63.

Petrie, G. (1857) Description of antiquities in Orkney recently examined, with illustrative drawings, *Proc. Soc. Antiq. Scot.* 2 (1854-7), 56-62.

— (1860) Notice of a barrow at Huntiscarth in the parish of Harray, Orkney, recently opened, *Proc. Soc. Antiq. Scot.* 3 (1857-60), 195.

— (1861) Notice of the opening of a tumulus in the parish of Stenness, on the Mainland of Orkney, *Archaeol. J*. 18 (1861), 353-8.

— (1866) Notice of a barrow containing cists, on the farm of Newbigging near Kirkwall ; and at Isbister, in the parish of Rendall, *Proc. Soc. Antiq. Scot.* 6 (1864-6), 411-18.

Petrie, G. (1890) Notice of the brochs or large round towers of Orkney. With plans, sections, and drawings, and tables of measurements of Orkney and Shetland brochs, *Archaeol. Scotica* 5 (1874-90), 71-94.

— (n.d. a and b) Sketchbooks 5 and 6, Soc. Antiq. Scot. MS 487, now housed in the National Monuments Record of Scotland.

— (n.d. c) Manuscript and notebook, Soc. Antiq. Scot. MS 550, now housed in the National Museum of Antiquities of Scotland.

Piggott, C. M. (1947) A late bronze age 'razor' from Orkney, *Proc. Soc. Antiq. Scot.* 81 (1946-7), 173.

Piggott, S. (1954) *The Neolithic Cultures of the British Isles*, Cambridge.

— (1972) A note on climatic deterioration in the first millennium BC in Britain, *Scot. Archaeol. Forum* 4 (1972), 109-13.

Plant, J. A. and Dunsire, A. (1974) *The Climate of Orkney*, (= Climatological Memorandum, no.71), Edinburgh.

Randsborg, K. (1980) *The Viking Age in Denmark*, London.

Radford, C. A. R. (1959) *The Early Christian and Norse Settlements at Birsay, Orkney*, Edinburgh.

— (1962) Art and architecture: Celtic and Norse, *in* Wainwright, F. T. (1962), 163-87.

Rae, D. A. (1976) *Aspects of glaciation in Orkney*. Unpublished Ph.D. thesis, University of Liverpool.

Rasmussen, H. (1974) The use of seaweed in the Danish farming culture. A general view, *in In memoriam António Jorge Dias*, vol.1, Lisbon, 385-98.

RCAMS (1946) Royal Commission on the Ancient and Historical Monuments of Scotland, *Inventory of the ancient Monuments of Orkney and Shetland*, Edinburgh. References to vol.2, *Orkney*.

— (1980) Royal Commission on the Ancient and Historical Monuments of Scotland, Archaeological Sites and Monuments Series, 11, *Sanday and North Ronaldsay, Orkney*, compiled by R. G. Lamb, Edinburgh.

Rees, S. (1977) The stone implements, *in* Hedges, M. E. (1977), 144-5.

Renfrew, A. C. (1973) Monuments, mobilisation and social organisation in neolithic Wessex, *in* Renfrew, A. C., *The Explanation of Culture Change*, London, 539-58.

— (1976) Megaliths, territories and populations, *in* de Laet, S. J., *Acculturation and continuity in Atlantic Europe mainly during the Neolithic and the Bronze Age*, (Papers presented at the IV Atlantic Colloquium, Ghent 1975), Brugge, 198-220.

— (1978) Space, time and polity, *in* Friedman, J. and Rowlands, M. J., *The Evolution of Social Systems*, London, 89-114.

— (1979) *Investigations in Orkney*, (= Rep. Research Comm. Soc. Antiq. London, no.38), London.

— (1983) The social archaeology of megalithic monuments, *Scientific American* 249 (1983), 152-63.

Renfrew, A. C. and Cherry, J. F. (forthcoming) *Peer Polity Interaction and the Development of Socio-Political Complexity*, Cambridge.

Reynolds, N. and Ralston, I. (1979) Balbridie, *Discovery and Excavation in Scotland in 1979*, 76.

Richardson, J. S. (1948) *The Broch of Gurness, Aikerness, West Mainland, Orkney*, Edinburgh.

Ritchie, A. (1972) Painted pebbles in early Scotland, *Proc. Soc. Antiq. Scot.* 104 (1971-2), 297-301.
— (1973) Knap of Howar, Papa Westray, *Discovery and Excavation in Scotland in 1973*, 68-9.
— (1974) Pict and Norseman in Northern Scotland, *Scot. Archaeol. Forum* 6 (1974), 23-36.
— (1977) Excavation of Pictish and Viking-age farmsteads at Buckquoy, Orkney, *Proc. Soc. Antiq. Scot.* 108 (1976-7), 174-227.
— (1984) Excavation of a Neolithic farmstead at Knap of Howar, Papa Westray, Orkney, *Proc. Soc. Antiq. Scot.* 113 (1984), 40-121.
Ritchie, J. N. G. (1969) Two new Pictish symbol stones from Orkney, *Proc. Soc. Antiq. Scot.* 101 (1968-9), 130-3.
— (1974) Excavation of the stone circle and cairn at Balbirnie, Fife, *Archaeol. J.* 131 (1974), 1-32.
— (1976) The Stones of Stenness, Orkney, *Proc. Soc. Antiq. Scot.* 107 (1975-6), 1-60.
Ritchie, J. N. G. and Adamson, H. C. (1981) Knappers, Dunbartonshire: a reassessment, *Proc. Soc. Antiq. Scot.* 111 (1981), 172-204.
Ritchie, J. N. G. and Ritchie, A. (1974) Excavation of a barrow at Queenafjold, Twatt, Orkney, *Proc. Soc. Antiq. Scot.* 105 (1972-4), 33-40.
— (1981) *Scotland: archaeology and early history*, London.
Ritchie, J. N. G. and Thornber, I. (1975) Small cairns in Argyll: some recent work, *Proc. Soc. Antiq. Scot.* 106 (1974-5), 15-38.
Robertson, W. N. (1969) The Viking grave found at the Broch of Gurness, Aikerness, *Proc. Soc. Antiq. Scot.* 101 (1968-9), 289-91.
Roe, F. E. S. (1968) Stone mace-heads and the latest neolithic cultures of the British Isles, *in* Coles, J. M. and Simpson, D. D. A., *Studies in Ancient Europe*, Leicester, 145-72.
Roussell, A. (1934) *Norse Building Customs in the Scottish Isles*, London.
Rowley-Conwy, P. (1983) The animal and bird bones, *in* Hedges, J. W. (1983b), 109-11.
Rymer, L. (1976) The history and ethnobotany of bracken, *Bot. J. Linn. Soc.* 73 (1976), 151-76.
Sawyer, P. H. (1976) Harald Fairhair and the British Isles, *in* Boyer, R., *Les Vikings et leurs civilisations: problèmes actuels*, Paris, 105-9.
Scott, L. (1948) The chamber tomb of Unival, North Uist, *Proc. Soc. Antiq. Scot.* 82 (1947-8), 1-49.
— (1951) The colonisation of Scotland in the second millennium BC, *Proc. Prehist. Soc.* 17 (1951), 16-82.
Scott, W. (1821) *The Pirate*, Edinburgh.
Sharples, N. M. (1981) The excavation of a chambered cairn, the Ord North, at Lairg, Sutherland by J. X. W. P. Corcoran, *Proc. Soc. Antiq. Scot.* 111 (1981), 21-62.
Sheldon, J. M. (1979) Analysis of charcoal fragments from Quanterness, *in* Renfrew (1979), 29-30.
Shennan, S. J. (1983) Monuments: an example of archaeologists' approach to the massively material', *Royal Anthrop. Inst. News* 59 (1983), 9-11.

Shepherd, I. A. G. and Tuckwell, A. N. (1977) Traces of beaker-period cultivation at Rosinish, Benbecula, *Proc. Soc. Antiq. Scot.* 108 (1976-7), 108-13.

Shetelig, H. (1940) *An Introduction to the Viking History of Western Europe, Viking Antiquities in Great Britain and Ireland*, vol.1, Shetelig, H., Oslo.

— (1945) The Viking graves in Great Britain and Ireland, *Acta Archaeologica* 16 (1945), 1-55, (reprinted in Curle, A. O., Olsen, M. and Shetelig, H., *The Civilisation of the Viking Settlers in relation to their old and new countries, Viking Antiquities in Great Britain and Ireland*, vol.6, Shetelig, H., Oslo, 65-111).

Sieveking, G. de G., Longworth, I. H. and Wilson, K. E. (1976) *Problems in Economic and Social Archaeology*, London.

Simpson, D. D. A. (1976) The later neolithic and beaker settlement site at Northton, Isle of Harris, *in* Burgess, C. and Miket, R. (1976), 221-31.

Skinner, G. W. (1964) Marketing and social structure in rural China: Part I, *J. Asian Stud.* 24 (1964), 3-45.

Small, A. (1965) *The Fourth Viking Congress, York, August 1961*, (= Aberdeen Univ. Stud., no.149), Edinburgh.

— (1966) Excavations at Underhoull, Unst, Shetland, *Proc. Soc. Antiq. Scot.* 98 (1964-6), 225-48.

— (1968) A historical geography of the Norse Viking colonisation of the Scottish Highlands, *Norsk Geog. Tidskrift* 22 (1968), 1-16.

— (1969) The distribution of settlement in Shetland and Faroe in Viking times, *Saga Book of the Viking Soc.* 17 (1966-9), 145-55.

— (1971) The Viking Highlands, *in* Meldrum, E., *The Dark Ages in the Highlands*, Inverness Field Club, Inverness, 69-90.

Small, A., Thomas, A. C. and Wilson, D. (1973) *St Ninian's Isle and its Treasure*, Oxford.

Smyth, A. P. (1977) *Scandinavian Kings of the British Isles, 850-880*, Oxford.

Soc. Antiq. Scot. (1892) Donations to the Museum and Library, *Proc. Soc. Antiq. Scot.* 9 (1870-2), 356-67.

Smith, I. F. (1965) *Windmill Hill and Avebury, Excavations by Alexander Keiller 1925-39*, Oxford.

— (1971) Causewayed enclosures, *in* Simpson, D. D. A., *Economy and Settlement in Neolithic and Early Bronze Age Britain and Europe*, Leicester, 89-112.

Smith, J. A. (1872) Notice of a cinerary urn, containing a small-sized urn (in which were the bones of a child), discovered in Fifeshire, with notes of similar small cup-like vessels in the museum of the Society of Antiquaries of Scotland, *Proc. Soc. Antiq. Scot.* 9 (1870-2), 189-207.

Spencer, P. J. (1975) Habitat change in coastal sand-dune areas: the molluscan evidence, *in* Evans *et al.* (1975), 96-103.

Steedman, K. A. (1980) *The Archaeology of the Deerness Peninsula, Orkney, unpublished* BA dissertation, University of Durham.

Steinnes, A. (1959) The 'Huseby' System in Orkney, *Scot. Hist. Rev.* 38 (1959), 36-46.

Stevenson, J. B. (1975) Survival and discovery, *in* Evans *et al.* (1975), 104-8.

Stevenson, R. B. K. (1946) Jottings on early pottery, *Proc. Soc. Antiq. Scot.* 80 (1945-6), 141-3.

— (1955) Pictish art, *in* Wainwright, F. T. (1955), 97-128.

— (1958) A wooden sword of the Late Bronze Age, *Proc. Soc. Antiq. Scot.* 91 (1957-8), 191-2.

— (1968) The brooch from Westness, Orkney, *in* Niclasen (1968), 25-31.

— (1976) The earlier metalwork of Pictland, *in* Megaw, J. V. S., *To Illustrate the Monuments*, London, 246-51.

Stoklund, B. (1980) Houses and culture in the North Atlantic islands. Three models of interpretation, *Ethnol. Scandinavica* (1980), 113-32.

Talbot, E. (1974) Scandinavian fortification in the British Isles, *Scot. Archaeol. Forum* 6 (1974), 37-45.

Taylor, A. B. (1938) *The Orkneyinga Saga. A new translation with introduction and notes*, London and Edinburgh.

Taylor, J. J. (1980) *Bronze Age Goldwork of the British Isles*, Cambridge.

Thom, A. and Thom, A. S. (1973) A megalithic lunar observatory in Orkney: the Ring of Brogar and its cairns, *J. Hist. Astronomy* 4 (1973), 111-23.

— (1975) Further work on the Brogar lunar observatory, *J. Hist. Astronomy* 6 (1975), 100-14.

— (1978) *Megalithic Remains in Britain and Brittany*, Oxford.

Thom, A. S. (1981) Megalithic lunar observatories: an assessment of 42 lunar alignments, *in* Ruggles, C. L. N. and Whittle, A. W. R., *Astronomy and Society in Britain during the period 4000-1500 BC*, (= British Archaeol. Reports, British Series, no.88), Oxford, 13-61.

Thomas, C. (1971) *The Early Christian Archaeology of North Britain*, Oxford.

Thomas, F. W. L. (1852) Account of some of the Celtic antiquities of Orkney, including the Stones of Stenness, tumuli, Picts-houses, etc., with plans, *Archaeologia* 34 (1852), 88-136.

Thorsteinsson, A. (1968) The Viking burial-place at Pierowall, Westray, Orkney, *in* Niclasen (1968), 150-73.

Tinsley, H. M. and Grigson, C. (1981) The Bronze Age, *in* Simmons, I. and Tooley, M., *The Environment in British Prehistory*, London, 210-49.

Tønnessen, J. N. and Johnsen, A. O. (1982) *The History of Modern Whaling*, London and Canberra.

Traill, W. (1868) On submarine forests and other remains of indigenous wood in Orkney, *Trans. Bot. Soc. Edinburgh* 9 (1868), 146-54.

— (1876) Notice of two cists on the farm of Antabreck, North Ronaldsay, Orkney, *Proc. Soc. Antiq. Scot.* 11 (1876), 309-10.

— (1885) Notes of excavations at Stennabreck and Howmae in North Ronaldsay, *Proc. Soc. Antiq. Scot.* 19 (1884-5), 14-33.

— (1890) Results of excavation at the Broch of Burrian, North Ronaldsay, Orkney during the summers of 1870 and 1871, *Archaeol. Scotica* 5 (1874-90), 341-64.

Traill, W. and Kirkness, W. (1937) Hower, a prehistoric structure on Papa Westray, Orkney, *Proc. Soc. Antiq. Scot.* 71 (1936-7), 309-21.

Turner, W. (1872) Additional notes on the occurrence of the sperm whale in the Scottish seas (notes from this paper), *Proc. Soc. Antiq. Scot.* 9 (1870-2), 360-6.

Wainwright, F. T. (1955) *The Problem of the Picts*, Edinburgh.

— (1962a) Picts and Scots, *in* Wainwright (1962), 91-116.

— (1962b) The Scandinavian Settlement, *in* Wainwright (1962), 117-62.

— (1962c) The Golden Age and After, *in* Wainwright (1962), 188-92.

— (1962d) *The Northern Isles*, Edinburgh.

Wainwright, G. J. (1969) A review of henge monuments in the light of recent research, *Proc. Prehist. Soc.* 35 (1969), 112-33.

Wainwright, G. J. and Longworth, I. H. (1971) *Durrington Walls: excavations 1966-1968*, (= *Rep. Res. Comm. Soc. Antiq. London*, no.29), London.

Wallace, J. (1700) *An Account of the Island of Orkney*, London.

Warner, R. (1976) Scottish silver arm-rings: an analysis of weights, *Proc. Soc. Antiq. Scot.* 107 (1975-6), 136-43.

Watt, W. G. T. (1882) Notice of the broch known as Burwick or Borthwick, in the township of Yescanbee and parish of Sandwick, Orkney, *Proc. Soc. Antiq. Scot.* 16 (1881-2), 442-50.

West, R. G. (1977) *Pleistocene Geology and Biology with especial reference to the British Isles*, 2nd ed., London.

Wheeler, A. (1977) The fish-bones from Buckquoy, Orkney, *in* Ritchie, A. (1977), 211-14.

— (1979) The fish bones, *in* Renfrew (1979), 144-9.

Whittle, A. (1980) Scord of Brouster and early settlement in Shetland, *Archaeol. Atlantica* 3 (1980), 35-55.

Williams, D. F. (1977) Petrological analysis of the pottery, *in* Hedges, M. E. (1977), 147-8.

Wilson, D. (1851) *Archaeology and Prehistoric Annals of Scotland*, Edinburgh.

Wilson, D. M. (1971) The Norsemen, *in* Menzies, G., *Who are the Scots?*, London, 103-13.

— (1976a) The Scandinavians in England, *in* Wilson, D. M., *The Archaeology of Anglo-Saxon England*, London, 393-403.

— (1976b) Scandinavian settlement in the North and West of the British Isles – an archaeological viewpoint, *Trans. Royal Hist. Soc.* 5th Ser., 26 (1976), 95-113.

Wilson, D. M. and Hurst, D. G. (1964) Medieval Britain in 1962 and 1963, *Medieval Archaeol.* 8 (1964), 231-99.

Wilson, G. V. *et al.* (1935) *The Geology of the Orkneys*, Memoir of the Geological Survey of Great Britain, Edinburgh.

Worsaae, J. J. A. (1849) *The Primeval Antiquities of Denmark*, London.

Young, A. and Richardson, K. M. (1960) A Cheardach Mhor, Drimore, South Uist, *Proc. Soc. Antiq. Scot.* 93 (1959-60), 135-73.

Young, A. and Lunt, D. (1977) Cremated bone and tooth identification, *in* Hedges, M. E. (1977), 146-7.

Youngs, S. M. and Clark, J. (1981) Medieval Britain in 1980, *Medieval Archaeol.* 25 (1981), 166-228.

Indexes